Werewolves and
Other Shapeshifters
in Popular Culture

Werewolves and Other Shapeshifters in Popular Culture

A Thematic Analysis of Recent Depictions

KIMBERLEY MCMAHON-COLEMAN *and*
ROSLYN WEAVER

Foreword by Gerry Turcotte

McFarland & Company, Inc., Publishers
Jefferson, North Carolina, and London

LIBRARY OF CONGRESS CATALOGUING-IN-PUBLICATION DATA

McMahon-Coleman, Kimberley.
  Werewolves and other shapeshifters in popular culture : a thematic analysis of recent depictions \ Kimberley McMahon-Coleman and Roslyn Weaver ; foreword by Gerry Turcotte.
      p.   cm.
  Includes bibliographical references and index.

  ISBN 978-0-7864-6816-4
  softcover : acid free paper ∞

  1. Metamorphosis in literature.   2. Shapeshifting.
3. Werewolves in literature.   4. Metamorphosis — Mythology.
5. Werewolves in motion pictures.   6. Metamorphosis — Religious aspects.   7. Fantasy fiction — History and criticism.
1. Weaver, Roslyn, 1979–   II. Title.
  PN56.M53M36 2012
  809'93353 — dc23   2012014929

BRITISH LIBRARY CATALOGUING DATA ARE AVAILABLE

© 2012 Kimberley McMahon-Coleman and Roslyn Weaver. All rights reserved

No part of this book may be reproduced or transmitted in any form or by any means, electronic or mechanical, including photocopying or recording, or by any information storage and retrieval system, without permission in writing from the publisher.

On the cover: The character George Sands in werewolf form on the British series *Being Human*, 2009 (BBC America/Photofest)

Manufactured in the United States of America

McFarland & Company, Inc., Publishers
  Box 611, Jefferson, North Carolina 28640
  www.mcfarlandpub.com

Acknowledgments

Inevitably in a project such as this there are particular people whose support and encouragement make an enormous difference. We would like to thank those conference audience members whose questions and comments prompted us to persist with exploring the trope of the shapeshifter, and the journal reviewers and editors who have offered feedback on our work in this area. Similarly, Professor Gerry Turcotte of the St Mary's College in Calgary influenced our early academic careers, and graciously agreed to write the foreword for this volume.

We would like to acknowledge and thank our colleagues at Learning Development and the Shoalhaven campus of the University of Wollongong and also the University of Western Sydney.

Our families instilled in both of us a love of literature and a belief that education was important and that a career in academia was a valid life choice — even when we found ourselves questioning the latter. Thank you to Alison and Barry McMahon, and Justin McMahon and his family. To Grace Bahamonde Neumann, Dany Coronel and Ellyn Leighton-Herrmann, thank you for continuing to enrich the lives of the Colemans. A special thank you to the next Ph.D. in the family, Ellyn, who assisted us in finding some texts we might otherwise have missed. And to Tony, Jamie and Robert Coleman, who often have to deal with a wife and mother whose head is elsewhere, but still celebrate our writing milestones enthusiastically, which we appreciate. Thank you to David and Kay Weaver, and to Carolyn Miller and Michael Weaver and their families, for their ongoing encouragement and interest in the work, and to Margaret Steinberger, for kindly offering her services as a proofreader.

Finally, we would like to offer our thanks to the following publishers for permission to reproduce previously published material which has been revised for this book:

Weaver, Roslyn. "Metaphors of Monstrosity: The Werewolf as Disability and Illness in *Harry Potter* and *Jatta*." *Papers: Explorations into Children's Literature* 40.2 (2010): 69–82.

Weaver, Roslyn. "Shapeshifting from the Margins: Ethnicity and Werewolves in the *Twilight* series." *Journal of Children's Literature Studies* 8.1 (2011): 67–86.

Contents

Acknowledgments	v
Foreword: Shapeshifters Know No Bounds (Gerry Turcotte)	1
Preface	3
Introduction	5
ONE • Dear Diary, I Become a Monster Once a Month: Shapeshifting and Adolescence	15
TWO • Wolf Boys and Wolf Girls: Shapeshifting and Gender Politics	41
THREE • Till Death Do Us Part and Beyond: Shapeshifting, Desire and Sexuality	68
FOUR • The Alpha Race: Racial and Social Politics of Shapeshifting	92
FIVE • Shapeshifting and the Body: Disability, Illness and Mental Health	117
SIX • Coping, Masking and Addiction: A Little Drinking Problem	140
SEVEN • What to Do with Eternity? Shapeshifting and Spirituality	161
Conclusion	184
Works Cited	187
Index	195

Foreword: Shapeshifters Know No Bounds
Gerry Turcotte

"I thought I would assume a pleasing shape"
— Martia, a shapeshifter, quoting from *Hamlet* (II.ii.612)
in *Star Trek VI: The Undiscovered Country*

The story of the twenty-first century is increasingly articulated through genres that challenge standard realism and explore the potentialities of narratives that cross boundaries. Such transgressions, understandably, take many forms, and this shapeshifting is very much at the center of the present volume. Shapeshifters, by definition, challenge boundaries of all kinds. Like ghosts, they are able to transcend physical limits, both constituting and troubling the limits of the known. A shapeshifter is a being that can move between worlds, identities, values and styles. In this sense, the shapeshifter is a perfect metaphor for our times, where concrete and abstract, good and bad, high and low culture seem always to revolve around and blur into each other, as the opening epigraph attests.

Having said this, it is critical to acknowledge that shapeshifters have always been with us, from earliest to postmodern times. They can be found in virtually every Indigenous creation story; in Fairy and Biblical tales; from medieval literature through to the present. Whether a frog prince, a beauty's beast, or a Janus-faced politician, from Shakespeare to *Star Trek*, from Arthurian courts to interplanetary constellations, the shapeshifter knows no bounds.

Like the figure of the vampire, shapeshifters writ large have expressed a wide variety of views that have been either consonant with or antithetical to particular cultures, with a shift in recent times to articulating more desired notions of otherness — or indeed, of reading otherness as desirable. Put another way, where vampires may once have been emblematic of a despised other —

the creature we feared becoming — in more contemporary stories the "monster" has become the "end goal," that which we want to be. This move from perhaps merely covertly desired object of fear to emblem of self says much about how writers have moved to speak of their own particular sense of disenfranchisement, either because of disability, sexuality, or even generational angst.

This volume, then, is a timely study of an important cultural phenomenon, a work that admirably canvasses the staggering growth in contemporary models of shapeshifting. What is especially useful in this volume is the way the authors, who have already produced significant and sensitive readings of popular texts, have managed to study the impact of shapeshifting across communities, styles, values. It is a necessary and relevant undertaking. There would be few people in the developed world who would not be touched by stories by J. K. Rowling and Stephenie Meyer, that would not know Buffy or Sookie Stackhouse, or understand the way the monstrous can speak in positive terms about identity and belonging. It is one thing to recognize and sympathize with a lonely vampire; quite another to wish to become one.

Werewolves and Other Shapeshifters in Popular Culture works to unravel this change in the narrative, itself a model of transformation. More importantly, it builds on isolated studies that have tended to focus either on historical or anthropological perspectives to locate the transformative tale into a larger and more sustained analysis. This more comprehensive approach to what is an obviously widespread phenomenon allows new connections to be made and new sensitivities explored.

This volume is an important new work by two exciting scholars. Since this is a book about transformations, it is fitting that it will change the way we look at many received ideas. As Percy Bysshe Shelley once wrote, "Nought may endure but mutability." As such, attention must be paid.

Gerry Turcotte is president and vice chancellor at St. Mary's University College in Calgary.

Preface

The figure of the shapeshifter has regularly appeared in popular fictions for adults and children over time, from King Lycaon and Dracula to the Wolf Man and the *Twilight* wolf pack. However, recent years have seen an increase in shapeshifting characters, with werewolves in particular taking a central role in many popular series, such as *Being Human*, *Buffy, the Vampire Slayer*, Maggie Stiefvater's *The Wolves of Mercy Falls*, Martin Millar's Wolf Girl novels, Stephenie Meyer's *Twilight*, and the *Underworld* films, with further texts released every month. In several of the recent texts, shapeshifting is not restricted to werewolves, with entire were-populations in Charlaine Harris's Sookie Stackhouse novels and the television series adaptation *True Blood*; and a return to vampires' shapeshifting capabilities in more recent incarnations of the genre, such as L. J. Smith's *The Vampire Diaries* novels.

This shift has been accompanied by an increased interest in the use of shapeshifting characters as metaphors, with novelists and critics identifying specific meanings and topics behind these characters, such as disability, ethnicity, gender relationships, queer theory, spirituality, addiction and adolescence.

Despite the growing popular interest in shapeshifters, there are few critical texts that explore this area at length. This book aims to unravel the shapeshifting trope in terms of its currency for diverse issues. Rather than pursue a case-based study, we have grouped works around specific themes — adolescence, gender, sexuality, race, disability, addiction, and spirituality — that are explored through the metaphor of shapeshifting.

With coverage of iconic fantasy texts and a specific focus on current works, this book engages with the shapeshifting figure in popular culture from the United States, Canada, the United Kingdom, and Australia.

The figure of the shapeshifter offers much of interest for readers and scholars alike. With its transformative possibilities and flexibility, the shapeshifter has the potential to change how we see our world.

Introduction

In early 2010 we both attended the International Conference for the Fantastic in the Arts, in Florida. Although we had completed our Ph.D. studies under the same supervisor and knew each other's doctoral work, it wasn't until we discussed our respective conference papers that we realized we shared more than an interest in fantasy literature and a burning mission to find a drinkable pot of tea in American hotels. Both our papers were on shapeshifting figures: Kimberley's on racial and sexual politics related to the Coyote figure in *The Cure for Death by Lightning* and Roslyn's on the racial, class, and disability implications of werewolves in *Twilight*, *Harry Potter* and *Jatta*. There seemed to be a great deal of potential in the shapeshifting figure, a character that was becomingly increasingly common in popular works.

A year later we attended a different conference, this time the Popular Culture Association/American Culture Association national conference in Texas. Our papers here were different again, but what struck us was the overwhelming scholarly attention to vampire literature. There were so many panels on vampires and *True Blood*, *The Vampire Diaries* and *Twilight* that it seemed possible to spend the entire conference attending vampire sessions and still miss some panels.

It wasn't a surprise that the scholarly world was so interested in what was by then a phenomenon in popular culture: vampires. But what we did wonder was why there was so little attention, in comparison, to those other supernatural creatures who had begun appearing in greatly increased numbers on the pages and screens of adolescent and adult texts: shapeshifters. Werewolves have been linked with vampires as far back as Dracula, who was himself a shapeshifter and who was seen in wolf form in the 1931 film, and they coexist—although not peacefully—today in *Twilight*, *The Vampire Diaries* and *True Blood*.

For every *Twilight* fan obsessed by Edward Cullen there seemed to be one just as loyal to Jacob Black, who proudly proclaimed an allegiance to

Team Jacob and the wolf pack with the reasoning that real men don't sparkle. Sookie Stackhouse can choose between vampire lovers such as Bill Compton or Eric Northman, shapeshifter Sam Merlotte or werewolf Alcide Herveaux (*True Blood*). The romantic relationship of Willow and werewolf Oz still had its supporters years after Oz left town and Willow had moved on to Tara (*Buffy, the Vampire Slayer*). And werewolves have since marked even more territory by taking center stage in series such as Jennifer Lynn Barnes's *Raised by Wolves*, Maggie Stiefvater's *The Wolves of Mercy Falls*, and Jackson Pearce's *Sisters Red*.

Most of these texts deal with werewolves. Where once lupine shapeshifters were monstrous creatures of the full moon, now they surf (Mason in *The Vampire Diaries*) and box, play lacrosse and basketball (*Teen Wolf* films and television series). They write songs and read poetry (Sam in Maggie Stiefvater's *Shiver*), enjoy musical theater (Devon in Barnes's *Raised by Wolves*), excel at artistic pursuits (Heather Davis's *Never Cry Werewolf*) and sail on the *Titanic* (Claudia Gray's *Fateful*). Other shapeshifters are entrepreneurs: they own bars (Sam in *True Blood*) and work as lawyers (Hal Hauk in Kevin Hearne's *Iron Druid* novels). Above all, they almost always appear shirtless and chiseled as they fulfill their duties as heroic male leads, now the objects of desire just as vampires have transformed from villains to heroes in many works. And this is not restricted to the boys, either: girl werewolves and shifters are starting to move in on the territory as well (*Ginger Snaps*, Jenny Hale's *Jatta*, Leah Clearwater in *Twilight*).

The wolf remains the most common form of shapeshifter in popular culture, and this is no surprise, given its cultural significance in Greco-Roman myths. The empire of Rome was founded by Romulus, a twin raised by a she-wolf. Indeed, the very word "werewolf" comes from the Latin and literally means "man-wolf" (see Noll 84, among others).

Zeus, the head of the Greek pantheon, routinely shifted shape and the word lycanthropy itself, meaning wolf-man, is most often associated with the figure of King Lycaon, werewolf and father of the shapeshifting nymph Callisto. Virgil's *Eclogues* are adapted from Theocritus's *Idylls*, and Damon's songs in both evoke wolf figures (Ward, *Cultural Contexts* 77–78). Aesop famously authored the "Wolf in Sheep's Clothing" and Ovid, *Metamorphoses*. This historical information is relevant as the contemporary texts do draw on that long literary history, in ways that are subtle and significant.

Of course, the figure of the shapeshifter is an international one, present in many cultures: the fox in Japan, tiger and crocodile in China, various jungle animals in tropical regions, and the bear in Canada and northern Japan (McMahon-Coleman *Comparison*; Poulakou-Rebelakou et al.). Denis Duclos draws parallels between American history and culture and Norse history and mythology, which may explain the resurgence of the use of words such as Fenris or its derivatives (*Harry Potter, Sisters Red*), and Duclos argues that "Anglo-American culture is polarized by the myth of the Odinic warrior" (212), which is evident in a number of the texts examined here, notably Kevin Hearne's *Iron Druid* novels. Given the dominance of the American publishing and screen market, most of our texts are from the United States, but we do discuss examples from the United Kingdom, Australian and Canadian markets as well. Our discussion does cover some of the racial implications of shapeshifters, but we do not attempt to argue that there are specific national differences in how shapeshifters are treated across countries.

Contemporary Gothic characters often need to explain the "rules" of transformation and/or undeath in each particular iteration. In other instances, nomenclature gives the nod to that history, as when one of the lead characters in *The Vampire Diaries* is named Damon, or similarly, in the use of the word "daemon" for the shapeshifters in Philip Pullman's *His Dark Materials* trilogy, both evoking the character from Virgil's *Eclogues* and the demonic capabilities one might expect from "creatures of the night, of darkness, death and duality" (Ward, *Cultural Contexts* 25).

And yet despite this slow change towards shapeshifters, scholarly attention still remains rather fixed on the undead. In Glen Duncan's novel *The Last Werewolf*, a rather tongue-in-cheek exchange between one character and werewolf narrator Jacob Marlowe neatly summarizes the larger meaning of werewolves as metaphors in society:

> "Werewolves are not a subject for academe," she said, "but you know what the professors would be saying if they were. 'Monsters die out when the collective imagination no longer needs them. Species death like this is nothing more than a shift in the aggregate psychic agenda. In ages past the beast in man was hidden in the dark, disavowed. The transparency of modern history makes that impossible: We've seen ourselves in the concentration camps, the gulags, the jungles, the killing fields, we've read ourselves in the annals of True Crime. Technology turned up the lights and now there's no getting away from the fact: The beast is redundant. It's been us along.'"
>
> "Yes," I said. "I keep telling myself I'm just an outmoded idea. But you know, you find yourself ripping a child open and swallowing its heart, it's tough not to be overwhelmed by ... the concrete reality of yourself" [119].

Vampires have been explored with respect to their links to race, class, American culture, and capitalism. Zombies are used to analyze international politics, terrorism in a post–9/11 world, and colonization. Werewolves and other shapeshifters are therefore also equally a subject for academe, and certainly their potential to represent particular issues in society has been highlighted by other critics. As Chantal Bourgault Du Coudray writes, "like other Gothic monsters, the werewolf has been thoroughly constructed as an alien 'other' threatening the social body; the negative of a normalized social identity" (*Curse of the Werewolf* 44). Du Coudray sums up these threats as spanning class, race, gender, sexuality, and human identity: "the werewolf, like other monsters, embodied a composite Otherness which gave expression to anxieties about working-class degeneracy, aristocratic decadence, racial atavism, women's corporeality and sexuality, and the human relationship to the animal world" (*Curse of the Werewolf* 50).

Many works take a historical overview of the genre, especially with regard to medieval werewolves. Du Coudray's research in *The Curse of the Werewolf: Fantasy, Horror and the Beast Within* has explored the werewolf figure across genres and from Gothic to more recent works, while her journal article "The Cycle of the Werewolf: Romantic Ecologies of Selfhood in Popular Fantasy" takes more interest in gender. Other works focus on the werewolf and its links to gender and queer theory, such as Phillip Bernhardt-House's book chapter on "The Werewolf as Queer, the Queer as Werewolf, and Queer Werewolves," Barbara Creed's *Phallic Panic: Film, Horror, and the Primal Uncanny*, and Tison Pugh and David L. Wallace's journal article "Heteronormative Heroism and Queering the School Story in J. K. Rowling's *Harry Potter* Series." Werewolves have been read in a range of ways as dichotomies of the human-monster: "representations of lycanthropy have also been consistently conceptualised around the related poles of civilized-primitive, rational-instinctual, public-private and masculine-feminine. In this sense, the werewolf has modelled the dualistic subjectivity that emerged through the Enlightenment in graphic, exaggerated — or monstrous — terms" (Du Coudray, *Curse of the Werewolf* 3).

Renée Ward, meanwhile, points out the possibilities of the werewolf in identity transformation in her Ph.D. thesis *Cultural Contexts and Cultural Change: The Werewolf in Classical, Medieval, and Modern Texts* and in her conference paper "Shape-shifting, Identity and Change in *Harry Potter and the Prisoner of Azkaban*." In her thesis, Ward discusses the werewolf figure in antiquity and in the Middle Ages, and analyzes the *Harry Potter* series in some detail for its construction of werewolf characters, arguing "lupine figures defy any single interpretation and must, therefore, be approached as sites of potentially varied meanings within their relevant historical and cultural contexts" (372). Shelley Chappell analyzes the racial and ethnic implications of werewolves in her journal article "Contemporary Werewolf Schemata: Shifting Representations of Racial and Ethnic Difference." In her Ph.D. thesis, *Werewolves, Wings, and Other Weird Transformations: Fantastic Metamorphosis in Children's and Young Adult Fantasy Literature*, Chappell explores shapeshifting figures in children's literature more generally.

Of these works, many are short or are solely concerned with werewolves. Of the longer studies, seminal works on shapeshifting such as Mircea Eliade's

Shamanism: Archaic Techniques and Ecstasy, Ioan Lewis's *Ecstatic Religion: An Anthropological Study of Spirit Possession and Shamanism* and Michael Taussig's *Shamanism, Colonialism and the Wild Man* observe shapeshifting from an anthropological perspective and only as a function of shamanism. Works that focus on the shaman in literature, such as Kirsten McKenzie's and Kimberley McMahon-Coleman's theses, are limited to discussion of one or two authors. A number of newer popular television series such as *The Vampire Diaries* and *True Blood* have prompted the recent publication of "companion" books such as Red and Vee's *A Visitor's Guide to Mystic Falls* and Harris's *The Sookie Stackhouse Companion*, but critical analysis is, as yet, scarce.

We remained convinced that shapeshifters deserved more attention, and decided to explore the topic on a larger scale in this book. As other scholars of popular culture have already said, it is vital to bring our attention to the contemporary texts that permeate our culture so that we can understand more about our society and how it shapes us and reflects us. We aimed to address a couple of main questions through our readings of this genre: why are shapeshifters so popular? And what are the possibilities — and limitations — of using the shapeshifting figure? Certainly the creators of these texts seemed to be employing them as metonyms for various social issues or categories.

Werewolves are, as we noted, the most popular type of shapeshifting figure in popular culture and accordingly much of our book deals with lycanthropes. Just like the contemporary treatment of vampires, modern werewolves do not always conform to traditional mythology. Creed summarizes the major tropes of the werewolf figure as: they transform at night usually during the full moon, infect others by biting them, run with a pack, and have no tail. Death is by a silver bullet or fire, and the werewolf has a "terrible fury" (126). Current fictions about werewolves sometimes conform to these tropes, and sometimes reject them. Recent werewolves may now be more at peace with their dual identities, as du Coudray notes, "no longer consumed by rage, fear, self-loathing or the desire for revenge" (*Curse of the Werewolf* 151). We have chosen to limit our analysis to contemporary texts, and primarily those from the last twenty years, although we do refer to earlier examples at times in order to locate modern shapeshifting figures within their histories. In so doing, we are noting how shapeshifting figures have themselves shifted shape according to sociohistorical contexts.

Although our primary interest is in shapeshifters, we acknowledge that vampires remain the favored supernatural creature in contemporary texts, if only because it is much easier to use pale makeup and teeth prostheses on a model/actor than convincingly represent lycanthropy on screen. And accordingly we allow space for the vampire figure in our discussions, which is a necessity anyway given that many texts recycle the idea of an eternal enmity between vampires and werewolves. This is not beyond the scope of our topic when we consider the original concepts of vampires as shapeshifters themselves, whether turning into bats, wolves, or the undead, or simply moving from human to monster by the baring of their teeth.

The ability to shift or morph shape is itself an area that is interpreted in vastly different ways by the various creators of the works. With the exception of the daemons within Philip Pullman's *His Dark Materials* trilogy and a few of the characters in C. S. Lewis's *Chronicles of Narnia*, in each case one of the forms is human. Building on Chappell's definitions in her doctoral thesis, *Werewolves, Wings and Other Weird Transformations: Fantastic Metamorphosis in Children's and Young Adult Fantasy Literature*, it is useful to think of dual-bodied metamorphoses as those that involve repeated transformations between two distinct forms (Chappell 10), such as the "weres" in the Sookie Stackhouse novels and television series. Multi-bodied shapeshifters have the ability to take on numerous forms, such as the "shifters" in Sookie Stackhouse's world. Unidirectional shifts into new permanent bodies (Bynum, *Metamorphosis* 175), terminal shifts signifying death (Forbes Irving 20, 96) or replacement bodies (Chappell, *Werewolves* 10) are not examined in this book. Modified bodies are those that are only partially transformed (Chappell, *Werewolves* 11), such as Caroline Forbes in *The Vampire Diaries* novels. There are also, of course, a wide range of other appearance-altering figures in speculative fiction; from the Vinvocci aliens who "shimmer" in order to present a less-frightening body shape in *Doctor Who: The End of Time*, and the shape-regenerating Doctor himself over the series; to the ignored students who become invisible in *Buffy, the Vampire Slayer* (1.11), to a seemingly endless array of body-swap films from *Freaky Friday* onwards, and even the introduction of a "were-car" in Matt Groenig's *Futurama*. We note also the different geneses of shapeshifting abilities, whether they be triggered by heredity, magic, virus, or some combination of the three. The variety gives scope for analysis of how individual shape-shifters view the world and their own identities.

In general, and in line with our topic, we avoid restricting ourselves to narrow definitions and categories where a broader, more flexible approach would better draw out the intriguing possibilities of this genre. In keeping with this principle, our analysis covers books, films and television shows that appear within the broad category of speculative fiction, which encompasses fantasy, horror, science fiction and other genres that depart from the commonly accepted version of reality (Irwin 4; Wagar 9). It is also worth noting that most of the works under analysis in this book are drawn from the Young Adult (commonly known as YA) and children's markets. This reflects the contemporary context of the popularity of the paranormal for YA and children, but we have not adhered rigidly to divisions along the lines of publishers' marketing categories for age-based markets. Instead, we recognize that adults will read and watch works promoted to adolescent and child groups, just as younger readers will consume texts from the adult markets. Our book therefore includes discussion of texts marketed to different ages.

There are new shapeshifting texts appearing monthly in publishing and other entertainment media. We do not attempt to analyze or even mention every shapeshifting text here: instead, we have chosen to focus on a smaller number of texts to read more closely. These naturally reflect our own interests as well as the limitations of writing about a genre that is ever expanding and changing—shifting shape, even. Moreover, some of the texts we discuss are themselves changing shape as they add new novels or seasons to what has already been released, and so our analysis is limited to those texts available at the time of writing in late 2011.

We have chosen to break up our exploration of this area by paying attention to several key readings: adolescence, gender, sexuality, race, disability and difference, addictive behaviors, and spirituality. Most of these sections cross over, inevitably, but each contributes another dimension to our overall argument.

In Chapter One, we analyze a number of shapeshifting texts that feature teenage protagonists facing adolescence. As Du Coudray argues, "the transforming werewolf body can also be understood (and is often presented as) an analogy for adolescent sexuality" (*Curse of the Werewolf* 84). Texts such as Stephenie Meyer's *Twilight* series (and its film adaptations), Maggie Stiefvater's *The Wolves of Mercy Falls* novel series, Ellen Schreiber's *Once in a Full Moon*, Ivy Devlin's *Low Red Moon* and Heather Davis's *Never Cry Werewolf*, deal largely with adolescent romance. Others focus more specifically on the onset of puberty, such as Jenny Hale's *Jatta* and Philip Pullman's *His Dark Materials* series. Some seem to straddle both, with supernaturally-induced identity crises mirroring family secrets and family dysfunction and impacting on other relationships, including romantic ones, as in *The Cure for Death by Lightning* by Gail Anderson-Dargatz, Jackson Pearce's *Sisters Red*, the *Lonely Werewolf Girl* and *Curse of the Wolf Girl* novels by Martin Millar, L. J. Smith's *The Vampire Diaries* novels and the television adaptation. A common theme throughout all, however, is the use of the metaphor of the werewolf for the adolescent's sense of feeling isolated.

This chapter has been located first not only to recognize that a significant number of these shapeshifting texts have teenage protagonists and are marketed to a YA audience, but also because adolescence is a period of transition when an individual's sense of self is established. This stage of life, then, informs ideas about the other areas of study examined.

In Chapter Two we explore works such as Jackson Pearce's *Sisters Red* and Jennifer Lynn Barnes's *Raised by Wolves*, which deal with gender by attempting to subvert traditional gender roles. Female protagonists are situated in terms of equality and empowerment, although mixed results are achieved in this endeavor. Although we might expect shapeshifters to move outside gender roles more easily than human characters, this is not always the case. The complexities of gender roles are also evident in the preponderance of male shapeshifters throughout many texts, such as *Twilight*, *Teen Wolf*, and *The Vampire Diaries*, and the dominant positions males hold within them. In many of these narratives, supernatural males are partnered with mortal females and their relationships follow the conventions of the romance genre. These characters reflect a more general shift within the genre to show a range of representations of women.

From Buffy Summers to Sookie Stackhouse, and Bella Swan to Scarlett March, these characters try to determine their own roles as not only partners, but also as waitresses, students and slayers, to name just a few. Within the genre, these women are defined by and challenged by their unusual relationships. This necessitates an examination of representations of desire and sexuality in Chapter Three. There is a long history linking vampirism with overt sexuality, from Bram Stoker's *Dracula* through to contemporary representations such as *True Blood*. Werewolves have also been linked to animal desires, but have received rather less critical attention. In keeping with modern representations of shapeshifting as a way of representing the Other, a small number of recent texts that promote unconventional romances between mortal humans and their supernatural partners have also moved beyond purely heteronormative representations of sexuality and desire. Non-heteronormative sexual relationships have become rather common in narratives such as *True Blood*, which are aimed at adult audiences, but adolescent texts seem to be almost exclusively heteronormative. Interestingly, shapeshifters (usually emblematic of identity fluidity) seem to be restricted to one gender and male/female pairings, and usually long term, committed ones at that.

This chapter explores these issues as represented in Philip Pullman's *His Dark Materials*, *True Blood* and Harris's Sookie Stackhouse novels, the 2011 film *Red Riding Hood*, *Buffy, the Vampire Slayer*, the werewolf "chick lit"—or should that be "vixen lit"?—novels Kathy Love's *My Sister Is a Werewolf* and Karen MacInerney's *Tales of an Urban Werewolf* series, and Amelia Atwater-Rhodes's *Wolfcry* from the *Shapeshifters: The Kiesha'ra of the Den of Shadows* series.

Texts that deal with romantic pairings, especially when the characters are avowing life-long partnerships, often implicitly deal with the perceived "suitability" of the match. Thus shapeshifting figures in contemporary texts often have clear links to race and class, where werewolves and vampires may represent different social groups or be constructed as "races." These are explored in Chapter Four. Such depictions seem to promote a negative model of society that reinforces rigid divisions between racial groups, and these representations warrant scholarly attention to unravel the issues at work in these texts. In Stephenie Meyer's *Twilight*, for example, the werewolves are from the Native American Quileute tribe with inherited shapeshifting abilities, while the vampires are almost all white characters. Larissa Lai's *When Fox Is a Thousand* also deals explicitly with race issues, and in particular, uses the shapeshifting fox as a vehicle for exploring the fusion of cultural traditions that is a function of the migrant experience. Similarly, Amelia Atwater-Rhodes's *Shapeshifters* collection, *The Vampire Diaries* and *True Blood* draw on ideas of race and class to delineate between shapeshifting groups. Texts such as these can also draw on the positive connotations of shapeshifting, by allowing shapeshifters to elude traditional boundaries and markers of identity and limitation.

Shapeshifting figures have also been deployed to represent difference in some works, often in werewolf tales, and more specifically to represent disability and illness. In Chapter Five, we examine popular texts where shapeshifting characters are linked to disability, illness, mental health disorders, exclusion and isolation. For instance, J. K. Rowling has said that her werewolf character Remus Lupin represents disability and AIDS in *Harry Potter*, while Jenny Hale writes that her werewolf protagonist in *Jatta* is a metaphor for disability and illness. Television programs *Being Human* and *The Vampire Diaries* have focused specifically on the physicality and pain of transformation. It is important to analyze these metaphors because of implications of conceptualizing disability and illness as monstrous. Moreover, the genre's tendency to glamorize shapeshifters and their bodies in many cases can undermine these intentions. Yet we explore in Chapter Five if the shapeshifting trope may also effectively challenge perceptions of identity and difference and provide parallels for understanding the experience of disability, illness, and mental health disorders.

All of these chapters deal with social categories of difference. The final two chapters of this volume explore some of the strategies employed in order to cope with these differences.

In Chapter Six, we discuss how masking strategies and the ability to "pass" as human have long been part of monster narratives. Characters such as Rowling's Lupin and the British *Being Human*'s George go to extraordinary lengths to mask their lycanthrope identities and protect the humans around them when they change once a month. Others, however, self-medicate, such as the werewolf cousins Kalix and Dominil in Martin Millar's *Lonely Werewolf Girl* and also *Curse of the Wolf Girl*, who are both laudanum users in order to cope with their complicated double lives. A variation on this theme is explored in television's *The Vampire Diaries*, where Stefan chooses to drink animal blood because he is a problem drinker on "the human stuff"; ironically, in the novels on which the program is based the ability to shapeshift is directly related to the amount of human blood consumed and Stefan's non-human diet precludes him from this ability. Thus his addiction is constructed as a limitation that must be managed, in much the same way as alcoholics need to continually monitor their own recovery. *True Blood* also configures blood as an addictive substance, and explores the idea of werewolves fueled by vampire blood, creating arguably the greatest control issues in popular culture since *The Hulk*.

The final chapter ponders the philosophical questions inherent in the eternal — or at least extended — life of shapeshifters and vampires. In an increasingly secular society, can one believe in a higher power when "cursed" to eschew the human soul and embrace the animalistic once a month? What impact do crucifixes and holy water have on vampires? Is salvation an option when the individual is genetically constructed to hunt and kill? We also examine the brief moments when non–Christian belief systems are presented in these texts, and the ways in which they are constructed. Many supernatural texts blend Christian and other elements such as paganism and the occult in a hybrid approach to spirituality. Yet the fantasy genre can provide an effective template for engaging with questions about life and death, and shapeshifting itself offers parallels with religious belief.

In short, the figure of the shapeshifter is employed in a variety of metaphorical ways to explore multi-faceted issues of identity. This book spans the fields of film, television, and literature, and engages with literary theory, gender, sexuality, fantasy, postcolonialism, ethnicity, disability, mental health, and spirituality, reflecting the diverse ways in which the trope of the shapeshifter is employed in contemporary popular fiction.

We hope that *Werewolves and Other Shapeshifters in Popular Fiction* begins to shift thinking away from the model where shapeshifters are the poor cousins within the family of supernatural beings; somehow less interesting, less desirable and less worthy of critical attention than the undead within their cohort.

One

Dear Diary, I Become a Monster Once a Month: Shapeshifting and Adolescence

> SCOTT: *It's complicated.*
> COACH: *Oh, those kind of problems. What is it? Drugs, girls? ...*
> SCOTT: *How can I put this? I'm going through changes.*
> COACH: *Oh, that. Don't worry about that. We all go through that.*
> — *Teen Wolf,* 1985

A significant number of shapeshifting texts feature teenage protagonists facing adolescence. Some, including Jackson Pearce's *Sisters Red*, Catherine Jinks's *The Abused Werewolf Rescue Group*, the *Teen Wolf* franchise and Philip Pullman's *His Dark Materials* trilogy, use adolescence as part of their mythology, suggesting that hormonal changes are what triggers (or, in the case of Pullman's works, stops) the ability to shift. Other texts focus on teenage romance where one party has the ability to shift shape, such as *The Vampire Diaries* by L. J. Smith and its television adaptation by the CW Network, Stephenie Meyer's *Twilight* series and its filmic adaptations, Ivy Devlin's *Low Red Moon*, Ellen Schreiber's *Once in a Full Moon*, and Heather Davis's *Never Cry Werewolf*. These then examine the implications of teenage angst and body dysmorphia of the supernatural kind on their romances. Maggie Stiefvater's *The Wolves of Mercy Falls* series develops this idea further, with both of the protagonists being able to shift, albeit at different times in their relationship. Martin Millar's *Lonely Werewolf Girl* and *Curse of the Wolf Girl* explore the motifs of abnormality and isolation from family through shapeshifting characters. Gail Anderson-Dargatz's *The Cure for Death by Lightning*, however, approaches a similar theme from a different angle, strongly suggesting that shapeshifting characters are drawn to vulnerable adolescents whose family lives are dysfunctional; that mutable characters are inexorably drawn to those most in need of change. In all of these texts, the isolation of adolescence and fear of bodily changes beyond the control of the individual are central concerns.

A subsection of the werewolf genre within YA literature presupposes that adolescence is a trigger or symptom of the ability to shift shape. This is a very visceral interpretation of the representation of adolescence as a time of turbulence. In some narratives, the teenagers' own bodies are fighting against them violently, in addition to the more obvious suggestions of hair growing where it previously did not and pubescent bodies changing shape. A number of contemporary texts explore the ability to shift into werewolf shape in terms of genetics, including *The Vampire Diaries, Sisters Red, The Abused Werewolf Rescue Group* and *Twilight*. All of these texts overlay extra trigger factors including race, family ordinance and the taking of a human life, to explain the apparent paucity of werewolves in the world.

Identity Formation

It is perhaps no surprise that vampires, werewolves and other supernatural creatures have become a focus of YA literature, television and film, since adolescence is itself something of a liminal space. Bennett and Royle refer to the uncanny as being a "sense of unfamiliarity at the very heart of the familiar, or else a sense of familiarity which appears at the very heart of the unfamiliar" (Bennett and Royle 34), a definition that can assuredly be applied to the significant psychological and physical changes associated with puberty. The figures of the shapeshifter in general, and the werewolf in particular, have been used as a metaphor for adolescence in popular television and film since the 1957 movie *I Was a Teenage Werewolf*, through the *Teen Wolf* movies of the 1980s, in a number of episodes of *Buffy, the Vampire Slayer* in the 1990s and beyond, to the recent spate of television series and movies featuring the supernatural, including *The Vampire Diaries, Twilight* and the current MTV remake of *Teen Wolf*. As Pappademas argues, "the teenage-monster movie works with more evergreen subtextual materials, making metaphorical the weirdness of adolescence — of waking up one morning with uncontrollable urges, new and troubling growth, and a sense that the world hates and fears you" (36). Chappell concurs, citing Northrop Frye's view that all literature is about the "loss and regaining of identity" (Frye 55), and noting that adolescence is often constructed as "the site of a major reconstruction of identity" (Chappell, *Werewolves* 119). These metaphors are also explored in a number of novels, television programs and films which include shapeshifting teens. The fantastic, the uncanny and adolescence intersect in a number of adolescent shapeshifter narratives, some of which will be examined in detail in this chapter.

Rosemary Jackson in her seminal text on fantasy noted that the genre is "free from many of the conventions and restraints of more realistic texts ... doing away with chronology, three dimensionality, and with rigid distinctions between animate and inanimate objects, self and other, life and death" (12), which presents some appeal to those in the throes of delineating their senses of self-identity. Further, the teenage years are often a period of rebellion and because fantasy requires the willing suspension of disbelief, the genre is arguably well suited to readers who may be resisting or rejecting the imminent responsibilities of adulthood. The teen vampire and werewolf genres allow for distinctions between self and other, and life and death, to be framed against distinctions between childhood and adult responsibilities.

Identity is often predicated on the notion of a single, coherent and essential self (Chappell, *Werewolves* 119). It may, however, involve a number of components of selfhood (Chappell, *Werewolves* 120). Teens, in particular, often attempt to locate themselves in terms of social groups to which they belong, in order to find ways to express their identities. Because adolescence is typically a time of radical physical, cognitive and social changes, it is often viewed as a time of metamorphosis (Chappell, *Werewolves* 122); a time when the childhood self becomes the Other, when decisions are made as to what kind of adult an individual will become. Some narratives construct this period as one of transition, as per the classic *Bildungsroman;* others construct it as a period of transformation. In either case, the metaphor of linking one version of self to an alternative version via shapeshifting is clearly a useful one for many authors.

As with any adolescent fiction or popular culture, "the action in a YA is in the turbulent psyche of the adolescent, with all the limitations of understanding and experience that implies" (Sutton 111). A number of the texts examined in this chapter, including *The Abused Werewolf Rescue Group, Once in a Full Moon, Sisters Red, Twilight, Shiver, Linger, Forever* and *The Vampire Diaries,* involve teenaged characters investigating unusual situations until they are able to move beyond the limitations of their knowledge and discover the truth about the supernatural. The characters also have limited agency as a result of their youth, having their actions and opinions mediated by the adult caregivers in their lives, with the exceptions of the orphaned characters in *Sisters Red* and *The Vampire Diaries.* At a time when teenagers in general have more agency and disposable income than ever before, and when adolescent fiction is now outselling mainstream fiction by a large margin (Sutton 113), it is perhaps ironic that this demographic is still being represented as disenfranchised.

Family Conflict and the Shapeshifting Teen

L. J. Smith's original four *The Vampire Diaries* novels (*The Awakening, The Struggle, The Fury* and *Dark Reunion*) were published in 1991 and focus on vampire brothers Stefan and Damon Salvatore. The brothers are configured as foils to each other who are eternally involved in two very similar love triangles. They first became estranged over their romantic involvement with the same woman — the vampire Katherine, who "turned" them both, and, later, by her descendant and look-alike, Elena (both played by Nina Dobrev in the television series of the same name). The "good" brother Stefan is marked by his refusal to drink human blood. The parallels between another "vegetarian" vampire who is besotted with a mortal teen seem obvious, although Smith, who claims not to have read *Twilight,* notes that her lengthy hiatus from writing coincided with her mother's long and ultimately terminal illness. Thus she argues that the timing of the *Return* trilogy of *The Vampire Diaries* books (*Nightfall* in 2009; *Shadow Souls* in 2010 and *Midnight* in 2010) is coincidental (Peterson), and not a reaction to the extraordinary popularity of the *Twilight* saga. (A third trilogy, *The Hunters*, is currently being published, but as of February 2011, L. J. Smith is no longer authoring the novels.) There is no such ambivalence about the origins of the television series of the same name, however, produced by Kevin Williamson and Julie Plec. In 2009 the CW Network picked up the series, which it had optioned some years previously, with a view to "filling the void between abstinence and orgies" (Calhoun 12) of *Twilight* and *True Blood*, respectively. In its third season at the time of writing, it has an ensemble cast of teens and young adults playing characters who are predominantly adolescents, but who are also vampires, witches, werewolves, and even *Doppelgängers*.

In the world of *The Vampire Diaries* novels, shapeshifters are figures to be mistrusted. Malevolent *kitsune* fox spirits cause trouble and carnage; a werewolf is an aggressive would-be rapist; and the "frenemy" character of Caroline Forbes is able to adapt her body into strange, insect-like configurations, yet retain her human facial features. There are significant changes to be found in the television adaptation of the show. In Kevin Williamson and Julie Plec's version of the story, Caroline is not a shapeshifter, but a neurotic member of one of the town's founding families, who is turned into a vampire as part of the cliffhanger between Seasons One and Two. In the first season Caroline is set up as the "mean girl" foil to Elena; she is vapid, pretty and often insensitive.

Unlike the self-confessed "gloomy graveyard girl" Elena (1.01), Caroline has a mother who is "very much alive, only occasionally present, and continually bewildered by and disappointed in her socialite of a daughter" (Barnes,

"Sweet Caroline" 151). Caroline is terrified of turning into her mother; after having her romantic overtures rejected by Stefan, she laments that she is never the chosen one. She fears that she will remain forever on the outer, watching as Elena gets the boys, the tiaras and the accolades. The girls' competition for Miss Mystic Falls becomes emblematic of their relationships with their mothers; Caroline is determined to win because her mother is the only female in the family not to have won it, and she wants to avoid that kind of ignominy; Elena is disinterested, as her now-deceased mother had entered her so that they could bond over the campaign. As Jennifer Lynn Barnes argues in her essay, "Sweet Caroline," "Caroline's relationship with her mother marks her as the 'normal' teen on the show, the one who struggles with hating and loving, disappointing and being disappointed by her mom. These conflicting desires — promising herself she won't turn into her mother while secretly wishing her mom would be proud of the person she is — are quintessentially teen" (153). It is because she is quintessentially teen, of course, that Caroline can be rude and brutal to her mother, cruelly rebuffing a rare overture with: "If I want to talk boys, I'll call Dad. At least he's successfully dating one" (1.05). Ironically, when she joins the undead the permanently-adolescent Caroline becomes more appreciative of her life. Her status as vampire, however, creates an even greater chasm with her mother, who is the town's chief vampire hunter and a member of the anti-vampire Founders' Council. Caroline's vampirism marks her as eternally different from her family and its traditions. It also means that her character has itself effectively shifted in the adaptation process from page to screen.

Caroline is closely aligned with Tyler Lockwood (known as Tyler Smallwood in the books) in both versions of *The Vampire Diaries* narrative. By the end of Season Two of the television series, Tyler has admitted to having feelings for his close friend Caroline, and each has confided in the other about their difficulties in adapting to their new identities as werewolf and vampire, respectively. In the world of Smith's novels, Caroline is one of a number of teenage girls in the township of Fell's Church who has been negatively impacted by the excesses of supernatural power drawn to the area by a convergence of ley lines. Caroline plays host to a Japanese shapeshifting fox spirit or *kitsune*, Masao. Masao and her twin Shinichi are tricksters with a penchant for sexual depravity and a keen interest in adolescents as vessels for their tricks. In *Nightfall* from the *Return* trilogy of *The Vampire Diaries*, teenagers Caroline, Kristen Dunstan, Isobel Saito and Tami Bryce all begin to behave provocatively and the latter two also engage in self-harming activities. Adolescent sexuality in the novels is constructed as deviant and a sign of evil at work; Caroline goes so far as to seduce Jim Bryce, Tami's older brother, and then taunt Isobel, his girlfriend, with that knowledge (285). The virginal Isobel's reaction to the news is noticeably out of character; she is described as looking "like some distorted goddess of piercing.... She was wearing only a pair of very brief bikini bottoms. Otherwise she was naked except for the blood and the different kinds of hoops and studs and needles she had put through the holes" (*Nightfall* 293). Similarly, Tami Bryce creates for herself an outfit that is described as being "close to nothing" (*Nightfall* 258).

> She had on a thong bikini bottom, but it looked handmade, as if she'd cut a regular bikini bottom with scissors — and it was beginning to come apart. On top she had two round decorations made of cardboard with sequins pasted on and a few strands of colored tinsel. On her head she wore a paper crown, which was clearly where she'd gotten the tinsel. She'd made an attempt to glue strands onto the bikini bottoms as well. The result looked like what it was: a child's attempt to make an outfit for a Las Vegas showgirl or stripper ... Tami was trying to be wicked [*Nightfall* 259–60].

This "wicked" outfit is later mimicked by thirteen-year-old Kristen Dunstan, who cuts "two big round holes just where Tami had had round pieces of cardboard" (*Nightfall* 401), a sight from which Elena's ex-boyfriend, Matt Honeycutt, feels compelled to turn away. Caroline and Tami both proposition Matt, much to his discomfort; he tells Elena that Tami is "only fifteen, but she acted like an adult woman" (*Nightfall* 191).

Throughout the novels, Matt is steadfast, loyal and "good-looking ... in a healthy American way" (*The Awakening* 37) and when asked to choose a colored candle which represents him, the suggested options are white for purity, or "American-flag patterned" (*Phantom* 326). As such, he is the established foil to Elena's vampire suitors. He is used to represent human decency, so his abhorrence of the adolescent girls' sexual assertiveness reinforces the novel's message that their behavior is unnatural and caused by spiritual possession. This is somewhat anomalous in the YA paranormal romances we have examined, which typically make some attempt to acknowledge the sexual desires of the characters, as will be discussed in more detail in Chapter Three. Here, the idea that adolescent females have agency in sexual experimentation is repeatedly rejected, with the point being made (albeit rather unexpectedly, in Book Six) that Elena saves herself for Stefan (*Shadow Souls* 130). Despite most of the school believing that her popularity with boys implies that there is truth to her reputation — one schoolmate even refers to her as a "whore" (*Shadow Souls* 140; *Nightfall* 260) — Elena never publicly refutes these accusations. Elena is upheld as a figure of purity, however, in stark contrast to Caroline; a dynamic which is echoed in the television series where Caroline blithely tells Elena to make a move on Stefan: "It's simple. Girl meets boy, girl likes boy, girl and boy have sex" (1.02). Interestingly, while Caroline follows this philosophy in her brief (and abusive) relationship with bad boy vampire Damon

Salvatore, she is more reticent in her potential romances with Matt and later Tyler. When the stakes are high, it seems, things are somewhat less simple.

The most (in)famous YA fantasy romance in recent years has been Stephenie Meyer's *Twilight* saga. This text is part of a subset of YA fantasy literature that focuses on mortal teenagers becoming romantically involved with supernatural characters. The marketing of YA fiction is intrinsically linked to the romance genre, for, as Bereska argues, YA literature was not profit-making until the introduction of adolescent series romance novels in the 1980s (Bereska 36). Bereska further notes that this trend was short-lived, as adolescent readers turned away from chaste romance, in favor of those which included sexuality as a component. In light of increased sexual activity in teenagers since the introduction of reliable contraception a generation previously, the denial of sexuality in these novels was effectively a denial of reality for many young readers. Distinct moral and ethical dilemmas arise from living in a sexualized society and hence narratives that failed to address these specific issues typically had shorter print runs (Bereska 40). Meyer's *Twilight* saga, despite the paranormal themes, discusses teenage sexuality but does so from a somewhat conservative framework. Protagonist Bella Swan, despite her acknowledged sexual desires for her boyfriend Edward Cullen, is a virgin on her wedding night.

In the second novel of the series, *New Moon*, Edward leaves Bella, and in his absence, she develops her relationship with her young Quileute friend Jacob Black. Bella is aware of Jacob's attraction to her, and at times admits that he could offer her a more conventional life than Edward. With Edward, she (incorrectly) assumes that she cannot become a parent. She also recognizes that being together in any practical sense requires her mortal death, which will in turn mean hiding her vampire nature from her friends and parents. Jacob, on the other hand, presents no such problems and indeed, a closer allegiance between the Black and Swan families would presumably be welcomed by their respective fathers. Yet, he, too, represents an omnipresent danger of physical violence because of his shapeshifting nature — as the scars on the face of Alpha wolf Sam's partner Emily attest, the wolf within can be unpredictable and savage.

Jacob is initially resistant to becoming like the other pack members, but once he understands that their apparent personality changes are due to their maturation into werewolves, he embraces the 'coolness' of his heritage. Jacob goes from referring to Sam Uley and his friends as being "like hall monitors gone bad" (*New Moon* 152) to cropping his hair to match theirs, and spending all his time with them and avoiding Bella. His genetic transformation, too, is triggered by puberty. In addition to the usual changes of additional height and bulk — Bella claims to feel like "a child hugging a grown-up" (*New Moon* 157) when she next sees him — she notes that the planes of his face seemed to have hardened subtly, tightened ... aged. His neck and shoulders were different, too, thicker somehow ... [but] It was his expression that made him almost completely unrecognizable. The open, friendly smile was gone like the hair, the warmth in his dark eyes altered to a brooding resentment that was instantly disturbing. There was a darkness in Jacob now [*New Moon* 231].

The loss of Jacob's childhood innocence thus coincides with his becoming a werewolf, and is represented through the physical changes to his body. There are less obvious changes as well, however; Jacob begins to live under a pack mentality, incapable of resisting an order from his Alpha, Sam, while he is a member. Jacob's resentment of the impact of his family legacy on his own free will is emblematic of complex family expectations and their influence on decision-making processes, which are a cornerstone of YA fiction.

Isolation, Dysfunction, and Vulnerability

Michael Millar's *Lonely Werewolf Girl* and *Curse of the Wolf Girl* are novels that focus on the feelings of isolation and dislocation experienced by its teenage protagonist, Kalix MacRinnalch, and, as in Heather Davis's *Never Cry Werewolf*, these are presented as arising from complex family dynamics. The texts are among the few British iterations of the shapeshifter in recent years, and much is made of Kalix's Scottish heritage and accent, and how these mark her as different when she seeks refuge in inner-city London. Kalix is a character who has been marked by difference from birth, however. The child of the Thane and his Queen was born on the night of the full moon when both she and her mother were in werewolf shape. This marks Kalix as unusual, and she is isolated from her much-older siblings throughout her childhood. The reader is told that Kalix shows unusual levels of passion, and that while her nature frees her from some traditional constraints — for example, she is less affected by lunar eclipses than her relatives (*Curse of the Wolf* 472) — her difference is, for the most part, a limiting factor. Kalix suffers from a form of "battle madness" when cornered, and her passionate love affair with a werewolf who is less than full-blooded earns her the rancor of her father; her revenge on the Thane leads to his death and her exile while still only in her mid-teens.

Kalix begins a new life in London after meeting Daniel and Moonglow, two unmotivated but kind-hearted college students, who take her in. Kalix is illiterate and her new flatmates find ways to motivate her to learn, offering her food both rare and raw, shelter, and access to educational computer programs and her new favorite television program, *Sabrina, the Teenage Witch*.

In the second novel, *Curse of the Wolf Girl*, Kalix moves in with the other two more permanently, so that she may attend a college which will improve her literacy and numeracy.

Kalix's cousin Dominil has also spent extensive periods of time in London, and is also marked by difference. She is the only MacRinnalch werewolf to have white fur (and platinum locks, when in human form). Constructed as a foil to Kalix, Dominil is as pragmatic as Kalix is impetuous. Late in the second novel it is revealed that the then-adolescent Dominil had been the only family member to show any affection to the young Kalix, reading her traditional werewolf fairy tales. The two cousins, both outcasts within the family, also share an addiction to laudanum. Their use of the narcotic in order to mask their difference will be examined in further detail in Chapter Six.

In Gail Anderson-Dargatz's 1997 Canadian novel *The Cure for Death by Lightning*, the adolescent narrator, Beth Weeks, is a displaced and uncanny figure. Beth lacks the ability to metamorphose herself, but her isolation and dislocation make her attractive to those who can, specifically, the Indigenous trickster spirit, Coyote. Beth is inexorably drawn into the bush near her home, despite dire warnings from all around her and her own experiences the previous summer, when she and her father were attacked by a bear. From this moment, the relationship between Beth and her father changes into something more sinister, with local Native Canadian matriarch Bertha Moses noting that John Weeks "didn't turn until that bear attacked…. Something got him in the bush" (Anderson-Dargatz 15). Beth is also hit by lightning when in the bush, and periodically loses power in her arm after this event. Whilst her wayward arm appears to do the bidding of her inner psyche—protecting her from harm, such as when it slaps her father across the face during one of his attempts to sexually assault her—the novel also presents the possibility that the arm is being controlled by supernatural means, the theory to which Beth herself subscribes. Beth's acceptance of the trickster Coyote, spirits, possession and haunting fit Australian critic Mudrooroo's definition of maban reality as being "characterized by a firm grounding in the reality of the earth or country, together with an acceptance of the supernatural as part of everyday reality" (98). Maban reality is a specific sub-genre wherein the fantastic is intrinsically linked with space and place.

Beth, as an adolescent, is a site of instability and of passion, and it appears to be this, as well as their shared quest to establish a safe "home," which excites and attracts the capricious trickster, Coyote. Coyote, we are told, partners for life but ultimately kills these wives. The desire to have or inhabit Beth is demonstrated by a series of characters: a schoolmate, Robert Parker, who leads a pack sexual assault on her; the bachelor Fowler from the town who offers to pay for her "company"; local hermit Coyote Jack, an embodiment of Coyote's spirit; local Indian cousins Dennis, Billy, and Nora; and most disturbingly of all, her own father. Even young Goat, a developmentally delayed boy who is figured as the stereotypical "village idiot," seems drawn to her (51–52). Goldman notes that *The Cure for Death by Lightning* is only one text in a long history of Canadian literature that features haunting and possession to examine "desires society deems unnamable, unacceptable, and unspoken" (Goldman 15). The maban realist world view explains Beth's heightened desirability as her being the result of Coyote's focus. The teenage Beth is living through a "time of turbulence, or 'storm and stress,'" which Violato and Wiley identify as the unchanging and defining representation of adolescence throughout literature in English (Violato and Wiley 254). Beth faces a series of confronting and damaging situations as she develops her adult identity and considers both the sexual and spiritual possibilities open to her. She is surrounded by dysfunction and depravity, and is sexually assaulted by her schoolmates and later her father. The attentions of Coyote scare her, but arguably the maban reality of accepting Coyote is, at times, preferable to her everyday experiences even though this will apparently lead to her doom. The text invites us to read her teenage sexual experimentation through the lens of Coyote possession. Beth has two main suitors throughout the novel, Nora and Billy, both of whom are grandchildren of local Indigenous matriarch Bertha Moses. Nora and Billy are also both closely linked with the figure of the shapeshifter, Coyote.

Coyote is traditionally a trickster figure, a shapeshifter who is neither good nor evil, and whose actions may be positive or detrimental, who is without a fixed gender or sexuality. Goldman notes that Coyote often "embodies, for the settler-invader society, the uncanny, aboriginal claim to the land" (Goldman 17). When Coyote is stalking Beth, Billy often appears, although it is initially unclear to the reader if he is protecting Beth from Coyote, or assisting Coyote in his quest to possess her. Beth, however, is accepting of Bertha's explanation that Billy, like his late father Henry Moses before him, sacrifices himself to protect others from Coyote. She further accepts Billy's repeated assertions that he is Coyote's "house," perhaps the ultimate symbol of home as the uncanny.

Nora is increasingly aligned with Coyote (Goldman 24), appearing and disappearing from the text, phantom-like. She even explicitly warns Beth about Coyote, saying: "Remember he's a shape-shifter. Takes any form he wants" (Anderson-Dargatz 259) before kissing her, only to have a Coyote appear in the entrance to the winter house above them. Nora then runs off, and Beth finds, a few minutes later, the body of a ewe, newly killed by a coyote (Anderson-Dargatz 260). The next day, Nora disappears out Beth's bedroom window, only to be replaced moments later by the spectral and threatening figure of

Coyote Jack, whom Beth has recently witnessed shifting shape between coyote and man, holding up his "hand in a wave or a threat" (Anderson-Dargatz 273).

Nora, who indulges in self-harm through the act of cutting, is last seen on Blood Road, her wounds bleeding into the snow on the road. With Beth's father in an insane asylum after setting fire to his neighbor's property, the most immediate threat to Beth's safety and well being is eliminated. Nora again asks Beth to join her in Vancouver, but Beth refuses, insisting that she must stay, with the uncanny argument: "'It's home ... I don't know anything else'" (Anderson-Dargatz 283). This is all the more troubling if we accept Sophie Levy's assertion that "the subaltern text makes a home for itself both inside and outside the dominant culture, using its liminality as a safe space. This becomes especially relevant for postcolonial and immigrant fictions that narrate incest. The home, these fictions demonstrate, is no longer a safe space" (864). Beth remains in her own "home," only to recall the vision of Nora's disappearance in the closing pages of the novel. Goldman argues that this is an image of Native resistance, with Beth watching a mixed-race girl leave, "chased by a trail of blood, the text juxtapos[ing] stasis with movement, the settled with the unsettled" (Goldman 33).

Nora is only one of three of Bertha Moses' grandchildren with whom Beth develops flirtatious relationships, however. Beth shares one passionate kiss in the barn with Dennis, employed by her father as a farmhand. She claims to have "planned ... [it] out in my daydreams that took over my nights. The surprise was that pleasure could push so far past fear as to make me reckless" (Anderson-Dargatz 208). Predictably, her father discovers them and is furious. In contrast, when her relationship with his cousin Billy develops, it does so through companionship and is marked by chaste hand-holding. In the face of extreme chaos, having fought a fire on the family property and heard a gunshot shortly after John Weeks went to confront his neighbor, the pair sits alone in the kitchen, ignoring the sirens and soot, "like an old couple past the clumsiness of romance, me rocking, him with his feet warming on the stove" (221). The novel closes with Beth and Billy holding hands in the middle of Blood Road, arguably an image of reconciliation and of moving forward, as her newly-reunited parents, facing the other way to represent the colonial past, also hold hands.

Throughout the novel, the reader is placed in an uncanny reading space, where supernatural events are portrayed as commonplace. Anderson-Dargatz positions the teenage narrator as a site of possibilities, struggling to find her place, sexuality and spirituality in a time and a region populated by shape-shifting tricksters. It is not only a novel about tricksters, but also a text that is uncanny in its very nature: a novel by a white Canadian who uses Native mythology as a central concern; a novel with some counter-feminist features but which is a female-centered text wherein female power is affirmed.

Nature or Nurture: Biology and Individual Choice

Conflicts between family expectations, biology and free will abound in these shapeshifting texts. Many use the metaphor of the werewolf to examine these conundrums within the adolescent identity-forming process. *Twilight*'s Jacob Black is initially resentful of his werewolf heritage, feeling that he doesn't have a choice in his identity, or later, the ability to make decisions unless they are sanctioned by his Alpha. Ultimately he chooses to begin his own pack in order to have some kind of autonomy. The notion of predetermination is further explored in *The Vampire Diaries*, where Tyler is from one of the town's founding families, a teenager whose father holds influence within the town, and a member of the school football team. In both iterations of the narrative, he is at times inappropriately aggressive, attempting to rape protagonist Elena Gilbert in the novels (Smith, *The Awakening*), and becoming involved in fights in the first season of the television series. This aggression is explicitly linked to his lycanthropic nature, even though there is an interesting nurture — or lack thereof — aspect clearly evident, at least in the television series; Tyler is very much the product of his father's own aggressive and often inappropriate Alpha-male tendencies.

In the Season One finale, Tyler and his father, Mayor Richard Lockwood, are both unexpectedly affected by a high-pitched noise which is inaudible to humans. Richard Lockwood is rounded up and killed as part of the vampire hunt, leaving Tyler in a single-parent family, but arguably much safer than he had been with his physically violent father living under the same roof. His hitherto absent paternal Uncle Mason returns to Mystic Falls after Richard's death, explains the Lockwood curse and unsuccessfully tries to help Tyler avoid triggering it. After Mason's untimely death for conspiring with the vampire Katherine, Tyler joins a pack of werewolves and finds his allegiances are torn between his new family and his old friends (most of whom are either vampires or aligned with them by Season Two). Tyler eventually decides that his family and friends are at risk if he stays, and so he leaves town with pack-member Jules, who had been a friend of Mason's and thus represents another connection to the Lockwood family.

Tyler's character embodies — quite literally — teenage concerns about physical and psychological changes as he tries to negotiate what it means to be a man. Similar issues are explored in Catherine Jinks's *The Abused Werewolf Rescue Group*, which follows the *Bildungsroman* model in that the teenaged protagonist undertakes a journey of maturation during a series of events related to his discovery that he is a werewolf. In this instance, the formerly wild child protagonist Toby Vandevelde decides that he no longer wants to be involved in "crazy schemes," remarking with noticeable irony: "I don't want to run with the pack anymore" (378).

The novel opens with the first-person narrator being admitted to hospital after being discovered, naked and suffering from amnesia, in the dingo pen at Sydney's Featherdale Wildlife Park. As Silver recognizes,

> [a]dolescence is a transitional point between childhood and adulthood during which adolescents cope with the often uncomfortable transformations of their bodies and with events that typically occur for the first time in teen years, including first sexual experiences, exposure to alcohol and drugs, and the complex social world of high school [123].

When Toby is found in such an odd location under unexplained circumstances, the first response of those around him is that it is somehow indicative of normal teenage experimentation. His mother assumes that Toby has been experimenting with drugs or alcohol, suspicions that she retains for much of the novel. His mate, Fergus, however, asks Toby if he took a girl with him to the dingo pen, observing that "[s]ome people are really strange with sex" (41).

Following media coverage of the incident, Toby is contacted by a priest and a young man, Reuben, who claims to suffer from the same as-yet undefined "condition" as Toby. Reuben asks Toby if he displays symptoms which include quick reflexes, fast-growing hair, and being jittery, before declaring, "It's genetic. Hormonal," and asking, "You've got six brothers, right? Six older brothers?" (47). According to Jinks's narrative, the werewolf gene is present in seventh sons of Portuguese or Spanish mothers, and is activated when puberty is reached. Toby, who is adopted and therefore unaware of his complete family history, is unable to answer these questions about his identity. Over the course of the novel, however, he comes to accept that he is a werewolf, and develops a stronger friendship group with fellow werewolves Reuben and Sergio than with his previous friends from school, Armin and Fergus. Thus his identity is formed through his shapeshifting experiences and the bonding experience of group therapy with Reuben and Sergio. The genetic ability to shift shape is depicted in the novel as merely the impetus for events; after all, Toby, as an adoptee, has no family members who can offer advice about their own experiences with the condition; Sergio was living in a foster care situation at the time of his kidnap, because his biological family, who were unable to deal with his difference, had incarcerated him in a pizza oven (179). In Jinks's novel, individual choice about identity is very much privileged over biological imperatives.

The idea of a "seventh son" having mystical significance has its origins in folklore. Various Celtic traditions name the seventh son as being lucky or gifted, and the seventh son of a seventh son is often considered to have healing powers. Interestingly, in Bulgarian folklore, seventh sons are rumored to be fated to be vampires (Rickels 3). It is a motif that has been utilized in other key YA fantasy texts, notably in Susan Cooper's *The Dark Is Rising* sequence where protagonist Will Stanton is destined to be the last of the Old Ones who fight the Dark.

Jackson Pearce's *Sisters Red* also utilizes the seventh son motif from mythology as a means of explaining which adolescent boys are potential werewolves. In this instance, the "Potential" is called to the "Dark" in the form of a Fenris, or werewolf. The Potential is always the seventh son of a seventh son, and must be bitten during a particular moon phase after a birthday which is a multiple of seven. Wolf-hunter Silas Reynolds, like Toby Vandevelde, is unaware that he meets the criteria, and could become the very thing that he and his companions have been fighting. He believes himself to be a sixth son, not realizing that his young Uncle Jacob is actually his eldest brother, born prior to his parents' marriage. His father, a werewolf hunter of some skill, suffers from Alzheimer's disease and has thus been unable to warn his youngest child, who has recently turned twenty-one. Silas's adolescent period between the ages of fourteen and twenty had been spent fighting the werewolf threat with his neighbors, Scarlett and Rosie March, themselves survivors of a Fenris threat. As the trio piece together the clues as to the Potential's identity, it is revealed that the Marches were attacked because the wolves were seeking the then-fourteen year old Silas, with a view to turning him. The attack changed the girls' lives irrevocably; Scarlett was horrifically disfigured, the girls' guardian, their grandmother, was killed, and both girls left school to hone their werewolf-fighting skills. Fenris-baiting and hunting have dominated their lives ever since, as we discuss in Chapter Two.

There are a number of modern lupine characters in popular culture who resist the ability to shift shape. Only Silas goes so far as to request that he be killed, rather than allowed to transition from Potential into fully-fledged werewolf (333). Most earlier representations of the werewolf (such as the 1985 movie *Teen Wolf*) show the characters embracing the animalistic other side of him (or occasionally her) self.

Another Self

Philip Pullman's *His Dark Materials* trilogy explores the notion of the developing self through characters he calls daemons. In Pullman's parallel universes, souls are separate entities — usually of the opposite gender to their human counterparts — which take on numerous and mutable animal forms in childhood, often according to mood. Humans and their daemons share their feelings and do not require speech to communicate. In children, the physical manifestation of the still-shapeshifting daemon is generally an indicator of the state of their intrinsically linked psyches, but the ability to change shape is lost when each pair reaches adulthood. Initially the protagonist, Lyra Belacqua, and her daemon, Pantalaimon, both express their desire that his shape never "settle." They are dismissive of the advice from the Able Seaman that there are compensations for having a settled form, such as knowing what kind of person you are (*Northern Lights* 167–68). Throughout the novels, the traits of particular animals are used to offer insight into their associated adults, or the emotions of the children's shapeshifting daemons. Servants' daemons, for example, are often dogs (*Northern Lights* 5); the glamorous but malicious Mrs. Coulter, revealed to be Lyra's birth mother, has as her daemon an exotic but nasty gold-colored monkey; and kind-hearted aeronaut Lee Scoresby's constant companion is the equally battle-hardened and pragmatic hare, Hester, whom Lee thinks of as his "center" (*Subtle Knife* 269).

The trilogy of novels centers around a complex plot that highlights adolescence as an important liminal space between childhood innocence and adult responsibility; a time when daemons can change shape because identity is not yet fixed; and children cannot yet attract the mystical particles of "Dust" that are associated with original sin and adulthood. Sexual experimentation is used as one of the markers of moving towards adulthood and fixing one's identity, as seen in *Northern Lights* when adolescent Tony Makarios is taken away for intercision immediately after spending time in a linen closet with a girl (*Northern Lights* 252). In the final novel, *The Amber Spyglass*, when Will and Lyra spend time alone in a secluded area together after declaring their love for each other, they return "holding hands, talking together, heads close, oblivious to everything else.... The Dust pouring down from the stars had found a living home again, and these children-no-longer-children, saturated with love, were the cause of it all" (*Amber Spyglass* 421).

The following morning the pair sees their daemons in the form of black and white matching doves, or lovebirds (*Amber Spyglass* 432), and Lyra discovers soon afterwards that she has lost her power to read the alethiometer, which is powered by Dust (*Amber Spyglass* 438–39). Lyra recognizes that other things are changing, too, and asks her daemon when he is a red-gold, graceful pine marten: "You're not going to change a lot anymore, are you?" (*Amber Spyglass* 446), noting that she is happy with his preferred form. Will then touches Pan. The scene is highly sexualized, with Lyra feeling breathless with pleasure, and reciprocating by placing her hand in the silky warmth of Will's daemon ... she knew that Will was feeling exactly what she was.

And she knew, too, that neither daemon would change shape now, having felt a lover's hand on them. These were their shapes for life: they would want no other [*Amber Spyglass* 447].

As Squires notes, the settling of the daemons thus marks the protagonists' "ultimate transition to adulthood" (64).

Even though daemons are constructed as "souls" in some instances, they are closely linked to bodily pleasures and bodily taboos throughout the trilogy. In stark contrast to the mutually pleasurable touching of daemons in this scene, in other instances the touching of a daemon without permission is configured as akin to rape. In the unnatural space of Bolvangar, Lyra and Pan are threatened with intercision, and the horror of having someone else touch her daemon is, as Hines argues, reminiscent of child molestation (42). It is

[a]s if an alien hand had reached right inside where no hand had a right to be, and wrenched at something deep and precious.
She felt dizzy, sick, disgusted and limp with shock.
... Pan was shaking, nearly out of his mind with horror and disgust [*Northern Lights* 276].

Identity Formation in the Absence of Family

Adolescence is a time of establishing autonomy, and can thus include rebellion against or rejection of family. In many of these texts, however, young people are isolated from family in rather more extreme ways. Lyra Belacqua, for example, is an apparently orphaned girl who learns that her parents are alive but have abrogated their responsibility for her. This is an example of the common trait within the genre, where adolescents are often not raised in functional nuclear family units. The CW Network's *The Vampire Diaries* and the exceptionally popular *Twilight* movie series, in particular, foreground adolescent angst and romance against a backdrop of the paranormal and a fracturing of traditional nuclear family units. Unlike *Twilight*, however, where the heroine eventually finds her post-adolescent identity and happiness as a young, married mother, not one of the main characters in *The Vampire Diaries* comes from or belongs to an unreconstructed nuclear family unit; nor do they appear to seek to recreate these frameworks. Yet, as Jennifer Lynn Barnes summarizes,

The Vampire Diaries is a show in which family matters: the entire premise revolves around Damon and Stefan being brothers; Elena's connection first to Katherine and later to Isobel propelled season one's dominant story arcs; Bonnie's character went through a witchy (and sometimes bitchy) metamorphosis almost entirely because of her grandmother's death; and even minor characters, like Tyler and Matt, struggled with abusive and absent parents, respectively ["Sweet Caroline" 150–51].

Greenburg has argued that postmodern vampire narratives replicate nuclear family units within contemporary settings in order to "expose the dysfunction beneath this veneer of stability" (166). *The Vampire Diaries*, however, deals with a wider range of supernatural beings and eschews the nuclear family unit completely. Family units depicted on screen include orphaned children, sole parent families, absent, irresponsible, and workaholic parents, and even a gay parent. Thus there is a focus on the feelings of dislocation or not adhering to the social norms and prevalent ideologies in the adolescents' mortal lives, even before they enter into the complexities of supernatural politics. For those characters attempting to negotiate the uncanny space of their new supernatural identities as witch (Bonnie), werewolf (Tyler), vampire (Caroline) or *Doppelgänger* (Elena), the fantastic space of their township — which appears to be something of a site of pilgrimage for the supernatural — allows them to develop their adolescent identities, supernatural strengths and limitations, and is a location in which to examine shifting family parameters.

The True Self: Animal or Human?

Teen angst, lifelong romance, and changing adolescent bodies are again explored through human-werewolf romances in Maggie Stiefvater's *The Wolves of Mercy Falls* trilogy. Again aimed at a female teenage audience, the series, comprising *Shiver*, *Linger* and *Forever*, focuses on the disconnections that can occur when one partner is human and the other a werewolf. *Shiver* is told in alternating first-person chapters, switching between the points of view of teenagers Grace Brisbane and Sam Roth. In the opening pages, Grace recalls being attacked by wolves in her backyard when she was a nine-year-old child. Grace remembers the intercession of a wolf with yellow eyes (*Shiver* 2). The subsequent chapter is Sam's recollection of the attack, told from his wolfish perspective. He describes her as "the most beautiful girl I'd ever seen, a tiny, bloody angel in the snow" (*Shiver* 5), a disturbing description which recalls the imprinting storyline of *Twilight*, wherein Jacob and Quil both imprint on much younger girls. Sam, even in his wolf state, identifies that his pack "were going to destroy her" and feels compelled to stop it (*Shiver* 5). Thus begins Grace's fascination with the local wolves, and "her" wolf with the yellow eyes, in particular. Grace notes that she only sees the wolves in winter, and as the narrative unfolds, it is explained that the cold triggers their ability to shift;

in the warmer months, the wolves are not seen because they are able to stay in their human forms.

As with many novels aimed at an adolescent audience, the trilogy is essentially a romance but also focuses on typical issues that may generate teenage angst, including conflicts with parents, rivalries at school, and questions about finishing school and matriculating into tertiary studies. These seemingly normal events are thrown into sharp relief when a local boy, Jack Culpeper, is attacked by wolves and disappears. Grace sees a wolf in the woods with hazel eyes, and thinks she hears Jack's voice, leading her to suspect that some, if not all, of the pack may be werewolves (*Shiver* 49–50). Jack's father Tom organizes a retaliatory wolf hunt, during which the yellow-eyed wolf is shot and injured, morphing back into his human shape to heal (*Shiver* 69). For Grace, the connection is immediate: "I still couldn't quite believe he wasn't my own invention—years of wishing made real. But whatever he was, he was here now, and I wasn't about to lose him" (*Shiver* 69).

The yellow-eyed Sam is often caught "between" selves. He can be human, yet smells "rich, feral, musky" (*Shiver* 83) and has enhanced senses. This leads him to assert that he does not belong on the night when Grace meets him in his human form. Grace's response, after helping him to escape from the hospital, is to invite him home. That night, she suggests that he leave his makeshift bed on the floor and sleep alongside her; an idea that Sam initially rejects. Although Grace presents the invitation into her bed as something innocent and practical, she notes that she feels "insulted that, apparently, I wasn't hot enough for him to charge the mattress like a bull" (*Shiver* 85). Here, sexuality is explicitly linked to an animal image, and is starkly contrasted with Sam's gentlemanly ways. Sam proves his romantic hero credentials by behaving in a chaste manner. Grace, for her part, is keenly aware that she has a "shape-shifting boy in my bed. Not just any shape-shifting boy, but my wolf.... A weird combination of excitement and nervousness tingled through me" (*Shiver* 85), clearly articulating that she finds Sam desirable, but conversely suggesting through the repetition of the word "boy," that she still sees him as a child, rather than a man.

On this first night, Sam also points out to Grace that because she was bitten, she should also have changed, which foreshadows the central questions of the series: who changes, and why? Under what circumstances can shifting be stopped, or indeed, might an individual want to stop shifting? These questions are closely linked throughout the series with the developing relationships between Grace and Sam, and, later, Isobel and Cole.

The benign neglect of Grace's parents allows Sam to essentially live in the house unnoticed for most of the first two novels. They share their first kiss in Grace's kitchen, and Sam describes it as "the barest brush of my lips against hers, nothing animal" (*Shiver* 97). The animal nature of the wolves, including their distinctive scents and ability to communicate wordlessly, are described in great detail throughout all three books. These observations are often made by their romantic interests. Grace notes that even when they begin the night sleeping chastely on opposite sides of the bed, she and Sam end up sleeping entangled with each other, where she could notice that he "smelled so good—like wolf, and trees, and home" (*Shiver* 109). That Grace is so attuned to his scent and that the wolves and pine trees represent home, however, are clues to her own true nature—that she, too, carries the wolf toxins because of the bite she sustained years earlier. These, it transpires, have been lying dormant because she became overheated when left alone in a car by her father shortly after the wolf attack. These events are the precursor to the narrative of the second book, *Linger*, wherein Sam is able to remain human after being infected with meningitis, but Grace finds that her own wolf toxins are no longer dormant. The opening lines of the novel are Grace's: "This is the story of a boy who used to be a wolf and a girl who was becoming one" (*Linger* 1).

The story is made more complex in the second novel with the introduction of new werewolf characters, including rock star Cole St Clair, the lead singer of a successful band. Cole provides the love interest to Jack Culpeper's sister, Isobel, taking shelter in her house after unexpectedly shifting and introducing himself to her with the line "Hi. Sorry. I'm naked" (*Linger* 81). Isobel offers him the shirt of her late brother, Jack, then realizes it brings back too many memories and removes it from him. Rather than explain her feelings, she kisses Cole, noting that "he was a good kisser.... This close, he smelt like Sam had on the first night that I met him, all mucky wolf and pine" (*Linger* 86). Thus Isobel, like Grace, immediately makes the connection between the young man and his werewolf alter ego. Cole leaves the house and the cold immediately makes him shift. Interestingly, when he is in this form, and not capable of "higher thought," Isobel is more able to demonstrate her vulnerability, confessing to the "gray-brown wolf with Cole's green eyes" that her brother died and that she is not a nice person, before apologizing for telling him that his kiss "sucked" (*Linger* 88–89). Later, she again confides, "My brother died" to Cole, this time when he is in his human form. Cole notes that the "words had a ring of familiarity about them, like I'd heard them before in her voice, although I couldn't imagine when" (*Linger* 135). Each shapeshifting character has two distinct selves who share uncanny almost-memories, highlighting the in-between status of adolescence and arguably, of teen romance. Grace believes in words like "*love* and *forever*" (*Linger* 168) while her mother warns her that Sam will "probably be nothing more than a prom picture" (*Linger* 169). Statistically, Grace's mother provides the more likely scenario, but Grace's position is privileged through first-person narration, her sensible nature and the general indifference of her parents. These strategies correlate with the similar storyline in *Twilight*, where Bella's first-person narration encourages readers to accept her becoming a wife and mother while still in her teenage years.

While Sam is emphatic that he is himself when he is human, Cole prefers to be wolf, telling Isobel that he is hoping to lose himself (*Linger* 121). Stiefvater makes it clear that the human Cole was hedonistic, promiscuous, suicidal and a drug-taker; like Isobel, he was angry at the world in general and his parents in particular. Isobel, too, notes the similarities, commenting that "his human eyes in that wolf face [had] looked as empty as I felt" (*Linger* 89).

As the novel progresses, a number of the characters notice that Grace is routinely running temperatures and Sam even smells "the tiniest trace of that sweet, nutty smell" they had previously found on a dead wolf (*Linger* 98). Grace's illness develops and her body attempts to shift, causing her to cry out in pain and finally alerting Grace's parents to Sam's presence in Grace's bedroom. Sam notes that she "stank of wolf. *Wolf, wolf, wolf*" (*Linger* 102). The completely human Isobel also notices (*Linger* 197), indicating the potency of the smell and thus the progression of the toxins.

As Grace shows new symptoms, including nose bleeds, Cole struggles to understand why Sam and Grace do not shift after having fevers, and why he can remain human longer than the others. He reasons that it is related to the hypothalamus, and that just as fever and adrenaline have affected the brains of Sam and Grace, so too has his past drug use affected his. He begins a series of experiments to prove his hypothesis and devise ways to trigger a shift in the third novel, *Forever*. The third novel begins with Cole and Isobel not speaking after Cole makes two uncharacteristic choices towards the end of *Linger*; the first being his attempts to resist shifting into a wolf (*Linger* 269), and the second being his rejection of the sexual advances of a willing female. Cole tries to deliberately eschew his animalistic nature first through the refusal to shift, and then through his insistence that it would be remiss of him to take the vulnerable Isobel's virginity, believing that she would hate herself for the rest of her life (*Linger* 272). Here we see another interesting trend in these adolescent paranormal romance books, wherein male characters — such as Cole, in this instance — or infamously, Edward Cullen in *Twilight*—effectively police the sexuality of their female, human partners.

Linger closes with the newly-reinfected lupine Grace escaping from the hospital bed in which her human form had been dying, and Sam echoing Grace's opening words: "This is the story of a boy who used to be a wolf, and a girl who became one" (*Linger* 360). He vows to find a cure and then find Grace. *Forever* opens with Grace remembering her human self and Isobel making contact with Cole, after refusing to answer any of his calls in the intervening winter months. In the Prologue, a girl has been torn apart by a wolf, and as the novel progresses, we learn that this was Grace's friend Olivia, bitten by Jack Culpeper in the first novel. Olivia's death is used as the impetus for a legal hunt of the Mercy Falls wolves, and so the novel becomes a race to save Sam's adoptive father Beck, the still-shifting Grace, and the rest of the pack.

For Grace, her desire for Sam is a sign of her humanity. She notes that when they kiss, "it didn't matter that I had been a wolf hours ago, or that I would be a wolf again" (*Forever* 152). Grace asks Sam if he is going to marry her, "instead of living in sin" (*Forever* 154), further developing the comments about eloping first touted in *Linger*. As with the *Twilight* novels, this seems to be an attempt to legitimize the sexual relationship, with the authors at great pains to establish these as eternal relationships, rather than passing teenage lust.

Sam's affection for Grace is marked as human and pure; Cole's for Isobel as animalistic and driven by lust. Isobel herself notes the difference, reflecting on how "Sam's hand looked, pressing against [Grace] as they kissed. I didn't think that was what it looked like when Cole and I kissed" (*Forever* 194). Indeed, the first time Sam and Grace re-consummate their relationship after her first winter as a wolf is precipitated by his gift to her of a simple white dress (*Forever* 198, 234–35). She calls it a dress a college student would wear, but its simplicity and whiteness also symbolizes the marriage they both desire, and she notes that when they make love, he touches the dress as though "he couldn't remember what shape I'd had before, and he was rediscovering it" (*Forever* 236).

As the novel progresses, Cole becomes more human, more responsible, more caring, and more understanding. Ironically, his adoption of these "human" positive traits over his previous impetuosity is facilitated by his involvement with the pack, and his loyalty to Beck and Victor, Grace and Sam. The changes in his personality are demonstrated through the changed nature of his desire for Isobel, who notes:

> It wasn't the sort of kiss I'd had with him before, hungry, wanting, desperate. This kiss was so soft it was like a memory of a kiss, so careful on my lips that it was like someone running his fingers along them. My mouth parted and stilled; it was so quiet, a whisper, not a shout.... It wasn't a touch that said *I need more*. It was a touch that said *I want this* [*Forever* 196].

Sam comes under suspicion for the disappearances of Grace, Olivia and Beck, and ultimately, for Olivia's death. An unexpected ally is discovered, however, in local police officer William Koenig. Koenig, who has been raised with stories of werewolves (*Forever* 226–27), has seen a wolf in Boundary Wood which appears to have Beck's eyes. This causes him to challenge the accepted wisdom that Sam is the only common denominator in these mysterious acts. Koenig goes so far as to offer Sam the use of a family property as an alternative to the now-unsafe Boundary Woods. Logistically, however, this is problematic. With the airborne hunt mere hours away, the pack must be moved to their new location. Despite his best efforts, Cole is, in his wolf-form, incapable of retaining enough of his human memory to undertake such a task. Sam, as the werewolf most able to hold onto part of his human identity, has to be reinfected in order to lead the pack.

In the carnage that follows, Grace and Sam are saved and Cole unexpectedly survives, despite being shot and his body appearing to be, in Isobel's view, "too ruined to heal itself" (*Forever* 362). He calls Isobel to tell her of his survival and the damaged, star-crossed lovers have a meaningful conversation about how he knows her better than most of her friends do. The novel closes with Sam and Grace together and human, and Isobel and Cole separated by geography but both human, with Isobel cautioning Cole not to lose her number. The series thus ends with the expectation that the adolescent romances may continue.

Ellen Schreiber's *Once in a Full Moon*, Ivy Devlin's *Low Red Moon* and Heather Davis's *Never Cry Werewolf* are relatively conventional teen romance novels, remarkable here only because the male love interests are werewolves. *Once in a Full Moon* draws self-consciously on the *Little Red Riding Hood* myth in yet another teen love triangle involving a slightly dislocated yet largely unremarkable mortal girl, a local boy, and a mysterious newcomer to their township of Legend's Run. The novel opens with Celeste Parker and her two best friends, Ivy and Abby, and their respective boyfriends, Nash, Jake and Dylan, telling ghost stories around a campfire (1). The friends adhere to teenage romance novel protagonist conventions in that they have access to money and popularity, and one of the characters, Ivy, articulates her sense of certainty that they are entitled to these privileges early in the novel, noting: "'This is how it always should be.... The six of us together.' She raised her latte for a toast. 'Forever'" (5). Somewhat unusually within this genre, Celeste's boyfriend Nash challenges this notion of "forever," suggesting that it is a long time, and far from being offended by his doubts, the first person narrator wonders whether she could really "see [her]self with someone who was usually more devoted to himself and to sports than others?" (5).

Indeed, Celeste values service to others to the point that she volunteers at the Pine Tree Village Retirement Community, where her favorite resident is Mr. Worthington, whom she describes as being "quite cute" for an eighty-nine year old (28). The reader first meets Mr. Worthington when Celeste visits the home on Halloween, dressed as Little Red Riding Hood, the name he uses to call her over. The *Little Red Riding Hood* trope is one which is used extensively in shapeshifting texts, and will be discussed in more detail in Chapter Two. He is dressed in "werewolf fangs, a brown-tipped nose, and a fluffy brown wig" (29), but despite the paucity of the costuming, she claims she does not recognize him at first. Mr. Worthington is famed for telling the story of the Legend's Run werewolf to anyone who will listen, later revealing to Celeste that the original werewolf in the town was his great-grandfather.

Celeste begins to research the local werewolf as part of a school assignment on American folklore. For the same class, her friend Abby decides to go to the poorer side of town and have a reading from a witch doctor, taking her friends with her. As they are leaving, Dr. Meadows warns Celeste, "Beware of a kiss under a full moon. It will change your life forever" (53).

Celeste opts to walk home, rather than return to the school, and is caught in an unexpected blizzard. She is bailed up by four snarling wolves, and unable to get a phone signal to call for help. She is rescued by a young man who attacks the wolves with a tree branch, and is bitten for his trouble. The young man in question is revealed to be newcomer Brandon Maddox, whose good looks Celeste has already noted (40), but who lives on the wrong side of town. He now appears to her to be "even more magnificent" (65). After she binds his wounds, he offers her "a terminally seductive smile. The kind used by A-list movie stars" (67).

Upon her return to safety, Celeste again visits Mr. Worthington, who offers more details about the Legend's Run werewolf, noting that the first one was an early settler who was bitten while protecting his baby. Thereafter, he disappeared whenever the moon appeared full. As her friendship with Brandon becomes romantic, she learns incrementally more about his family, finally realizing that Mr. Worthington's errant granddaughter and Brandon's missing mother are one and the same, which makes Brandon a direct descendant of the original Legend's Run werewolf.

Schreiber does not eschew adolescent sexuality in this novel, commenting repeatedly on Brandon's sexiness and the passion of his and Celeste's kisses. After their first kiss, which made Celeste wonder whether she had "gone to heaven" (134), Brandon begins to feel odd and starts to take off his clothes. Celeste seems more concerned about Brandon's health than she is worried about his intentions, however, noting that he was "standing in thirty-degree weather in several inches of snow in just his jeans. He was barefoot and shirtless. And he wasn't shivering" (136). He insists that she is in danger and must leave, and she notes that his voice is so deep as to be "animal-like" (137). When he steps from behind the tree, he has transformed, and Celeste sees him not as a figure of horror, but in highly sexualized terms:

Brandon's short, wavy brown hair was now savagely wild and shoulder-length. His normally clean-shaven face sported a goatee. His once-smooth chest was now lined with a thin layer of hair. His stomach was ripped as an Olympic swimmer's, and his biceps were cut like a triathlete's. His eyes were a gorgeous gray. He was breathing heavy, as if he'd run a marathon. Brandon had fangs like a wolf ... [he] glared at me with the frailty of a human and the intensity of an animal [138].

One of the after-effects of his transformation, however, is that he has no memory of his actions or indeed, of having been a werewolf at all. At the next full moon, Celeste insists on witnessing his transformation, and finds herself drawn "to Brandon, to this strange and powerful figure, something more than just his magnetic muscles and chiseled abs. It was his soul" (203). He enlists her help to lock him away from society during the nights of the full moon, but during his third transformation, she goes to him and declares that she wants them to be together under any conditions (285). When he tells her that he loves her, she ignores the warning of the witch doctor not to kiss under the full moon, as it will change everything forever, noting: "I had to kiss Brandon because I knew that if I didn't, I wouldn't be able to breathe. I'd never loved someone or something as much as I did him, and I knew that at that moment I had to let him know how much" (286).

The consequences of that kiss are far from dire, however. Rather, the fact that she still desired him, even in his werewolf form, brings his two worlds together and offers some sort of *Beauty and the Beast* cure, in that Brandon is suddenly able to remember his life as a werewolf. Even though the novel closes with Brandon under threat, for Celeste's ex-boyfriend Nash has recorded his transformation on film, the final lines offer hope for the pair:

> Brandon drew me into him and playfully nuzzled his stubbly cheek against mine and then nibbled my neck softly with his fangs. Then he kissed me with the roaring passion of a pack of werewolves and the romance of many full moons [Schreiber 292].

Ivy Devlin's *Low Red Moon* is the story of a teenage girl, Avery, who has been raised an only child by her nature-loving parents in the woods on the outskirts of town. Avery's parents are brutally murdered and she is found with the bodies, but the trauma of the event is such that it invokes amnesia. The subsequent events of the novel are as much about Avery's transition to living with her grandmother in town and attempting to remember the circumstance of her parents' death as they are about her romance with newcomer Ben Dusic. In the world which Devlin creates, Ben and his uncle Louis, as werewolves, are people of the forest in a way that is inextricably linked with Avery's family and its history. The romance between Avery and Ben is thus depicted as being inevitable and natural, as is, by extension, their overwhelming sexual desire for one another. Indeed, Avery and Ben are able to feel each other's emotions (100), and Ben argues that Avery is herself a mythical creature, because humans are not supposed to be able to see the wolf within, yet she can see his eyes in their wolfish silver state, as well as the more natural-seeming but "masked" brown version that he usually shows the world (166).

Despite this simpatico, Avery does at least have the agency to insist that Ben not make decisions on her behalf, insisting: "You might sense what I feel, but they're my feelings. *Mine*" (139). The narrative does conform to the convention of eternal romance, however, with Ben insisting that if the couple separates, Avery will be fine, but he will not, because "[o]nce a bond happens, it can't be undone, just ... broken if the other person is human" (140). Ben's animal nature is brought to the fore by his lust for Avery, with him warning her that he may lose control of his physical form. As they kiss, Avery can feel the "muscles of his back twitch, felt them become longer, leaner" (142) and Ben fears that their passion for each other could trigger a shift in shape: "'If I touch you now, I'm afraid I could change,' he said, and that primal wanting was still there" (169). Thus the virginity of the mortal teenage character is again protected, against her own wishes and desires. Interestingly, no long-term solution is offered to the conundrum of the instability of Ben's shape when affected by his sexual desires, so it would appear that the pair could never safely consummate their relationship.

The connection of Avery and her family to the woods was the impetus for her parents' murders, and marks her as different. Local police officer and family friend Ron was seeking to develop the area, but Avery's father refused to sell his land. Ron presents throughout the novel as the loyal friend who was first on the scene, but he was actually the perpetrator of the crime, armed with a silver ax in an allusion to *Little Red Riding Hood*. Avery's role as the protector of the natural habitat is marked by her ability to communicate psychically with Ben, and physically through the blood red strand of hair which appears overnight after the murders of her parents, and subsequently her neighbors.

In Heather Davis's *Never Cry Werewolf*, Shelby is the female narrator attending "brat camp" because of her troubled relationship with her father and stepmother. Shelby attends Camp Crescent and meets werewolf Austin. The camp is explicitly the site of shapeshifting given its Transformation Ceremony, with the camp brochure explaining: "Transformations happen every summer at Camp Crescent through traditional camp activities and a variety of artistic expression exercises" (14). The parallels between adolescent turmoil and lycanthropy are clear: the troubled teenagers must confront their problems, such as denial, family conflict, or feeling like they do not belong, and make some progress into maturity. When Shelby is able to at last admit her feelings about her father's withdrawal and remarriage since her mother's death, she says, "I felt like something in me had changed" (161). Austin learns that he is not alone and friendless despite his lycanthropy, and Shelby's friend Ariel blossoms in the attention of a boy and develops more social connections. Thus their transformations in their adolescence are allied with shapeshifting.

Shapeshifting texts about adolescents vary from those that focus on a conventional romance, albeit with one partner being afflicted by lycanthropy or similar, to texts wherein the ability to shift shape is integral to character development; many attempt to bring these two extremes together. Each of the texts examined in this chapter focuses on the experience of adolescence as much as the supernatural elements.

Two

Wolf Boys and Wolf Girls: Shapeshifting and Gender Politics

> GILES: *The point is that our wolfman could also be a wolfwoman, or anyone who was bitten by a werewolf.*
> —*Buffy, the Vampire Slayer* 2.15

Although shapeshifting in popular texts is not always linked to a particular gender, a glance at many contemporary works shows a high proportion feature male shapeshifters, and, more specifically, male werewolves. In most cases, lycanthropy is either solely or primarily restricted to men. In popular novels we find Lupin and Fenrir Greyback in J. K. Rowling's *Harry Potter* series, Sam and Cole in Maggie Stiefvater's *Shiver*, *Linger*, and *Forever*, Callum and Chase in Jennifer Lynn Barnes's *Raised by Wolves* and *Trial by Fire*, and the werewolves of Jackson Pearce's *Sisters Red* and *Sweetly*. In works appearing across media we can see Jacob and his Quileute friends in Stephenie Meyer's *Twilight* series, Tyler and Mason in *The Vampire Diaries*, and Sam Merlotte and Alcide Herveaux in *True Blood*. We find Oz in *Buffy, the Vampire Slayer*, George, MacNair, Josh and Ray in the United Kingdom and United States versions of *Being Human*, and Scott, Todd, Derek and Peter in the *Teen Wolf* movies and television series. Although there are female wolves in some of these texts, they are more usually characterized as rare or aberrant.

The previous chapter discussed the intersections between adolescence and shapeshifting. Here, the focus is on gender and gender relations in shapeshifting works. Given the symbolic power of shapeshifting, there is obvious potential for shapeshifting characters to step beyond or resist more stereotypical or traditional depictions of male-female roles to inhabit a new space. This chapter surveys how several popular texts negotiate male and female roles and identities in the context of shapeshifting.

"Your Typical Male": Shapeshifting and Masculinity

In many contemporary texts, shapeshifters are not villains but are attractive and desirable characters despite the danger they pose. Indeed, in some cases they even function as the romantic hero. In modern texts, the formerly villainous male werewolf has transformed into an array of sorrowful poetry-reading teenage boys, noble defenders of humans, and confident and alluring men. In *The Curse of the Werewolf,* Du Coudray writes that

> the body of the monster still tended to be coded in terms of excessive masculinity, as the visible extension of the aggressive potential contained within the body of an ordinary human male. Indeed, the aggression implicit in the masculine physique has been consistently emphasized in werewolf films by the casting of powerfully built actors in the role of the werewolf [85].

Schell has described more generally of werewolves that there has been a shift "from a villainous victim into a sexy role model: the alpha male" (110), and we can certainly see the evidence of this in contemporary works. Vampire Stefan Salvatore describes a vampire-wolf conflict with werewolf Mason Lockwood as an "Alpha male fighting thing" (*The Vampire Diaries* 2.05); actors of werewolf characters on screen are just as likely to be models strolling around shirtless (and hairless) in ways that almost approach objectification. So much has lupine shapeshifting transformed into the site of romance that there is now a subgenre of chick lit focusing on werewolves, such as Ronda Thompson's *Confessions of a Werewolf Supermodel,* Karen MacInerney's *Tales of an Urban Werewolf* series, and Molly Harper's *How to Flirt with a Naked Werewolf* and *The Art of Seducing a Naked Werewolf.*

There are fairly obvious connections between shapeshifting and masculinity. Many works relate lupine shapeshifting to male aggression and uncontrolled, unprovoked violence, from Tyler Lockwood's anger on *The Vampire Diaries* to Jacob's surly behavior in the *Twilight* series. As dialog from *Buffy, the Vampire Slayer* has it:

> GILES: While there's absolutely no scientific explanation for the lunar effect on the human psyche, the phases of the moon do seem to exert a great deal of psychological influence. And the full moon is — it seems to bring out our darkest qualities ...
>
> You see, the werewolf is such a potent extreme representation of our inborn animalistic traits that it emerges for three full consecutive nights: the full moon and the two nights surrounding it ... it acts on pure instinct. No conscience, predatory and, and aggressive.
>
> BUFFY: In other words, your typical male.
>
> XANDER: On behalf of my gender, hey.
>
> GILES: Yes, let's not jump to any conclusions [2.15].

In *Buffy, the Vampire Slayer,* Xander initially proclaims a kinship with werewolves because of his shapeshifting experience as a hyena and its aggression: "I know what it's like to crave the taste of freshly killed meat, to be taken over by those uncontrollable urges" (2.15). Xander's comment might be false bravado, but the notion of "uncontrollable urges" recurs throughout many shapeshifting texts, whether it is anger, lust, or revenge. In the high school setting of texts such as *Teen Wolf, The Vampire Diaries* and *Buffy,* male adolescence is linked to shapeshifting as a fitting metaphor. Oz tells Willow he is "going through some changes" (*Buffy, the Vampire Slayer* 2.15), dialog also appearing in the original *Teen Wolf* film. Shapeshifting is often a metaphor for the hidden male aggression lurking beneath the surface. In television's *The Vampire Diaries,* Mason instructs potential werewolf Tyler to manage his aggressive tendencies by strenuous physical activity such as running and athletic sports. This contrasts with television's *Teen Wolf,* where sports can actually provoke, not manage, lycanthropy:

> STILES: It's like I told you before. It's the anger, it's your pulse rising. It's a trigger.
> SCOTT: But that's lacrosse. It's a pretty violent game, if you hadn't noticed.
> STILES: Well, it's gonna be a lot more violent if you end up killing someone on the field. You can't play Saturday, you're gonna have to get out of the game [1.02].

The same theme is evident for female lycanthropy in *Ginger Snaps,* where Ginger attacks popular girl Trina during a field hockey game. Many of the werewolf confrontations and dangerous moments happen in the boys' locker room in *Teen Wolf,* and Scott's anger during lacrosse leads to his partial transformation: his fingernails morph into claws, his teeth extend, and his eyes turn yellow. Older werewolf Derek Hale teaches Scott self-discipline that allows him to remain human, to harness the aggression instead of allowing it to control him:

> DEREK: Getting angry? That's your first lesson. You want to learn how to control this, how to shift? You do it through anger, by tapping into a primal, animal rage ...
> SCOTT: I can get angry.
> DEREK: Not angry enough! [1.05].

Not all texts adhere to this theme, of course. Indeed, *The Mummy: Tomb of the Dragon Emperor* suggests quite the opposite, when heroic male lead Rick O'Connell implies that authentic masculinity is only in human, not shifted, form as he provokes the shapeshifting Emperor to fight as a human: "Where's your honor? Fight like a man!"

Perhaps in some ways the modern versions of werewolf tales draw on Prokofiev's musical composition and tale of *Peter and the Wolf,* later adapted into film by Walt Disney and by others, in which the boy Peter declares that he has no fear of the wolf, and captures the wolf and puts him on display in a parade. This tale of overcoming the monstrous threat is perhaps evident in the modern version of wolf tales in which the dangerous lupine side is often subdued by the human male. Peter is, as well, a name that recurs in werewolf tales (for example, the romantic interest in Catherine Hardwicke's *Red Riding Hood*, and the Alpha Peter Hale in television's *Teen Wolf*).

"Just That Time of the Month": Shapeshifting and Femininity

Despite the preponderance of male shifters, and particularly werewolves, scholars have noted that there are folkloric and historical traditions linking the werewolf with the female gender (Creed 140). Creed sums up this as a blurring between the gender lines:

> the werewolf is linked to the primal uncanny (woman, nature, death) ... a creature who literally gives birth to himself: his fur covers the inside of his skin. Thus, like woman, he carries the signs of nature within his body at all times.... The werewolf is a feminised male monster, a queer creature aligned to the primal uncanny. Yet, strangely, the horror film almost always depicts the creature as male, despite the fact that myth and legend valourise the she-wolf [140].

Du Coudray writes that female werewolves gradually became more popular in fictions and were often treated in sinister, unnatural terms, reflecting the historical changes related to suffrage, sexuality, and women's growing social power (*Curse of the Werewolf* 46–49). Although contemporary texts often point out the rarity of female werewolves, it is nonetheless possible to see more female shapeshifters emerging in popular fiction.

Just as some texts make links between masculinity and lupine aggression, others point to associations between shapeshifting and femininity, a point that has been raised by many critics (Creed 140; Du Coudray, *Curse of the Werewolf* 122–23). Du Coudray points to earlier beliefs that associated women and the body, the material element, compared to men's supposed connection with the mind, which was reflected in an earlier configuration of female werewolves as demonic and male werewolves as suffering (*Curse of the Werewolf* 55–56). Schell's discussion of masculinity and werewolves notes the significance of the adolescent theme in werewolf tales in that "the tragic wolf man resonated with the coming of age of not just men but also women, with his loss of control, his recurring monthly 'curse,' and suddenly hairy body" (112). Evans claims that "the werewolf's bloody attacks — which occur regularly every month—are certainly related to the menstrual cycle which suddenly and mysteriously commands the body of every adolescent girl" (357).

For instance, although *Buffy, the Vampire Slayer* references the idea that shapeshifting has connections to male aggression, dialog also suggests a link to female hormones. Willow's decision to pursue a relationship with werewolf Oz despite the danger makes this explicit: "Well, I like you. You're nice and you're funny. And you don't smoke. Yeah, okay: werewolf, but that's not all the time. I mean, three days out of the month I'm not much fun to be around either" (2.15). In novels such as Jenny Hale's *Jatta*, shapeshifting emerges for female protagonists in adolescence. Jatta's move into her teenage years is accompanied by her transformation into a wolf—her wolf "emerged at puberty, when it should" (334)—which suggests obvious parallels with female adolescence. Holly Bennett's *Shapeshifter* explicitly notes this in that Sive is only able to shapeshift after her first "moon-cycle" begins (5). When Lydia is attacked by Alpha Peter Hale in the *Teen Wolf* television series, Stiles says: "once a month she'll go out of her freaking mind and try to tear me apart," to which Peter replies rather disturbingly, "Well, actually, considering that she's a woman, twice a month" (1.12). Jennifer Lynn Barnes's *Trial by Fire* implies the link again: "it was probably nothing—just that time of the month, with emotions running high and my heart beating with the power of the impending full moon" (6–7). "Just that time of the month" is, of course, a cultural reference to menstruation, here substituting for the lunar cycle. The film *Ginger Snaps* takes this association further, with Ginger Fitzgerald bitten by a werewolf and experiencing her first period at the same time; and the dialog points to the connections between the two: lupine shapeshifting and female puberty/menstruation are both known as "the curse" and involve pain and physical and emotional changes. As her sister Brigitte puts it, "Something's wrong, like more than you being just—female" (see A. Miller for an analysis of gender in the *Ginger Snaps* films).

A Legacy of Gender Politics

Beyond these more straightforward links between shapeshifting and particular gender traits, we want to take a closer look at the ways in which shapeshifting works handle gender and power relations. Although shapeshifting offers space for resisting or reframing gender stereotypes, not all authors choose to do this. Here we discuss several recent, popular works that address gender and shapeshifting in different ways.

In recent shapeshifting novels by Jackson Pearce and Jennifer Lynn Barnes, no female protagonists are shapeshifters. This might seem to have the result of limiting the female characters' capacity to truly move beyond their gender roles, but this is not necessarily the case.

Before discussing these novels in any detail, it is important to acknowledge the inheritance of fairytales in many texts about lupine shapeshifting, and specifically the legacy of the traditional folktale *Little Red Riding Hood*, which we mentioned briefly in Chapter One. The image of a hooded red figure recurs in numerous texts that include shapeshifting characters; so iconic is the red cloak that even the Pilot episode of the 2011 *Teen Wolf* television program includes footage of Scott in a red hoodie walking through the forest before he is attacked by a werewolf. In *Buffy, the Vampire Slayer*, season villains are known by the generic name as "the Big Bad," which seems to offer a reference to *Little Red Riding Hood*'s Big Bad Wolf, and dialog between Spike and Dawn also draws on the tale. As Spike tells Dawn, "All number of beasties between here and there. Bet they'd really go for a little red riding hood like you" (5.13). This is fairly appropriate given that both are shapeshifters in more abstract, symbolic ways rather than literal: vampire Spike is attempting to change his nature and become a new man; Dawn is not the ordinary human girl she appears on the surface. At one stage, Buffy is even seen to have a *Little Red Riding Hood* Halloween costume (4.04). Meanwhile, the cover image of Heather Davis's YA novel *Never Cry Werewolf* depicts a girl in a red hoodie, representing the female narrator Shelby, who is dressed in the clothes when she first witnesses her love interest Austin shifting into wolf form.

Jack Zipes argues that gender is a particularly important aspect of this ongoing interest in the *Little Red Riding Hood* folktale. As Zipes writes,

> [*Little Red Riding Hood*] raises issues about gender identity, sexuality, violence, and the civilizing process in a unique and succinct symbolic form that children and adults can understand on different levels. All the issues raised in this tale are crucial for establishing principles of social justice and gender equality that have not been satisfactorily practiced in Western societies and are thus continually readdressed in different versions of *Little Red Riding Hood*. For instance, if we take several of the more recent versions ... we shall see how the tale is still closely connected to shifts in social and political attitudes toward gender identity and rape [343].

Du Coudray points out that there was a shift from earlier works depicting lycanthropy as monstrous to twentieth-century approaches depicting "the lycanthrope as a manipulative and darkly charismatic male figure, seducing innocent women" (*Curse of the Werewolf* 71). Although not all shapeshifting texts are primarily or even at all interested in rewriting or referencing *Little Red Riding Hood*, it is nonetheless evident that gender remains a key interest in many of the current shapeshifting texts. Since Zipes's work, many more versions of the tale have been produced, and here we explore how some of these deal with gender in the context of shapeshifting.

"I Will Not Wait to Be Rescued": Human Heroines and Lupine Villains

Sisters Red by Jackson Pearce is one such retelling of the fairytale of *Little Red Riding Hood* in a modern setting. In Pearce's version, the central character of the original *Little Red Riding Hood* tale is now shared between two sisters, Scarlett and Rosie. The wolf is now a werewolf, and there is not one wolf but many. The novel retains the red hood of the original tale in several ways, with the names of Scarlett and Rosie and also their wearing of red cloaks. The novel begins with the murder of Scarlett and Rosie's grandmother, Oma March, and then moves forward seven years in a dual first-person narrative, alternating between Scarlett's and Rosie's perspectives as Scarlett battles against the wolves and Rosie attempts to live a so-called normal life outside hunting wolves. The third main character is woodsman and childhood friend Silas, who becomes Rosie's romantic interest and Potential werewolf. The sequel to *Sisters Red* is called *Sweetly*, and although this novel draws on the tale of *Hansel and Gretel*, we find the same werewolves and this time the main characters of Gretchen and her brother Ansel are joined by woodsman hunter Samuel Reynolds, apparently brother to Silas, and Sophia, who acts as the witch of the fairytale by luring girls to the Fenris at her annual chocolate festival.

As we discussed in Chapter One, the werewolves of *Sisters Red* and *Sweetly* are the Fenris, men who can transform at will into wolves to attack humans, primarily young women. The Fenris are members of wolf packs called Arrow, Bell, and Coin, which are led by Alpha wolves. In the lupine mythology of Pearce's work, shapeshifting has gender and genetic connotations because only certain people can be turned into werewolves: men who are the seventh son of a seventh son. In *Sisters Red*, we learn that the Fenris do not age (14), do not have a human soul (12), and are between human and animal: neither human nor wolf (19). The mythology becomes even more complicated in *Sweetly*, when Gretchen discovers that the Fenris have a special interest in surviving twins such as herself, who have absorbed a second soul when the twin died. These surviving twins with their dual souls are taken by the Fenris to the ocean, where they become "ocean girls—they're dark, they're kindred evils" and thus more suitable as lovers for Fenris than mortal girls, who would die (291–92).

Sisters Red engages with gender issues in several key ways. Scarlett and Rosie are wolf hunters, which is itself a shift away from the passive female victim of other werewolf tales. Silas also hunts, but he is very much a useful addition rather than the heroic male lead. Instead, there is a theme that women must protect themselves and each other rather than rely on men to save them. The opening scenes show that women must be their own defenders, as Oma

March dies and Scarlett is severely injured defending her younger sister Rosie from a wolf's attack, while waiting for the local woodsman, Pa Reynolds, to arrive—too late. Scarlett is a self-appointed guardian of other girls when she and Rosie and Silas move to Atlanta to track down wolves who hunt young women; Scarlett likens girls to Dragonflies in their glittering beauty, and watches over them for their safety. In a scene when Rosie cries because of conflict with her sister, Silas tells her, "Stop.... You're in control here; you don't need to be rescued" (212), a theme that is repeated elsewhere when Rosie is kidnapped by the wolf pack and decides she must escape rather than hope for rescue: "I am confident, I am capable, and I will not wait to be rescued by a woodsman or a hunter. I will escape" (301). In this she mimics Scarlett, who "has never wanted to be rescued. Not from hunting, not from Fenris" (251). We see the same sentiment in *Sweetly*, the sequel to *Sisters Red*, where protagonist Gretchen wants to move on from childhood trauma—she lost her twin sister to a Fenris—to "a future where I know how to shoot, how to kill them. How to keep myself and other girls from vanishing" (118). Not only this, but although Samuel teaches Gretchen to shoot, she comes to take more control in their plans, as he says, "Just tell me what you need me to do, Gretchen. You lead, I'll follow" (275).

The novels' use of American Gothic reinforces the peril of the lone female in a hostile landscape. Although the first novel shares its location with the city, both books are set in small towns that hide sinister secrets:

> The town's not bustling, by any means, but a few families push strollers and groups of middle-aged women window-shop along the sidewalk. Ellison is the sort of place that people move to when they want a slice of Americana, though the entire place turns rather shady after the sun sets: BBQ restaurants become bars; coffeehouses transform into dance clubs; and, of course, the monsters come out after dark [*Sisters Red* 52].

In *Sisters Red*, when the three characters travel to Atlanta their new address is in a street that is "dark, as if a thunderhead is hovering over us despite the sunny day," in a building where "white paint peels off the boards, rusted sconces swirl by the door with a sort of Victorian air, and an octagonal cupola on the roof reaches to the sky" (106). Scarlett and Rosie's ability to defend and attack themselves transforms the gendered spaces of this Gothic landscape because they are not victims. In *Sweetly*, Gretchen's fear of the woods around Sophia's gingerbread-like house is overtaken by her determination to learn to shoot so she can defend herself. This is a rather different outcome to Zipes's comments that "the hope in the best of the more recent re-framings of the Red Riding Hood story ... is that women do not have to reproduce the violence of men to change the rhetoric of violence" (381). In *Sisters Red*, Scarlett's violence surpasses rather than reproduces Silas's; indeed, Scarlett's need for fighting the wolves is contrasted to his (and Rosie's) desire for a more peaceful, ordinary existence. The dual narrative structure leaves both sisters pursuing their different destinies, with the suggestion that both choices are equally valid.

The ideal of feminine beauty is also critiqued in a minor way in these two novels. Gretchen is configured as different to other girls because of her (former) piercings and "clown-coloured hair" (*Sweetly* 128); in part this is a failed rebellion against being forgotten or lost as was her sister. *Sisters Red* more explicitly deals with this theme: in the initial werewolf attack that kills Oma March and injures Scarlett, Scarlett takes a mirror, shatters it, and fights the wolf with the broken mirror. From this moment she bears the visible traces of her ordeal: one eye missing, scars marking her hands and face. Her symbolic rejection of the focus on feminine beauty is a theme that is undermined, however, particularly when Scarlett feels jealousy of her sister or other girls. Scarlett's identity is so bound up in her attack that she can imagine no life beyond hunting; nor does she view her life in terms of choice, which is an essential tenet of modern feminism. When Scarlett considers Rosie's desire for a normal life, she thinks: "I'm not stupid — I'd choose tango over werewolves any day — but I have no choice. I'm scarred, tied to the hunt. But Rosie ... she's half Dragonfly" (240). Later, when she discovers Rosie and Silas are romantically involved, Scarlett's anger stems partly from her loss of connection with her sister and friend, and her own inability to enter into the romantic sphere: "'You didn't tell me. You kept it a secret, because ... because I ...' I look down at my scars. 'Because I'm an outcast. A freak because I hunt. Because I do what's *right*. Because I ... I fight. I don't let people die, while you two are here, like this ... taking dance classes and ... and kissing ... and' I'm losing control" (246–47). Scarlett's words and actions here draw together her scarred appearance as an "outcast" and "freak" with her role as a Fenris hunter, and clearly distinguish between these aspects and the possibility of romance, which is outside her world. Scarlett's identity is thus linked with her appearance in inseparable ways: what she looks like determines her role and destiny in life, just as Rosie's beauty gives her romance and a normal life. The connection between appearance and role seems to complicate the empowering messages. A later scene between Scarlett and Silas attempts to move beyond this rather narrow conception of female roles, suggesting Scarlett is able to choose to have another life:

> "You could have more too [than the hunt], you know."
> "Come on, Silas," I say flatly ... "Can you really see me as a wife? A mother?" My frustration becomes desperate pleading, and I realize how badly I want Silas to have an answer to my questions.
> Instead, he looks surprised. "Lett, you've got to be kidding me" [255].

Silas here confesses to Scarlett that he loved her before he loved Rosie, but it was unrequited. Since this declaration may seem to undermine the integrity of Rosie and Silas's romance, the narrative offers a rather convenient solution by having Silas and Scarlett kiss to prove both feel "nothing" for each other (257). Silas then suggests that this means Scarlett might only feel "that kind of love in the hunt" (257), which seems to contradict his insistence she is not limited to that role.

The configuration of male wolves preying on young women in these two novels has obvious implications for gender relations. Scarlett and Rosie wear red because the color attracts wolves, and other cultural or traditional markers of femininity become bait: glossy hair, perfume, a helpless attitude, giggling, batting eyelashes, swaying hips (*Sisters Red*). Scarlett nicknames the young women Dragonflies because of their sparkling makeup and hair; the missing girls' photos also show them to be "happy, smiling, tanned and sparkly girls" (*Sweetly* 63) who were wearing shades of red when they disappeared, clothed in "party dresses, all of them: Whitney in a scarlet one, Allie in cherry, Taylor in rose" (*Sweetly* 64). Girls aged eighteen are most appealing for the Fenris because their blood is the most potent at that point (*Sweetly* 284). The *Sweetly* Fenris act more strategically to capture their prey because they are "from the South ... from farmland. It's the first key to successful farming.... Wait until your crop is mature to harvest" (284). In general it appears that the Fenris can exercise discipline over their transformations but choose not to, primarily adhering to their lupine desires. Yet they can decide not to transform and can abstain from hunting, particularly under Alpha orders. Their control appears imperfect, however, with most Fenris transforming in partial ways in every scene. The wolves' transformations are primarily triggered by lust. For instance, in a scene at a bowling alley in *Sisters Red*, Scarlett and Rosie realize that the boys in the next lane are Fenris. It is not until Rosie deliberately flirts with them that they start to lose control and start transforming: "A waitress sets another pitcher of beer down on to the wolves' tables, but their eyes are all on Rosie. A few shove their hands into their pockets, I'm certain in an effort to hide the claws that are beginning to grow" (196). As the pack later carries off Rosie, the other wolves bite her in apparently masochistic ways: "every now and then one bites at my legs or waist, just enough teeth to break the top layer of my skin, not enough to seriously wound me. Still, the cuts sting and ache, and I snarl as I hear their joyous howls at my expense. The Alpha's breathing is guttural, almost sexual" (276). The novel thus clearly depicts the werewolf as the predatory male and its victim as the human girl.

This is no surprise when we consider popular critical readings of the original fairytale *Little Red Riding Hood* itself, which claim the red cloak and wolf as symbols of female adolescence and the threat of male sexuality. Steven

Swann Jones writes that "the wolf's wolfness ... may be read as a thinly veiled metaphor of masculine virility since the distinguishing wolf's features may also apply to mature men" (103). Hanks and Hanks reject modern versions that excise what they call the central "erotic metaphor" and tragic ending (68) of Perrault's version. They cite Perrault's tale with its metaphorical seduction and accompanying moral that young, beautiful women must be wary of wolves/men seeking to do them harm. And this appears to be a lesson, even if implicit or unintentional, for girls reading Pearce's version, with the difference that young women must learn to protect themselves.

Zipes suggests that the Perrault and Grimm versions became "a narrative about rape in which the heroine is obliged to bear the responsibility for sexual violation" (78). And if the wolf is a predatory male whose attack of women operates as a metaphor for rape, there are several potentially disturbing implications in *Sisters Red*, particularly in an apparent rehearsal of a rape myth. In a scene where Scarlett watches Dragonfly girls at a nightclub, she is frustrated by their clothes and appearance and wonders if she should abandon them to their inevitable fate:

> The Dragonflies laugh, sweet and bubbly, and I groan in exasperation. They toss their hair, stretch their legs, sway their hips, bat their eyes ... everything about them luring the Fenris. Inviting danger like some baby animal bleating its fool head off. *Look at me, see how I dance, did you notice my hair, look again, desire me, I am perfect.* Stupid, stupid Dragonflies. Here I am, saving your lives, bitten and scarred and wounded for you, and you don't even know it. I should let the Fenris have one of you. No. I didn't mean that.... Ignorance is no reason to die. They can't help what they are, still happily unaware [115–16].

Readers might see in Scarlett's feelings a familiar rape myth of blaming victims because of the clothes they wear, with the associated sense that they "asked for it." As research shows, this attitude is already evident in society when it comes to blaming women for rape for wearing so-called provocative or suggestive clothing (Workman and Freeburg; Whatley). Johnson, Kuck and Schander write that "typical myths revolve around ideas that victims somehow contribute to their own victimization or that the perpetrators are not really responsible for their actions" (694). In *Sisters Red* and *Sweetly* we can see some evidence of both: the female victims invite danger because of their clothing and behavior; the male predators are excused because of their inherent, inevitable lusts that cannot be controlled. Of course, this second element is only evident in novels that position the werewolf as uncontrollable. In other works, wolves are able to control themselves in their transformed state, either before (by willingly restraining themselves) or during (by having the mental discipline) their shift; given such a scenario, the wolves could not escape blame for their actions. In *Sisters Red*, the wolves appear entirely incapable of controlling themselves and thus cannot be held responsible for their actions. Indeed, the only answer to the wolf problem is to kill them. Thus readers have no opportunity to blame the wolves in any real sense and instead it is the victims who must shoulder some of the blame. These implications sit uneasily in a novel that otherwise seems to seek to empower women and provide strong female characters. *Sweetly* offers a slightly different perspective in that the wolves of the second novel do appear to have more control: they plan their attacks in concert with a human girl, Sophia, whom they blackmail into cooperation by holding her sister hostage. This seems to then attribute the blame to the attackers.

The overall message of female independence is one that appears to be growing in the genre post–*Buffy*. In television's *Teen Wolf*, Scott's romantic interest Allison tells her aunt, Kate Argent, that when she and her friends were under siege in the school by the Alpha, she resolved: "I want to not be scared. That night, in the school, I felt utterly weak, like, like I needed someone to come and rescue me. I hate that feeling. I want to feel stronger than that. I want to feel powerful" (1.09). Kate assures her that she will, which is fitting given that Kate is one of the most enthusiastic wolf-hunters in their family to the point of breaking their "moral code" by killing human children and other innocent people in her attempts to murder werewolves (1.12). Kate's introduction to the series is in Buffy-esque terms: a beautiful blonde is stalked by a monster only to pull out a weapon and shoot it (1.04). Allison does not learn of her family's hunting identity or Scott's lycanthropy until the end of the first season, and Kate then attempts to empower and train Allison to kill werewolves, despite Allison's parents' wishes to keep their daughter away from their world until she is older. Kate tortures werewolf Derek in a sadistic manner, taking pleasure in his pain and mocking their earlier romance, but her treatment of protagonist Scott is seen as a betrayal of the code, which Chris Argent describes as "We hunt those who hunt us" (1.12). Ultimately Kate is killed by the Alpha Peter in revenge for her attack on him and his family.

Davis's *Never Cry Werewolf* also reflects this message of female empowerment and independence. When werewolf Austin asks Shelby to trust him, she tells him that this approach "didn't really work for Little Red Riding Hood," and he then asks if he resembles the Big Bad Wolf (176). Whereas in Pearce's *Sisters Red* and *Sweetly* the girls have a woodsman by their sides as they fight, in *Never Cry Werewolf* Shelby points out that she has no woodcutter to rescue her, to which Austin replies, "You're not about letting other people save you, Shelby" (176). Although Austin (in lupine form) later rescues Shelby from a cougar, she returns the favor by saving his life as well. During this scene she is bitten by him, a mark that does not heal over time, and the inference is that she has been infected with lycanthropy, although this is not confirmed. It is clear that these texts draw on traditional ideas of gender and *Little Red Riding Hood* to reflect the contemporary focus on female independence.

"*I Wasn't Some Weak Little Human Girl Anymore*": Heroic Male Werewolves and Human Girls

Like *Sisters Red*, Jennifer Lynn Barnes's *Raised by Wolves* directly engages with gender issues, this time through the prism of domination and submission in the lupine pack context. The teenaged heroine this time is Bryn, who occupies a unique position within a powerful American wolf pack because she has been adopted into the pack despite being a human girl. Like Scarlett, Bryn is scarred by a wolf and has since valued independence for her life. Yet unlike *Sisters Red*, Barnes's use of werewolves is sympathetic; they are Bryn's family and friends. Aged four, Bryn was rescued and adopted by Callum, Alpha of the Stone River pack, when her parents were murdered by a Rabid, a wolf without a pack who kills humans. Callum killed the Rabid and took Bryn with him to live with their pack under the care of Ali, another human woman.

Werewolves in *Raised by Wolves* and its sequel *Trial by Fire* are sympathetically portrayed. Becoming a werewolf is almost always governed by genes: wolves pass down the shapeshifting gene to their children. Others can become werewolves but only if they hold a special kind of power that Bryn calls Resilience, a particularly strong survival instinct that means adaptation to any situation. Most wolves are male; female wolves are rare because they can only be born if they are one of twins, and their twin must be male. Apart from the possible allusions to the legend of Romulus and Remus, this state has implications for gender in its inference that a female needs a male to protect her even before birth. Other werewolf lore is more conventional: silver is deadly for all wolves except a rare few with immunity; strong emotions and full moon can trigger the desire to transform, although shapeshifting occurs at will. Despite this control, wolves can be threatening: "Wolves in sheepskin had nothing on werewolves masquerading as men; shape-shifters were dangerous when their beasts were loose on the inside but contained on the surface. As wolves, they were hunters. In human form, they could be deadly" (*Raised by Wolves* 5). When Bryn meets a newly created male werewolf, Chase, she discovers Callum has lied to her and the Rabid not only still lives but has been changing children into wolves and holding them captive. This revelation is the catalyst for Bryn to break pack law; she is then violently punished under Callum's instructions and Ali takes her away in protest. Bryn is joined by Chase and other pack friends Devon and Lake to hunt the Rabid and free his wolves. Although Bryn is human, she has unique Resilient abilities to resist the psychic pack bond that connects the pack and compels the wolves to obey the Alpha; not only this but she also changes the bond between Chase, Devon, Lake and the Rabid's wolves to connect with her into a new pack. Bryn offers them the choice of freedom — perhaps ironic given she changed their pack bonds with neither their prior knowledge nor consent (331–32) — but they accept her as Alpha and form a new pack, Cedar Ridge, living in former Stone River territory ceded by Callum, and the sequel, *Trial by Fire*, finds them under attack from a coven of human psychics as well as a hostile neighboring pack.

In Barnes's world, werewolves exist in packs with strongly defined hierarchies and protocols. Alphas lead the packs and exercise absolute control over their wolves' actions and thoughts, and they cannot be challenged except in rare circumstances or by purebred or Resilient wolves (*Trial by Fire* 73). The packs operate in different territories with strictly defined and enforced boundaries; wolves may not cross from their pack's territory to another's without the permission of both Alphas. Even the Alphas coexist within limits: Callum initiated a Senate of Alphas who rule territories across the United States and meet to vote on particular issues, and each Alpha adheres to the rules governing pack conduct. This is not dissimilar to the rigidity of werewolf pack rule in Amelia Atwater-Rhodes's *The Shapeshifters*, where strict rule is a necessity to ensure the pack's survival (662).

Aligned with this power structure is the patriarchy in the packs; all Alphas are male until Bryn. Indeed, almost every wolf is male, which makes female werewolves such as Lake and others in Bryn's pack not only rare but highly valuable as potential mates for other wolves. This becomes part of the reason Bryn's pack is attacked and also causes Lake to flee at times from the threat of unwanted advances from other wolves: "As long-lived as werewolves were, most wouldn't have batted an eye at the idea of taking possession of a female [wolf] and waiting a decade or two for her to grow up" (*Trial by Fire* 37). Although this is perhaps akin to Stephenie Meyer's notion of lupine imprinting in her *Twilight* series, where male wolves will "imprint" with a young female girl and wait for her to age before moving into a romantic relationship, Barnes's treatment is decidedly less positive, with Bryn rejecting this state as intolerable: "If I had to, I'd tear this intruder to shreds with my bare hands to keep our girls safe" (37). Human girls do not fare better, either, with Bryn acknowledging that most packs — save hers and Callum's — saw human women as "for breeding" only (*Trial by Fire* 89).

There is a strong theme of possession in the series. When Callum brings Bryn and Ali to his pack, he gives them his Mark, a scar of his claws, in their skin: "For most of my childhood, the Mark had been a visible symbol to the pack that had raised me that I was one of their own, that anyone who messed with me messed with the werewolf who'd dug his fingers into my flesh hard enough to leave scars" (*Trial by Fire* 8). This physical and symbolic mark positions them as a member of the pack, and not just a member but a possession, owned by Callum. Ali marries a Stone River wolf and bears twins to him but Bryn, younger, occupies a close position to Callum, who is her "legal guardian, the executor of my estate, and the closest thing I had to a brother, uncle, or mentor, all rolled into one" (*Raised by Wolves* 2). Bryn sees Ali as her primary parental figure, taking her last name as her own and living with Ali and her children. Callum occupies a somewhat ambiguous position with respect to Bryn, where he seems to function as a rather unapproachable figure in that he "would always make me feel like a kid" (*Raised by Wolves* 410) yet also has a closer relationship with Bryn than with anyone else: "His words were laced with unspoken warmth, an affection that — in his human form, at least — he showed only to me" (*Raised by Wolves* 12). Their relationship undergoes a change when she becomes an Alpha, placing them on more equal terms, although this is still at Callum's advantage given his greater age (centuries), political status, experience, and abilities.

In some ways Bryn's relationship with Callum echoes the traditional gender dynamics of women under the protection of men. As Bryn tells the reader, "by Pack Law, [the Mark] made me his" (*Raised by Wolves* 7–8), and Callum's name protects her (*Raised by Wolves* 59) because anyone who might wish to harm Bryn will fear Callum too much to do so. Callum conforms to the traditional heroic pattern of powerful male; he is the most powerful wolf in North America politically, and he is a strong and competent leader of his pack. He also has a psychic gift of foreknowledge allied with a devotion to protecting his pack and particularly Bryn, which in a sense legitimizes his control of other people because his actions, however dubious or apparently uncaring, are inevitably proved justified by later events. As a narrative strategy, this does work to allow several disturbing events to be excused, with the most obvious example of this being Bryn's beating in *Raised by Wolves*. When she breaks the pack law and is subjected to a brutal beating under Callum's authority, this is legitimized by two aspects: that Bryn knew the consequences for disobedience and was in fact given a lighter sentence than the usual death because of her relative human frailty; and that Callum knew about Bryn's destiny because of his foresight and that the beating was somehow facilitating events to unfold to best protect her own interests.

It is this physical abuse that complicates the obvious overtones of female empowerment, even if Bryn is characterized in terms of her independence and her fierce resistance to the dominance hierarchy of the pack world. Ali offers a clearer rejection of male/lupine hierarchy because she abandons Callum's pack and also her werewolf husband because of the attack, to take Bryn away from the wolf pack to start a new life with her own children elsewhere. Bryn, in contrast, despite her rhetoric of independence and resistance, is rather accepting of her attack. The novel cannot solve this dilemma no matter how much it naturalizes the pack rules because Bryn has insistently rejected pack law throughout the text, so her acceptance of pack vengeance seems contradictory.

Moreover, there is an irony of Bryn rejecting hierarchies and power only to form her own pack. Bryn does operate differently to some extent to other Alphas, which can be attributed to her humanity, but hierarchy is inevitable in any pack because of the supernatural Alpha authority. The second novel, *Trial by Fire*, makes some attempt to address the intriguing power issues at work in Bryn's romantic relationship with Chase, who is her subordinate, although Chase is rather a ghost of a character without much development or even narrative space, compared to Callum's far more complex characterization. Bryn's own Alpha leadership, however, is constructed as different to others as she seeks to both incorporate and exclude particular aspects of Callum's (and other Alphas') leadership into her own management of her pack. Indeed, her conception of leadership relies on change, on transformation, to evade expectations: "I'm whatever kind of alpha I need to be" (*Trial by Fire* 260).

Bryn's humanity may be a positive element in allowing her to reject the power hierarchies of pack life, but the second novel closes with her implied decision to become a werewolf (*Trial by Fire* 355). She asks Callum to perform this action, trusting him to do so without injuring her beyond what is necessary for the transformation (*Trial by Fire* 356). Thus the idea that Bryn's humanity places her in a powerful position beyond the patriarchy and hierarchy of wolf pack law is somewhat altered at this stage of the series. Moreover, it is interesting to consider that Bryn's feeling of power is realized after her initiation into the rigid divisions of the werewolf hierarchies: "I wasn't some weak little human girl anymore. For that matter, I'd never been some weak little human girl. I was a survivor, I was their *alpha*, and I could take care of myself" (*Trial by Fire* 33).

Romances with Wolves

Given that these novels are almost all about the romantic lives of their heroines, it is important to contextualize this discussion of gender within the framework of romantic fiction generally. Readers of these paranormal romances will find a familiar trope in *Raised by Wolves*; Bryn meets Chase in dangerous circumstances because his first reaction is animalistic violence: he transforms and tries to attack her, to kill her. This theme of male hero and female victim is familiar: as with the plot of dozens of paranormal romances, the hero is initially attracted to the heroine because of his desire to kill her, an instinctive, integral violence that he must learn to control as he seeks to win her love. The same is true of Edward and Bella in *Twilight*—with one commentator at least arguing that Edward appears to meet the criteria for compensated psychopathy (Merskin). Of course, this theme is not unchallenged. In *True Blood*, for instance, flashbacks show that Bill Compton became a vampire after rejecting the advances of vampire Lorena because he wished to be faithful to his family; Lorena attacked him regardless (1.05). Yet the predatory female character is much less common than the dangerous male.

Although in one respect this simply recycles the message of fairytales such as *Beauty and the Beast* that a woman's love can redeem a monster into a man, in another way the theme might be seen as disturbing and dysfunctional, suggesting as it does that violence and dominance are at the heart of true romance, where the weaker female partner is always at risk of the male losing his self control and attacking her. This is not the province of fairytale alone, however, for the threat (if not occurrence) of male violence has been a common theme over decades of romance novels. As Hubbard wrote of 1950s romances, "Dominance is placed at the root of masculinity and nurturance at the core of femininity" (122). Even in later decades, as feminism began to emerge in popular culture,

> the hero is cast as superior to the heroine in wealth, position, and education. In the 1970s novels he must use these advantages to battle the new feminism and to preserve the old ways. As the militant heroine tests his mettle, he resorts to exhibitions of power. Earlier heroes frequently subdued heroines physically when in the grips of passion, often bruising flesh.... And along with these physical displays, he also educates the heroine with insults, exasperation, and argumentation until she recants. Thus he provides a counter-statement, both verbal and nonverbal, to her liberation rhetoric [119].

Hubbard suggests that 1980s romance novels reflected a shift to gender equality and negotiation of power provoked by contemporary feminism. It seems fairly clear, however, that many current paranormal texts instead rehearse earlier gender relationships where males are aggressive, powerful, and dictatorial, and the females' attempts to assert their own individuality are eventually subsumed by their great love for the hero.

Of course, one key point here is that these modern versions of *Beauty and the Beast* invert the original formula: the human girls meet and fall in love with the handsome, princely hero, only to then discover that he is, after all, a beast. More than this, today's heroes are more likely to be both beauty and beast. Davis's *Never Cry Werewolf* directly references the *Beauty and the*

Beast tale as a parallel for the relationship between Shelby and Austin. Shelby meets Austin while attending a "brat camp" for troubled teenagers, Camp Crescent, and they work together painting scenery for a talent show production of *Beauty and the Beast*. Austin is the son of a famous rock star, and is handsome, glamorous, and dangerous, an alluring combination for Shelby, who sees him as "more than a boy — he was also a beautiful, dangerous creature" (163). Part of Austin's danger for Shelby is not just his lycanthropy but also his masculinity and her fears of getting into more trouble than she already has experienced with boys (151). Ultimately Shelby rejects her fears and helps Austin, and the novel concludes that "love works the real magic in the world. Only love" (212), a theme that aligns with the *Beauty and the Beast* fairytale. Other texts draw on the theme more literally: when Allison kisses Scott after discovering he is a werewolf, his lupine features fade to his normal visage (*Teen Wolf* 1.12), and when Jena kisses her frog companion, Gogu, he turns into a boy and later becomes her husband in Juliet Marillier's *Wildwood Dancing*.

Perhaps this pattern is even more evident in the vampire genre, where the contemporary vampires are even more so handsome princes who turn out to be beasts. Buffy's interest in Angel and Bella's attraction to Edward both follow this theme, although Buffy's romance with Angel inverts the fairytale even more by Angel truly turning into a monster because of his curse: a woman's love does not save him but in fact turns him from man to beast. In television's *The Vampire Diaries*, human Elena is intrigued by vampire Stefan, but then refuses to become involved with him because of the danger and her doubts about him. Perhaps somewhat ironically, her decision to sleep with him for the first time after she changes her mind is accompanied by Plumb's song "Cut," about self-harm, which can be a symptom of mental illness. Deliberate or otherwise, this seems a rather fitting metaphor for the self-harm that these human girls inflict on themselves in their choice of dangerous boyfriend. Elena's doubts about Stefan seem validated by his later fall into human blood addiction and violence; more worryingly, Elena repeatedly apologizes and insists that she is to blame for his violence for forcing him to drink her blood thereby breaking his abstinence — her reason for this was so that he could protect her from a threatening vampire. At every turn we are confounded with layers of gendered romantic relationships that shapeshifting texts seem unable to dissect.

Joanna Russ points out that uncertainty about the dangerous male drives much of the narrative of what she calls Modern Gothics. Russ cites the comment of editor Terry Carr, who spoke of "a simultaneous attraction/repulsion, love/fear going on [in the genre]. Most of the 'pure' Gothics tend to have a handsome, magnetic suitor or husband who may or may not be a lunatic and/or murderer" (667). Modleski similarly writes more generally that romance fiction can "perpetuate ideological confusion about male sexuality and male violence" (440), where "Male brutality comes to be seen as a manifestation, not of contempt, but of love" (439). Transferring these themes across to the paranormal romances of werewolves and vampires, it is not surprising that these lupine and vampire heroes are characterized in ways that underscore their violence lurking just beneath the surface. As Lee puts it, "Paranormal romance novels, however, are often closer to their fairy-tale counterparts in that they frequently depict male protagonists who are literally beasts or monsters, often vampires, werewolves, or demons of various sorts" (59; see also M. Miller; Torkelson). Marion Rana highlights this fusion of sex and violence in the *Twilight* and *The Vampire Diaries* novels: "The intertwining of sexuality and violence in the novels both normalises and eroticises violence, making the role of the sexual assailant a sexy and glamorous one and romanticising and sexualising the role of the female victim" (101).

In some cases this theme of male threat is treated rather comedically, as in *Buffy, the Vampire Slayer* when Willow discovers Oz is a werewolf:

> BUFFY: Certainly gonna put a strain on Willow and Oz's relationship.
> XANDER: What relationship? I mean, what life could they possibly have together? We're talking obedience school, paper training, Oz is always in back burying their things, and that kind of breed can turn on its owner.
> BUFFY: I don't know. I kinda see Oz as the loyal type.
> XANDER: All I'm saying is she's not safe with him.
> ...
> WILLOW: I'm sorry about how all this ended up. With me shooting you and all.
> OZ: It's okay. I'm, I'm sorry I almost ate you.
> WILLOW: It's okay [2.15].

Despite this exchange, Oz's inability to control himself and his potential danger to Willow is the catalyst for him to later break off their relationship and leave.

For some of the male creatures in romantic texts, female characters are the moral compass directing and redeeming them. This is evident enough in vampire-focused texts, as when Lexi and Elena help Stefan renounce his "ripper" lifestyle just as Elena has a positive influence on Damon (*The Vampire Diaries*); Buffy influences Angel and more particularly Spike to perform heroic, redemptive actions (*Buffy, the Vampire Slayer*). We also find this in werewolf characters: Tonks gives Lupin hope for his future because of her love for him (*Harry Potter*), and Bryn is able to calm Chase's anger to stop him transforming into a wolf (*Raised by Wolves* 351). In *The Vampire Diaries* television series, Caroline is Tyler's only source of support when he undergoes his first transformation. Werewolf Jules conforms to some feminine stereotypes as the voice of moral reason: she cautions fellow wolf Brady against harming (vampire) Caroline Forbes beyond what is needed to win back their wolf Tyler; insists they have a duty of care for Tyler to teach him as a fellow werewolf; and aids Tyler's departure from Mystic Falls as he seeks to reconcile his newfound knowledge of his lycanthropy with his identity. In the *Teen Wolf* television program, Scott's love interest Allison is his "anchor" (1.06); she helps him maintain control over his anger and thus his shifting (yet, contrarily, provokes him into shifting in their romantic scenes). Her last name is Argent, which means silver. Although Derek scorns the idea of silver bullets (1.04), which suggests silver has no effect on wolves in this mythology, the Argent name encapsulates the broader theme of women as a softening effect on these violent males — even to the point of being a weakness for some, as was Kate Argent for Derek (and the Argents are a family of werewolf hunters). Scott even says that Allison "makes me weak" (1.06), although Stiles parodies this theme: "this whole women make you weak thing is a little too Spartan warrior for me" (1.06). Scott's lacrosse rival and popular boy in school, Jackson, is the one to point out the significance of the Argent name to Scott (1.09).

In some cases the human and lupine girls in these works subvert the original message of *Little Red Riding Hood* because of their assertive sexuality. Ginger's transformation into a werewolf comes with behavioral changes where she is sexually aggressive and predatory (*Ginger Snaps*). Allison initiates many of the romantic scenes with Scott in television's *Teen Wolf*, unaware that he is a wolf. In Catherine Hardwicke's 2011 *Red Riding Hood*, Valerie actively seeks the attention of her romantic interest, Peter, and is a willing partner in their interludes, even to the point of suggesting they leave the village for a new life elsewhere, together. Although the film includes dialog referencing the original tale's moral guidance of not stopping to talk to strangers, it appears to either subvert or ignore the original meaning of the tale and its warnings against young girls acting foolishly around men who might compromise their reputation and chastity. At one stage Valerie attempts to kill Peter when she (wrongly) thinks he is a werewolf, only to embrace him later when she knows he is one. It is her father who is the werewolf terrorizing the village, and Valerie discovers that she too carries the genetic gift of lycanthropy, which she rejects. Valerie shows some initiative when she decides to visit her grandmother after deciding she is the wolf, although her move beyond gender norms is limited in that it is Peter who rescues her from her father. Shapeshifting is subject to somewhat rigid and inexplicable rules in the film, where it is both contagious — passed on by a werewolf biting a human during a blood moon every thirteen years — and genetic, where Valerie inherits lycanthropy from her father, and he from his, although the film does not explain why she never becomes a werewolf or how the genetic gift manifests itself.

In contrast to the reservations about gendered norms in romance fiction, others suggest that the genre can reveal less conservative aspects. Radway, for instance, questions whether romance reading might rather uncover "significant discontent with the institutions the books purport to celebrate" (69). Modleski also raises the possibility that the audience of such romances may find some appeal in the narrative where "the woman is bringing the man to his knees" (441), while Swan writes that Disney's *Beauty and the Beast* emphasizes a unity between human and animal traits: "Ultimately, it is the integration of dualities which allows the main characters to be transformed into mature Selves able to love from wholeness instead of separateness" (353): "Belle and Beast model the growth of Self that is required to avoid the trap of mindless tradition. They each find a balancing of the Animal and Human aspects without losing either masculine or feminine energy. Belle combines deep intuition with firm self-assertion; Beast merges his strength with tenderness and relational responsibility" (366). And so it is in many of these shapeshifting texts, where the males must change in order to be worthy of the heroine.

And yet, rather than negotiating their relationship on equal terms, in some of these novels the women are forced to move into the male sphere: Bella, for example, must become a vampire like her boyfriend in order to fulfill her romantic goals. Rarely does the male lead have the choice to change his life. Despite the supernatural premise of this genre, which could allow more complex power relationships, authors rarely give the same choice to their male and female leads; in most cases, the possibility is never imagined for the hero to move outside his life and join the female in her sphere. In short: Bella must always become what Edward is; she can never expect him to become what she is, human. Unlike Spike in *Buffy*, who fought to win a soul in the hopes it would prove him worthy of Buffy, these female protagonists are never given the option of the men adapting to them, instead they must adapt to their men. Elena similarly has to decide if she retains her humanity or abandons it for love (*The Vampire Diaries*); even Bryn is unable to envisage a future as a human (*Trial by Fire*). So for many of these human girls, their human state may give them power that the shapeshifters do not have, but it is not a position they seek; indeed they abandon it. Despite these limitations, perhaps another way to read this is that these human girls have choices that the shapeshifters do not, and this might be seen as offering them a modicum of power over their lives.

Shifting Shape to Elude Gender Norms

It is harder to find many female shapeshifters as main characters of popular recent texts, but those that do exist have the obvious potential for occupying a more powerful position in gender relations. Jenny Hale's *Jatta* tells the story of a princess named Jatta in a fantasy kingdom called Alteeda. Jatta's mother was killed by wolves ten years ago, and now, as Jatta enters adolescence, she realizes that she has become a werewolf— at each full moon she turns into a bloodthirsty wolf; in the morning she awakes, unable to remember. Like the traditional werewolf, Jatta suffers from an inability to control herself when inhuman. She is a danger to those around her, even — and particularly — her family, who are closest to her. Unlike so many other angst-ridden emotive werewolves that populate children's and YA texts today, Jatta's wolf is fierce and violent: brutal and malicious with no redeeming qualities, and Jatta does not retain her human side in her shifts. Despite this, shapeshifting has transformative potential because it leads Jatta to a freedom of sorts, as she leaves the castle and discovers new confidence and independence, and even as her lycanthropy is removed by the conclusion of the novel, it appears that she may have gained (or discovered hidden) different powers.

This is not unlike the possibilities of shapeshifting for Sophie in Diana Wynne Jones's *Howl's Moving Castle* and Miyazaki's film version. *Howl's Moving Castle* is replete with characters whose appearances are deceptive, from scarecrows and dogs to wizards and schoolteachers. Shapeshifting is rather symbolic of self-identity: protagonist Sophie sees herself as dull and cannot envisage a better future, feeling instead "as if the past months of sitting and sewing had turned her into an old woman or a semi-invalid" (20). And shortly after this, Sophie is cursed into the form of an elderly woman by the Witch of the Waste. This causes Sophie to leave the hat trade and seek the infamous Wizard Howl for his help. Part of Sophie's own transformation into an old woman appears to be linked to her sense of self, because even if the Witch of the Waste enacted the change with a curse, Howl insists that Sophie is the one maintaining her "disguise" (261), so much so that he cannot break it despite his own considerable magical gifts. Formerly a rather reserved and quiet girl, Sophie changes through her experience, becoming more confident in herself and assertive towards others. Where once she was shy with men, she eventually falls in love with Howl and discovers he loves her. Sophie becomes a girl again by the story's end, which becomes representative of her confidence in herself after realizing she has her own magical abilities.

"The Coolest Thing": Hot Werewolf Boys, Harpy Werewolf Girls, and the Possibilities of Being Human

In television's *The Vampire Diaries*, the second season introduces a female wolf for several episodes, Jules. Along with Jenna and Elena, Jules ultimately becomes a sacrifice for Klaus to access his lupine abilities, and Klaus notes the three sacrifices (wolf, vampire, *Doppelgänger*) are all women: "I rather appreciate the symmetry of three women — three goddesses — sacrificed at nature's altar" (2.21). Klaus is also assisted by a witch, Greta, and although there may be some power attached to these roles, the use of women as sacrifices and servants for Klaus while male characters attempt to save them cannot be overlooked. In Maggie Stiefvater's *The Wolves of Mercy Falls* series, Grace becomes a werewolf, as do Shelby and Olivia, but given that Cole and Sam are the main focus of the action and Shelby and Olivia are both killed, this is in keeping with the male-dominated trend of the genre.

In Stephenie Meyer's *Twilight* series, werewolves are primarily male, and are heroic rather than villainous. Shapeshifter Jacob Black is the boy competing for Bella Swan's affections against vampire Edward Cullen and he has gained significant popularity among fans of the books and films, many of whom identify themselves as Team Jacob. The film versions go further by explicitly positioning the wolf pack in publicity stills in ways akin to male underwear models in advertising, the objects of desire; publicity around the films even included interviews with Taylor Lautner about his fitness regime. This is not simply *Twilight*, of course, for we can see a similar focus on Hugh Jackman's body as he plays the wolverine/human mutant with wolf-like claws in *X-Men Origins: Wolverine*. Natalie Wilson also notes this element of characterization and representation in *Twilight*, but argues that the focus on the bodies of the wolf pack in both novel and film versions owes a debt to colonial tendencies to sexualize Native American groups (*Seduced* 174). A glance at any film still of the wolf pack shows them to be remarkably unusual werewolves by their conspicuous lack of body hair. Du Coudray suggests that the "hairiness" of werewolves marks them with "inferior masculinity" by its links to animals and notions of evolutionary theory (*Curse of the Werewolf* 86). In modern werewolves, however, hairiness seems to have been replaced by hairlessness, with another example being *Teen Wolf* Scott's evolution from his furry film self to his television incarnation with hairless chest and abs constantly on display in the television series, conveniently enabled by his now partial-transformation of face and fingernails only. Thus we have come so far from the monstrous hirsute wolf-men of tradition that the Quileute characters in *Twilight* actually describe their transformations as "the coolest thing" (*Eclipse* 102) and "exciting" (*Eclipse* 430) rather than a horrifying transformation, despite the initial trauma. Even Meyer ("The Story") has written that her choice of werewolves was "cool"; in this way, the werewolf characters are not subjects of exclusion and fear as they are in other contemporary fantasy texts such as J. K. Rowling's *Harry Potter* series.

The *Twilight* wolves diverge from werewolf tradition in that they are shapeshifters who take a lupine form, meaning they can transform into wolves at will instead of being bound to shift at full moon. In one way, the shapeshifting is linked to romance when Jacob experiences his first shifting and his father, Billy, claims that he has "mono" (*New Moon* 199) in an attempt to hide his son's true condition. Mono is, of course, known as the kissing disease because it is spread by saliva, and its links with adolescent romance perhaps serve as (unintended) reminders of the dangerous allure of contemporary male werewolf characters for young female human protagonists.

The *Twilight* series seems to promote a traditional patriarchal structure where the males are leaders, as in werewolf (Sam and Jacob), vampire (Carlisle) and human (Bella's father Charlie and step-father Phil) groups, and the women are the loving and supportive wives. In Meyer's work the werewolf is bounded by masculinity; in traditional and contemporary times the Quileute wolves are all male. The modern exception is Leah Clearwater; however, Leah appears to function as the exception that proves there is a rule, because her presence is uncomfortable for the male wolves and causes friction. Meyer's creation of a predominantly male pack does reflect the male gendering of other key werewolves in contemporary texts, including the use of a male as Alpha. Even when Jacob breaks away from Alpha Sam Uley's pack, the only result is that he forms a new pack with him as Alpha. Leah, who has the most to gain from breaking free from her enforced mental connection with Sam and the other wolves, is unable to exercise the same freedom. Instead, she follows Jacob as her new Alpha. However unwilling Leah is to submit to Sam or Jacob's authority, the novels do not give her (nor the other non–Alpha wolves) the opportunity to exist outside this hierarchy. This excess of masculinity in the wolf pack negatively differentiates the wolves from the Cullen vampires, whose ranks are comprised of equal male and female numbers in romantic partnerships, thereby achieving the ideal state promoted in the series, a topic discussed at more length by other researchers (see, for example, Silver).

Leah is, for the most part, defined by her failed romance with Sam. As the sole exception to the otherwise all-male wolf pack, Leah receives dubious treatment as a stereotype of the scorned woman embittered by a failed love affair — her unrequited love has made her a "bitter harpy" (*Eclipse* 552). Bella calls Leah "beautiful in an exotic way" (*New Moon* 131–32) before later telling readers Leah's beauty has been lost because of her unsuccessful romance with Sam (*Eclipse* 552). Her failure in romance thus marks her physically and also emotionally, which becomes a problem given the mind connection shared by the pack. Her shortcomings as a woman are reinforced twice more: she remains almost the only single person in the wolf or Cullen groups, which is signaled as a negative state in a series that prizes the notion of soul mates (or imprinting, as the wolves call it); and she loses the essential marker of young femininity, menstruation, because of the (ironically) frozen state of shapeshifters. Leah is unhappy and sees herself as a "genetic dead end" (*Breaking Dawn* 291), seeing a connection between shapeshifting and her inability to have children (*Breaking Dawn* 291). Yet if a nuclear family is a prized state in this series, Bella's willingness to forgo childbearing to secure her future with Edward, and Leah's depression over her inability to have children, suggest that Leah is portrayed in a positive way, to some extent, although ultimately Bella does have a child and Leah remains alone.

In *Twilight*, then, we can see again a theme that humanity offers more scope for gender shifting than paranormal creatures. Bella occupies a privileged position because of her humanity in contrast to Edward's vampire existence. For the female characters, the human state is the only one in which they can attain the privilege of motherhood. Neither Rosalie Hale (a vampire whose body cannot accommodate change) nor Leah (a shapeshifter whose body apparently changes too much) can have children, and this is very much configured as a loss. Averill argues that "female reproduction is a limitation of the female body" in the novels, where the series "portrays female reproduction as a hurdle to overcome. Meyer celebrates the vampire state, an overt patriarchal worldview, and portrays it as perfection so much so that her readers are literally rooting for Bella's change, rooting for Bella's death and the death of her biologically female state" (235). Yet we suggest that the opposite is true. These novels privilege flexibility and change as markers of freedom and new life, particularly in *Breaking Dawn*. It is part of Jacob's appeal to Bella that she can imagine their future life with their children (*Eclipse* 469); when she decides to become a vampire she knows she will lose this option. Rosalie, a Cullen vampire, continually mourns the loss of the human ability to bear children, and she thus becomes an unexpected ally when Bella becomes pregnant with Edward's child. Vampires can only attain families artificially, either by newborns (newly transformed vampires) or choice (the Cullen family is an artificial arrangement of like-minded vampires choosing to live together). Bella's ability to conceive a child would be impossible if she were already a vampire, because pregnancy and childbirth require change, transformation, even shapeshifting:

> Of course Rosalie could not conceive a child, because she was frozen in the state in which she passed from human to inhuman. Totally unchanging. And human women's bodies had to *change* to bear children. The constant change of a monthly cycle for one thing, and then the bigger changes needed to accommodate a growing child. Rosalie's body couldn't change. But mine could [*Breaking Dawn* 114].

The repeated emphasis on change and transformation is important. Here, the series seems to privilege a natural, human state of flux over the unnatural, inhuman fixed state of the vampire. The werewolves' shapeshifting and fluid identity offer similar possibilities of change and renewal, but, crucially, not for the female shapeshifters. What is especially intriguing here is the significance of childbirth. Children represent the future and the potential for a generational continuity of legacy and tradition. The renewal of the Cullen family is never certain. They cannot reproduce without death (changing humans to vampires by ending life). They may live forever, but they can be killed. The continued legacy of the wolves is assured in that they can have children, and their children can inherit the same gift.

The same theme presents in *The Vampire Diaries* television series, where werewolves can bear children but vampires cannot. Caroline reasons that Elena and Stefan cannot expect their relationship to last: "You're a human, he's a vampire. You're going to be seventy and in diapers and he's still going to be smoking hot. And you will never have his children, Elena, and you are too maternal to not have children" (2.04). When she faces the prospect of being forced to become a vampire in Season Two, Elena mourns her loss: "I was supposed to grow up, decide if I want to have kids, and start a family, grow old. I was supposed to have a lifetime of those choices and now? It's all gone. I don't want to be a vampire, Stefan, I never wanted to be one" (2.20). Although Elena would have still lived in a sense after being killed by Klaus, her father John wants to give her a human existence and the ability to have a child plays a key part in his decision to give his own life up so that Elena may achieve this. As he writes in his farewell letter,

> It's no easy task being an ordinary parent to an extraordinary child. I failed in that task. And because of my prejudices, I failed you. I'm haunted by how things might have played out differently, if I'd been more willing to hear your side of things. For me, it's the end. For you, a chance to grow old and someday do better with your own child than I did with mine. It's for that child that I give you my ring [2.21].

However, unlike *Twilight*, the ability of werewolves to bear children is not a positive mark in *The Vampire Diaries*. Instead, it is negative because it perpetuates a genetic "curse," as Mason Lockwood refers to it, whereby the children are condemned to the same torment should they activate the particular lupine gene (by killing someone).

Shapeshifting in these series, then, is contrarily a fixed and limited state. It is generally only the human women who can move outside traditional gender roles, such as Scarlett or Gretchen, or who can experience the physical changes of mortal women, a theme that is reinforced when Bella or Elena can envisage becoming pregnant as a human while Rosalie and Leah are confined to their identity as supernatural creatures, unable to change. This restriction is not just physical but also psychological; Leah is unable to exercise free will, bound to follow either Sam or Jacob as her leader. Human women have the choice of existing outside the patriarchal pack system, as Bryn does.

It is therefore interesting that in many of these texts it is the female human characters with stable bodies and boundaries who offer the most resistance against the traditional stereotypes and restrictions of gender roles. Instead, it is often the shapeshifting characters, the male and female werewolves with their unstable bodies, who seem more likely to be bound to conform to unchanging gender norms and hierarchies.

Three

Till Death Do Us Part and Beyond: Shapeshifting, Desire and Sexuality

> *She could be attracted—well, obviously she could. And she could have sex with one, again an obvious statement. But she couldn't go into heat with a human, and a mated werewolf always bred with its mate.*
> —Love, *My Sister Is a Werewolf* 53

There is a long history linking vampirism with overt sexuality, from Bram Stoker's shapeshifting vampire *Dracula* through to contemporary representations such as *True Blood*. Similarly, werewolves have also been linked to animal desires. It is no great surprise, then, that a large number of shapeshifting texts focus on sexual relationships involving supernatural characters. Recent representations of shapeshifting have begun to move beyond purely heteronormative representations of sexuality and desire, although perhaps not as much as one might reasonably expect of characters whose identity is not fixed. This chapter explores these issues as represented in HBO's *True Blood* and Charlaine Harris's Sookie Stackhouse novels (on which the aforementioned television series is based), the *Red Riding Hood* film, Kathy Love's novel *My Sister Is a Werewolf*, Karen MacInerney's *Tales of an Urban Werewolf* trilogy, and Amelia Atwater-Rhodes's *The Shapeshifters: The Kiesha'ra of the Den of Shadows (Volume 4: Wolfcry)*, and contrasts these representations with those in the YA market. In the latter context, L. J. Smith's *The Vampire Diaries* and its CW network television adaptation, and the groundbreaking television series, *Buffy, the Vampire Slayer*, will be examined.

Punter and Byron have argued that the "Gothic always remains the symbolic site of a culture's discursive struggle to define and claim possession of the civilised, and to abject, or throw off, what is seen as other to the civilised self" (15). Exploration and representations of sexuality have thus always been a significant focus when examining Gothic texts. In Victorian England, vampires were an encoded means of discussing sexuality, power relations and penetration; werewolves and alter egos such as Mr. Hyde were a means of examining the baser side of humanity. Queer figures such as Joseph Le Fanu's Carmilla threatened the "established patriarchal hierarchical distance of sanctioned relationships" (Auerbach 260). Auerbach also notes the links between vampires and their animalistic desires, which manifested in early works such as Bram Stoker's *Dracula* in an ability to shift into an animal form (295). These elements are to be found in contemporary shapeshifting texts, albeit in modified forms.

Justin Edwards notes that Gothic literature is fundamentally about breaking down stable identities and unsettling "the smooth surfaces of selfhood" (xviii). It is, at its core, about questioning fixed identities and assumptions about binary differences (Edwards xviii). It is perhaps unsurprising, then, that questions around sexuality are central to a number of paranormal texts, and those aimed at a YA audience, in particular. What arguably is somewhat less predictable is that the majority of these texts do not move beyond traditional, monogamous lifelong heterosexual pairings, with only a handful acknowledging the full range of expressions of human sexuality.

The figures of the vampire and the werewolf have again been linked in stories which have risen to prominence in recent times, with Stephenie Meyer's *Twilight* series the flagship of the current *Zeitgeist*. Modern Gothic texts have explored the tension between traditional representations of the vampire, which were located within these very particular social and cultural structures, and the ways in which these are problematized by modern life. Meyer's male protagonist, Edward Cullen, for example, is viewed by his mortal love interest, Bella Swan, and legions of fans as a gentleman, representative of the morals and manners of an earlier time. A 106-year-old virgin, Edward actively discourages Bella from demonstrating her desire for him, and ultimately will only consummate their relationship within marriage. *Twilight* suggests that the awkward Bella finally becomes all she can be through the social institutions of marriage and motherhood. In this respect, *Twilight* is highly unusual within the current spate of supernatural texts, which typically include sexual relationships outside of marriage, and occasionally include non-heteronormative representations of sexuality.

Sex and the Single Shifter: Letting the Good Times Roll in Bon Temps

The phenomenally popular character of Sookie Stackhouse, for example, is one who seeks physical intimacy as much as romance and agency. Throughout Charlaine Harris's eleven novels to date and the first three seasons of Alan Ball's screen adaptation for HBO, Sookie seeks to reconcile her decisions and behavior around her Christian beliefs and ideas about civility and propriety (Poole 82), even in the face of an ever-increasing array of supernatural monsters and her own burgeoning sexuality.

When readers first meet her, she is a virginal twenty-something waitress who lives with her grandmother, having been orphaned as a child. Sookie is also psychic, a gift that she configures as both a liability and a disability. She is clearly working class and is viewed with some suspicion by others in the town of Bon Temps because of her unusual abilities, yet she continues to define herself as a lady, and demands to be treated as such. Her values are largely shaped by what Wilcott describes as "the conservative social codes that still linger in the Deep South" (115). Sookie is fiercely loyal to her family and friends, and respects her elders even when she is not convinced that they deserve it.

Although the novel series focuses largely on her two vampire paramours and her own uniqueness, Bon Temps and the settlement on its outskirts known as Hot Shot both contain significant populations of shapeshifters. In Harris's world, "shifters" are multi-bodied shapeshifters who are able to transform into an animal of their choice at will; they must, however, change shape at the full moon. Only the first-born child of two shifters will carry this trait. Weres, on the other hand, are dual-bodied shapeshifters, only able to transform into that one animal shape. Sookie has shapeshifter-suitors throughout the series, in the form of her loyal friend, boss, and sometime admirer Sam Merlotte, werepanther Calvin Norris and werewolf pack leader Alcide Herveaux. In the middle books of the series, *Definitely Dead, From Dead to Worse*, and *Dead and Gone*, she has her only sexual relationship with a non-vampire to date, during her relationship with weretiger John Quinn.

Over the course of the series Sookie becomes increasingly aware of the gamut of supernatural creatures — or "supes"— as they are termed in the series (*Living Dead in Dallas* 168). Shapeshifting characters are inherently "queer" subjects in that their identities are fluid. The ultimate border crossers, they place their audiences in unfamiliar reading positions. Theorists such as Alexander Doty and David Buchbinder argue that while the term "queer" is generally understood as a signifier of "non-heterosexual, non-traditionally gendered individuals or groups" (Buchbinder 149), "queerness as a theoretical concept is rather more elusive" (Buchbinder 149). Doty argues that

> [h]omosexuals as well as heterosexuals can operate or mediate from within straight cultural places and positions ... and basically heterosexual, straight-identifying people can experience queer moments. And these people should be encouraged to examine and express these moments as "queer" ... the cultural "queer space" recog-

nizes the possibility that various and fluctuating queer positions might be occupied whenever *anyone* produces or responds to culture [3].

In other words, as Buchbinder asserts, readers experience queer moments when "reading texts or understanding situations from a reading position which one would not normally occupy" (Buchbinder 166).

Sookie's whole world is effectively queered when she becomes aware of the existence of shapeshifters. The first shifter of whom she becomes aware is her boss, Sam Merlotte. Sookie typically exerts an effort to stay out of his thoughts, suggesting via first-person narration that she has lost jobs before because of inadvertently reading the minds of her employers (*Dead Until Dark* 24). Early in the first novel, Sookie hears the thoughts of the Rattrays, a couple who are planning to drain the first vampire Sookie has ever met, Bill Compton, and sell his blood as an illicit drug. Although she saves Bill in an altercation, she earns Sam's ire in the process. He grabs her by the shoulders and gives her "a little shake" (*Dead Until Dark* 25) when he warns her not to play vigilante in future. First-person narrator Sookie notes that the sense of touch "accelerates [her] disability" (*Dead Until Dark* 25) and she learns not only that Sam desires her, but that she "couldn't hear his thoughts as clearly as ... other people's ... [it was m]ore like wearing a mood ring than getting a fax" (*Dead Until Dark* 25). Later, Sam invites her to listen to his mind sometime, assuring her that whatever she hears, she will have a job at Merlotte's while ever she wants one (*Dead Until Dark* 62). She later describes his thoughts as a "semiopaque snarly tangle" (*Living Dead in Dallas* 180), neither the same as the absence of thought that she feels around vampires nor the more obvious thoughts of humans. Having saved Bill from "Drainers," Sookie herself becomes a target, and Sam, in the form of a collie dog, accompanies her home and offers her protection. Several references to popular culture are made when Sookie struggles to find a name by which to call the dog, which she believes to be a stray, beginning by asking if she should call it Buffy (*Dead Until Dark* 248), before finally settling on Dean (*Dead Until Dark* 249) (which appears to be an allusion to the brothers Sam and Dean Winchester, who are the main characters in *Supernatural*). When "Dean" wakes on her bed as a naked and human Sam, Sookie is shocked and it is only then that she learns of the existence of shifters (*Dead Until Dark* 251). This also precipitates Sookie admitting that her new boyfriend and first lover, Bill, is "really dead," rather than affected by a virus which renders him sensitive to sunlight, silver and garlic, as the vampire spin doctors have led the public to believe (*Dead Until Dark* 252).

Despite his stated (and subliminal) desire for Sookie and his dislike of Bill, Sam demonstrates true loyalty and friendship to her when Sookie spends one very long day waiting to discover if the fourth and unidentified body of a vampire killed in a house fire by local vigilantes is Bill's. Sam distracts her thoroughly with a bout of extreme house cleaning which includes polishing all the wood finishes and her late grandmother's silver, and washing all the blinds and curtains so that "[b]y the time the light was growing dim, [Sookie] had the cleanest house in Renard parish" (*Dead Until Dark* 178). He then excuses himself, stating that he realizes that Sookie will want to be alone. This vignette from the novel demonstrates traits that are constructed as essential components of Sam's personality—loyalty, companionship, intelligence and a strong work ethic, and are reflected in his preferred animal shape, that of a collie dog.

Sam further demonstrates understanding and compassion in *Living Dead in Dallas*, noting that Merlotte's murdered short-order cook, Lafayette Reynolds, who was African American and openly gay, "wanted to be accepted for what he was more than anything else" (*Living Dead in Dallas* 17). In the second novel, Sookie and her friends find themselves under the threat of a maenad, an ancient Greek creature who takes a particular interest in bars and who chooses to maim Sookie as a warning to the Viking vampire Eric Northman, owner of the nightclub, *Fangtasia* (and the other apex of the vampiric love triangle in which Sookie becomes involved throughout the series). Sookie, in turn, warns Sam, because he is a supe and owns a bar, and she also notes that he "had been wonderful to me when I'd lost my grandmother, and I counted him as a good friend, a great boss and (every now and then) a sexual fantasy" (*Living Dead in Dallas* 51–52). Sookie repeatedly links this particular shapeshifting character with sexuality and desire.

As a fellow supe, Sam is evidently well-informed on maenads, telling Sookie that they prefer large game, like bears and tigers, prompting Sookie to note that it is "[h]ard to find a tiger in Louisiana" (*Living Dead in Dallas* 54), foreshadowing the arrival of her love interest and weretiger, Quinn, in subsequent novels. To Sookie's surprise, Sam enters a sexual relationship with the maenad, and Bill points out to Sookie that it must be hard for Sam to "find someone who can accept his true nature" (*Living Dead in Dallas* 281), echoing Sam's earlier sentiments with regard to Lafayette. Sexuality and shapeshifting are thus linked as fundamental components of identity which are necessary in order to find acceptance.

The early Sookie Stackhouse novels are characterized by the inclusion of a murder mystery that Sookie helps to solve, and in this novel, she determines to find out how Lafayette met his death. As part of this agenda, she agrees to attend a local sex party. Owing to the prolonged absence of her boyfriend Bill, Sookie does not have vampire protection, and thus she asks Eric to attend as her faux lover. As someone who has had to reconstruct his identity many times over the centuries, he apparently has no issues with the role-playing aspect of this, arriving in pink and black lycra and cheerily suggesting: "I could be bisexual?" (*Living Dead in Dallas* 252). The reader learns in *Dead and Gone* and *Dead in the Family* that although Eric clearly considers himself to be heterosexual, he has indeed been in at least one long-term sexual relationship with a male, his maker, Appius Livius Ocella. He tells Sookie that "when you're a new vampire, anything sexual seems exciting, so even that I enjoyed" (*Dead and Gone* 89), although he does qualify this statement with the afterthought: "eventually" (*Dead and Gone* 89). Upon Ocella's arrival at Sookie's house, with another wayward vampire "child"—the psychologically damaged tsarevitch Alexei Romanov—in tow, Eric further notes that if Ocella were to make a sexual request of him again, he would be required to comply, regardless of his feelings for—or indeed, by this late stage of the sequence, his marriage to—Sookie (*Dead in the Family* 244).

Similarly, in the third novel, *Club Dead*, Bill returns to his maker, Lorena, and finds himself once again in her sexual thrall, leaving it to *Fangtasia* vampires Eric and Pam to protect Sookie from seemingly ever-present supernatural threats. Sexual orientation is also represented as being very fluid within the television series, although here it is not limited only to vampires. Sookie appears to accept the news that her lifelong best friend Tara is in a homosexual relationship unreservedly, although this does provide one of the series' many queer moments:

TARA: I didn't plan it. Just kinda fell for her.
SOOKIE: And these years we've been friends, you never—
TARA: It's not like that with you.
SOOKIE: I was gonna say, you never knew you liked girls [4.05].

Those who have consumed vampire blood also find themselves bonded in extraordinary ways, providing some of the queerest moments in the series. In dream sequences, we see erotic fantasies: Tara's is of her abuser, Franklin Mott; Sam and Bill have a shirtless conversation about showering together, and Jason fantasizes about his best friend Hoyt's girlfriend, Jessica, before her visage shifts into that of Hoyt himself.

Becca Wilcott has argued that *True Blood* is "as queer as they come.... Everything the show discusses, from the persecution of minorities in society to the challenges faced by an independent woman in the South to straight sexual addiction, is filtered through a queer lens" (Wilcott 87). This "queer lens" challenges notions of labeling from the outset. Notions of identity are further explored in the repeated questions around what—not who—Sookie is; a question that she neatly and uncannily sidesteps for the first two-and-a-half seasons with the naive response: "I'm a waitress." Viewers' reactions to queerness, labeling and prejudice are largely determined through the character of Sookie Stackhouse, whose narrative viewpoint is the focus of the series. She is herself an outsider, as are her lovers (Lima 38). Sookie encourages the reader to move beyond heteronormative romances and accept particular partnerships on their merits, regardless of the individuals' minority status. Bigotry and labeling are routinely rejected throughout the series.

True Blood is graphic and often confronting in its depictions of sexuality and desire, but it is effectively drawing on a long tradition of homoerotic vampirism; as Nina Auerbach notes in *Our Vampires, Ourselves*, "in the nineteenth century, vampires were vampires *because* they loved. They offered an intimacy ... that threatened the hierarchical distance of sanctioned relationships" (60). Clearly attitudes to sexual morality have changed markedly in the twenty-first century, and Michelle Belanger suggests that "[h]omosexuality, bisexuality, and pansexuality are all topics that can be freely explored within the vampire trope, because the vampire's needs are redirected to something everyone, regardless of gender or orientation, has: blood" (qtd. in Wilcott 18). Within the vampire world, definitions around orientation are particularly fluid, as Makers and Progeny appear to often enter intimate relationships even with those to whom they are not attracted. Indeed, in the actions of Bill and Lorena we see that a vampire who absolutely loathes his or her Maker finds it difficult to reject their sexual advances. We also see that "straight" vampires such as Eric have clearly had and/or are prepared to enter into homosexual relationships. Pam clearly has a deep love for Eric and the television series intimates that it has been physical in the past. Her apparent lesbianism is confirmed in the novels wherein she is described as being omnisexual but preferring women. Similarly, when predominantly gay vampires Russell and Sophie-Anne marry for political purposes in the third season of the television series, the level of hysteria with which this is greeted by Russell's consort, Talbot, strongly implies that very real sexual jealousy is at play. In the world of the novels, it is a requirement that there is at least one conjugal visit between royals and their consorts each year, regardless of the individuals' sexual preferences or personal desires, and a consort may not be shared with a human lover (*Dead Reckoning* 252, 260).

While Sookie is under his care, Eric assigns her protection in the form of Alcide Herveaux, whom she immediately identifies as a werewolf (*Club Dead* 57). It is Alcide who explains to Sookie — and by extension, the reader — the rules of shapeshifting genetics in Harris's world; for example, that only purebred weres can create a were-child, and that infant mortality is high (*Club Dead* 67). Only the eldest child can carry the trait, which, in the tradition of many werewolf narratives, manifests at puberty (*Club Dead* 67). Sookie poses as Alcide's girlfriend as part of her plan to locate and rescue Bill. In the process, she draws the attention of his ex-girlfriend, Debbie Pelt, a shapeshifter who, along with her sister, Sandra, become Sookie's enemy throughout the book series. Sookie and Alcide share a kiss towards the end of the novel, despite her growing conviction that he "would never be happy with anyone but another Were" (*Club Dead* 280). At the end of the novel, she rescinds her invitations to both Bill and Eric, leaving her house vampire-free for the first time in months, and seemingly paving the way for a romance with one of her shapeshifter suitors. The next novel, however, *Dead to the World*, focuses almost exclusively on the development of her relationship with Eric, who suffers from personality-changing amnesia as the result of a witch-induced spell for most of the book.

Concurrently, her brother Jason develops a relationship with Crystal Norris. Despite his resistance to all things supernatural, he quickly becomes deeply involved with Crystal, who is revealed to be a werepanther from the liminal small community of Hot Shot. The close-knit community becomes a metonym for sexual deviance, with Sam warning Sookie: "That's an old settlement. An inbred settlement" (*Dead to the World* 130). Sookie is unfamiliar with the ways of the Hot Shot community until her brother Jason disappears and she seeks information from Crystal. Crystal's uncle, Calvin Norris, is the leader of the community, and forces Crystal to share what she knows. He confides to Sookie that Crystal is as flawed in her animal persona as she is rude in her human one; she is only able to change at the full moon, and even then, not very effectively (*Dead to the World* 141). He then makes Sookie an unexpected offer, saying that since she is a woman without protection in the absence of both Bill and Jason, he could be "her man" (*Dead to the World* 140). He has heard that she is different, and notes that although the community needs "an infusion of new blood, new genes" (*Dead to the World* 141), an "ordinary woman" would not survive long in Hot Shot. Among the werepanthers, as among the vampires, Sookie's difference is viewed as desirable.

Jason is eventually discovered in a shed owned by Felton Norris, a rival for Crystal's affections. Felton had held Jason captive and bitten him on a nightly basis, so that Jason would also be a werepanther. He hoped that in so doing, he would remove Jason's intrigue and appeal as an outsider, to make Crystal less interested in him. Ironically, Felton made Jason more of an outsider, in that those who were "bitten, not born" (*Dead as a Doornail* 4) "changed into the half-man, half-beast creatures who populated horror movies" (*Dead to the World* 273). Jason will thus wear the stigma of this cross-cultural relationship for life, alienated from the non-were and were-communities alike by his difference; he is no longer truly human, but is also an outcast even within the Hot Shot community. Here long-established cultural paranoia about miscegenation is played out in the fantasy context. Jason's apparent inability to control his bodily desires is likewise extrapolated in the loss of control over his body's shape, which is now dictated by the lunar cycle.

Jason's relationship with Crystal is as ambivalent as his identity; after one miscarriage to him and when pregnant again, the couple marries (*All Together Dead* 44, 49–53), only for her to cheat on Jason while the child is still *in utero* (*From Dead to Worse* 250–51). Although this causes a rift between himself and Sookie, who, along with Calvin, is witness to Crystal's infidelity, Jason quickly establishes a new relationship with Michele Schubert (*From Dead to Worse* 315). Later in the pregnancy, Crystal is found murdered on a wooden cross, with silver nails keeping her hands and feet as panther claws (*Dead and Gone* 58–9).

Sookie's loving (and serial) monogamous relationships are privileged throughout the series over Jason's often transitory ones, and in this instance, she rejects the possibility of a relationship with Calvin because of his commitments to other women in the community; that is, he has fathered four children in the Hot Shot to four mothers (*Dead as a Doornail* 251; *Definitely Dead* 82). Although he tells her he has done his duty and can now be hers exclusively, Sookie claims to be "just too human to think of having my husband's children all around me ... knowing my husband had had sex with almost every woman I saw day-to-day" (*Definitely Dead* 83). She immediately contrasts herself with Jason, noting that he should be able to fit in to Hot Shot, because of his own promiscuous history (*Definitely Dead* 83), presumably implying that even before his brush with the werepanthers, his behavior — at least in the eyes of his sister — is somewhat less than human.

The other significant relationship between a human and a shapeshifter is the one between Sookie and weretiger Quinn, who first appears in *Dead as a Doornail*. Well known throughout the supernatural community, Quinn is an event manager who asks Sookie to use her psychic abilities when witnessing the competition for packmaster between Alcide's father Jackson and his rival Patrick Furnan. After Sookie uses her telepathy to understand that Furnan is cheating in one of the tests, Sookie is injured by Furnan and Quinn licks her leg wound to heal it, an action they both find sexually stimulating (*Dead as a Doornail* 275–76). During this interlude, Quinn loses physical control of his body and he begins to move subtly towards a more animalistic version of his human self, reflected in his eyes, which change to their golden tiger color. He promises Sookie that they will see each other again (*Dead as a Doornail* 277).

Furnan wins the competition, and kills Jackson Herveaux. As the winner and new packmaster, Furnan is brought a teenage girl, with whom he will undertake the public and "ceremonial gesture of breeding" a "whelp" in addition to his legitimate shapeshifter son and non-shifter daughter (*Dead as a*

Doornail 281). Sookie finds the public nature of the interchange and the infidelity to Furnan's wife distasteful, but is told by her fairy relative, Claudine, that she must remain, even if she chooses not to watch. In a later novel, *From Dead to Worse*, Alcide and other members of the Long Tooth pack defend their territory against a refugee from Hurricane Katrina, Priscilla Herbert, and a group of her followers. When Furnan dies in the skirmish, Alcide declares himself leader of the pack and is "very excited. All over" (*From Dead to Worse* 140). Sookie's non-werewolf friends who are also present, Claudine and Sam, this time advise her to leave while the pack "celebrate[s] their victory and the ascension of a new packmaster" (*From Dead to Worse* 144), and Sookie worries that she cannot tell whether Alcide is going to rape the hostages or kill them (*From Dead to Worse* 140). Interestingly, the reader does not learn the fate of the two females and one male, either, because Sookie "tried not to listen to the noises" as she was escorted away (*From Dead to Worse* 140), and, as the first-person narrator and focalizer, the limits of Sookie's knowledge are shared by her readership.

Quinn returns in *Definitely Dead*, and on their first date, they are attacked by "a brand-new, fresh half Were" (*Definitely Dead* 97) and his accomplice, both of whom Sookie thinks were on drugs (*Definitely Dead* 99). Sookie notes that going through this ordeal together "had probably accelerated our relationship the equivalent of four dates" (*Definitely Dead* 101) after they share a passionate post–adrenaline-rush kiss. Sookie, who believes that both her previous sexual relationships — with the vampires Bill Compton, who cheated on her with his maker, Lorena, and with the amnesiac Eric Northman — were ultimately ill-considered, has vowed to herself to be less impulsive in her future sexual relationships, yet when she and Quinn are later interrupted by a telephone call, she claims to have been: "within an ace of chucking [her] good resolutions out the window" (*Definitely Dead* 247). She tells him that she "'never set out to be a one-night stand kind of a woman'" and he reassures her by asking, "[w]ho would want just one night with you?" (*Definitely Dead* 248). Lust is linked to the animal within in both characters; in Sookie, through her loss of logic and resolve, and in Quinn through the emergence of his tiger-like qualities.

The pair is kidnapped by the family of Debbie Pelt, causing Quinn to partially change at least twice as a means of fighting more effectively, before he finally decides that he needs to change completely. Sookie views the naked Quinn before his transformation and notes that "[e]very conjecture I'd had about Quinn's body was absolutely on target ... [it was] a work of art, though a scarred work of art" (*Definitely Dead* 275). With the assistance of Quinn as a tiger, and Eric who appears in response to Sookie's distress, the Pelts are overcome. Sookie decides to go in search of the clothes of the now human–

again and naked Quinn, after deciding that she is "not sophisticated enough to be comfortable in a room with a naked guy, an unconscious guy, a real horrible girl, and another guy who's been my lover" (*Definitely Dead* 283).

Quinn and Sookie attend a party in honor of the Queen of Louisiana, Sophie-Anne Leclerq, and her new husband, the King of Arkansas, Peter Threadgill, which rapidly descends into carnage, prompting Quinn to once more assume his tiger form. At the end of the evening, they return to the home of Sookie's late cousin, Hadley, and are greeted by Hadley's downstairs neighbor, the witch Amelia Broadway, who confesses that she has turned her fellow witch, Bob, into a cat during some adventurous sex. Amelia asks if she and the feline Bob can come and stay with Sookie for a while and she responds in the affirmative, noting that she likes cats. Quinn is delighted to hear that, given that he was too tired to completely transform, and now has a tail. Sookie tells him that he will be sleeping on the floor (*Definitely Dead* 317), as though he is as much a pet as the hapless Bob. In the next book in the sequence, *All Together Dead*, Sookie agrees that they may consummate their relationship after Quinn assures her that he is planning to take a month off after the vampire summit they will both be attending, and asks to spend his vacation time with her. Sookie, whose previous two lovers have been vampires, finds the experience novel; firstly, she has never made love in the daytime before, and secondly, she has to consider birth control (*All Together Dead* 33–34). Quinn's animal nature is highlighted during the sex scene, with Sookie noting that his "tongue was just a bit raspier than a regular man's" (*All Together Dead* 35). Despite all her insistences that she is not a one-night stand kind of a person, however, Sookie is separated from Quinn during a bomb-blast at the vampire conference, and Quinn's younger half-sister, Frannie, takes him home to Memphis to recover (*All Together Dead* 317). Sookie admits to Eric in the next book that she has not seen nor heard from Quinn since (*From Dead to Worse* 52). Quinn has become beholden to Victor Madden, a vampire from Nevada who has assassinated all the vampire sheriffs bar Eric as an emissary for the Nevada King, who is trying to take over Louisiana and Arkansas. Eric and Bill reluctantly accept the sovereignty of the new King, Felipe de Castro, and Sookie expresses anger at watching Quinn, in his tiger form, on the side of the enemy vampires. He discusses his situation with her the next day, and while she concedes that he was only trying to protect his mother and sister, she breaks up with him, saying that they will always come first, and she is selfish enough to want to be his priority (*From Dead to Worse* 187).

The overarching thesis of the book series is that individuals should be judged according to their actions, rather than classified according to race, gender, sexuality or other innate traits, such as the ability to shift shape, yet although Harris attempts to critique these beliefs, some of them appear to be reconstituted in order to uphold accepted moral norms. Sookie's morals with regard to were-breeding practices are certainly conservative, for example. Alan Ball's adaptation of Harris's novels, *True Blood*, is arguably less morally conservative; it does, at least, establish loving homosexual relationships, in stark contrast to the noticeably shortened life spans of the majority of the gay and bisexual characters in the novels. As such, it does a more convincing job of arguing that an individual should be judged on his or her choices, rather than ethnicity, class, gender or sexuality. The main villain in Season Two, the maenad is reconstructed as a shapeshifter, rather than merely a foil to the shapeshifting Sam. Known as Callisto in the novels, the television version of the maenad is named Maryann, evoking the innocence of the *Gilligan's Island* favorite, and is given an altered backstory which includes a sexual history with a then-adolescent Sam. She is also given an accomplice in Daphne, another shapeshifter and love interest of Sam's. Temptation and lust are thus constructed as forces with the ability to obfuscate the truth and lure a predominantly 'good' individual towards evil.

Sex and the Southern Belle

The television series has become synonymous with sex and violence, and Sookie's sexuality as depicted within it is, as in the novels, inextricably linked with the mythos of the Southern belle. The television incarnation of Sookie is arguably more feisty and independent than the Sookie of the novels; for example, whereas the novel iteration of Sookie constantly laments that she and Bill could not marry even if he were to propose, the television Sookie faces no such legal impediment, yet hesitates when Bill proposes in the Season Two finale. Sookie has more social and political power than Southern women of previous generations (Rogers 58), and is, as Lillian Craton and Kathryn Jonell have noted, "truly a woman of her times, living out all of the complexities and ambiguities of contemporary feminism while maintaining a tough, spunky, 'girl power' appeal" (110).

As in the novels, Sookie is introduced as a Christian who is horrified by the baser side of humanity. She deems swearing and sexual innuendo to be "nasty," and her love life has been nonexistent because she can read her dates' minds and realize their intentions early in the evening. She flees in an embarrassed fluster when her colleagues Lafayette, Dawn and Arlene indulge in a lascivious conversation in the pilot episode, "Strange Love." When the vampire Bill Compton enters Merlotte's Bar and Grill, he seems like the answer to her prayers; she cannot read his thoughts, and he appears to be a Southern gentleman whose manners hearken back to an earlier time. He is the first temptation she has met that she has not been able to conquer (Poole 82), but she has significant qualms about their relationship, which are later shown to be well-founded.

When introduced to the world of the supernatural, however, Sookie ultimately comes to behave with more agency. Rather than avoiding listening to nasty language, she begins to use it herself when fighting back against vampire threats. While it is true that initially this could be construed as being a side-effect of the increased libido that comes with drinking vampire blood, Sookie is eventually revealed to have supernatural powers of her own, when her fairy heritage is discovered. Fairy blood, according to Harris and Ball, is particularly intoxicating to vampires and thus the degree to which Bill and Eric can excercise free around their desire for her is compromised. In Ball's mythos, vampires who have ingested fairy blood are able to withstand sunlight, albeit briefly. Just as Nosferatu required the blood of a pure woman as a cure for the plague (Gelder 95), so too is the blood of the nice-natured fairy-human-hybrid Sookie a cure for the ills of vampires; namely, being bound to the darkness. No longer, however, are the vampires' fangs an erotic metaphor and a means of making inferences about sex (Auerbach 84), as they were in Victorian times; rather, sexual relationships are an integral part of the contemporary televisual vampire narrative. Nowhere is this more pronounced than in *True Blood*.

Pansexuality, Penetration and Paws: Keeping One's "Inner Cool"

The suggestion that contemporary vampires are pansexual is an extrapolation of the representation of their literary maker, Lord Dracula, who was a sexual predator. Even though most modern vampires do not share his ability to shift shape, they do retain the representations of animalistic and unfettered desire. The Gothic is noted for its ability to interrogate stable identities, and the vampire tradition has thus been reshaped for a twenty-first century audience; ironically, the shape and form of the vampire has been significantly altered to the point where such figures have typically lost the physical ability to do so. Television representations of the vampire as in *Buffy, the Vampire Slayer* and *The Vampire Diaries*, however, pay homage to this history by showing the vampires' faces change form when they are at their least human.

In the late 1990s, *Buffy, the Vampire Slayer* dealt explicitly with teen sexuality, with lead character Buffy facing unexpected consequences after sleeping with her boyfriend, the vampire Angel. Characterized as a vampire with a soul, Angel was cursed to lose it again if he were ever to experience a moment of pure happiness (2.13). Consequently Buffy literally wakes to find a young man who has completely changed since she made the decision to consummate their relationship (2.14). Later, vampire penetration as a metaphor for sex is employed when Buffy's younger sister, Dawn, goes parking with a boy she barely knows. He assures her that she is special and he just wants to "taste" her. Dawn's first kiss is rudely interrupted when his passion causes an involuntary bodily reaction — he shifts into his vampire-face, alerting her to his true intention, which is to go "all the way" and make her a vampire, too. His dialog through the episode is that of a teenage boy trying to talk around a girl in whom he is interested, and is interrupted by the appearance of father-figure Giles, who acidly remarks: "I bet you say that to all the girls" (6.06).

Although a number of shapeshifting characters were used throughout the *Buffy* series, as noted in the Introduction, the most obvious example was the character of Daniel "Oz" Osborne, who was involved in a complex love triangle which also included witches Willow and Tara. Appearing in Series Two through Four, with further appearances in the comic book series *Buffy, the Vampire Slayer Season Eight* and the spin-off television program *Angel*, Oz becomes a werewolf after being bitten by his young cousin. As noted in Chapter Two, an explicit correlation is drawn between Oz's monthly "affliction" and that of his girlfriend, Willow. Oz voluntarily locks himself in a secure part of the school library each month, to render himself incapable of hurting any innocent people whilst in his primal form. In Season Four when Buffy and her friends — also known as the Scooby Gang or the Slayerettes — enroll in college, however, Oz finds himself inexplicably drawn to a singer in a rival band, named Veruca (4.05). When Willow is concerned by Oz's apparent interest in Veruca, Buffy's words of comfort echo the animalistic phrasing which is typical of expressions of sexuality, reassuring her that "Oz just isn't the type to stray" (4.06). Oz escapes his incarceration and meets a female werewolf, and when the two grapple with each other it is at first unclear whether the confrontation is antagonistic or sexual. When he wakes the next morning, naked, in human form and beside an equally naked Veruca, it becomes apparent that he has indeed "strayed," although he has no clear memory of what transpired while in his shifted form.

Veruca is a werewolf who has embraced her animal side, and insists to Oz that the animal inside is omnipresent and omnipotent. She tells him that she feels sorry for other people because they cannot feel as alive and free as they, with their animal natures, can; she further accuses him of having allowed himself to be "tamed" (4.06). A clearly conflicted Oz entices Veruca to join him in his cage, claiming that he is trying to keep her safe, because Buffy and her friends are aware of the existence of a second werewolf and will be hunting for it that night. His motives come under scrutiny, however, when they kiss, and the viewers see a close-up of their linked hands transforming.

Willow finds the pair the next morning, and is understandably devastated. When Oz tries to explain his actions, she asks "But you wanted her? Like, in an animal way? Like, more than you wanted me?" (4.06). Here lust and love are being delineated as categorically different processes. Veruca confronts Willow on the third and final transformative night of the month, but Oz interrupts, protecting Willow and, whilst in his werewolf form, killing Veruca. At the end of the episode, he tells a traumatized Willow that he is leaving town. Dressed in a sheepskin jacket, he tells her that Veruca was right about one thing: "The wolf is inside me all the time. And I don't know where that line is anymore, between me and it" and that he needs to be away from her until he figures out both sides of his identity (4.06). By the time of his unexpected return in Episode Nineteen of that season, "New Moon Rising," Willow has fallen in love with her fellow Wiccan, Tara, and she is confused as to where her loyalties lie. With Willow also wearing a sheepskin-lined jacket, which aligns her with Oz, her wolf in sheep's clothing, the pair walks around the college campus, discussing their situation. Oz asks for confirmation that Willow had "no new guy," unaware that her sexuality is no longer strictly heterosexual (4.19). He then points out to her that it is a full moon. Willow realizes that she has ceased to keep track of the lunar cycle, which indicates that she no longer thinks of him as she once had, and is genuinely confused when he earnestly tells he that he is a different person and has returned because he can now be what she needs (4.19).

Through meditative practices, Oz has learned to "keep his inner cool," and tame the animal side of himself, which had been explicitly linked to sexuality through his interactions with Veruca. When Oz bumps into Tara and smells Willow's scent on her, however, he loses his control over the animal side of his personality. Primitive lust and jealousy overtake him, and immediately after asking, "Are you two *involved?*," he begins to morph, warning Tara to run. As Tara fends him off in a lecture theater, two military agents, one of whom is dating Buffy, capture Oz and take him away for experimentation in their secret facility where they attempt to render demons harmless. After being rescued by Buffy's boyfriend, Riley, and the Scoobies, led by Spike, Oz confesses to Willow: "The one thing that brings it out in me is you." Producer Marti Noxon explained in the Season Four Overview DVD featurette that the werewolf storyline was deliberately developed as a means of consciously exploring the repression of the id; the simplified, subconscious and primal features of identity and sexuality.

The idea of keeping one's "inner cool," as explored in *Buffy, the Vampire Slayer* is again played out in Catherine Hardwicke's 2011 film, *Red Riding Hood*. Valerie is in love with a woodcutter named Peter, but her parents have organized her betrothal to Henry, who has better prospects. In an over-complicated plot, Valerie learns that the local werewolf feared by the villagers can speak to her, and it has brown, human eyes. She suspects first her grandmother, who has given her a red cloak as an early wedding gift, and later Peter, who sustains a burn on his right arm the same night as the wolf burns his right front paw by stepping onto consecrated ground. Ultimately, Valerie discovers that the wolf is her father, and he encourages her to become a wolf and come away with him, meaning that she has to choose between Peter (who has already made the same request of her) and the wolf, in one of many rather obvious allusions that are used throughout the film. During their final struggle, Valerie's father is killed, but Peter is bitten. Like Oz in *Buffy, the Vampire Slayer*, who ostracizes himself from society, Peter sails away, telling her, "I have to leave. You won't be safe with me. 'Til I learn how to protect you." Valerie pledges to wait for him and the film closes with her coyly smiling when the werewolf reappears in the woods.

Earlier in the film, sexuality had been explicitly linked to animal-like tendencies in a number of notable ways. Firstly, the opening scenes show Valerie as a young girl, claiming that she tried to be a good girl but was always tempted by Peter. This is illustrated when the pair play in the woods, hunting and slaughtering a rabbit. Later, when a villager erroneously believes that he has slain the werewolf, all the inhabitants of the village of Daggerhorn celebrate in a drunken, orgiastic party, during which a number of the townsfolk wear pig and sheep masks, both notable nemeses of fairytale wolves. Seeing Peter dancing suggestively with her friend Rose, Valerie quickly downs some alcohol, and leads her friend Prudence in a similarly robust dance. This attempt to titillate Peter appears to be effective, as Valerie and Peter soon share a lustful interlude in the hay of the granary, which is interrupted only by the werewolf's appearance in the village square.

Why Must I Be a Teen Werewolf in Love?

Contemporary questions about when it is permissible for teenagers to have sex, how lust and love interrelate, and what impact the decision to engage in sex may have on others' perceptions of the individual are explored in the current spate of supernatural romances in a myriad of ways. L. J. Smith's novel series *The Vampire Diaries*, for example, contains a number of characters who shift shape, and the evil supernatural characters often focus on adolescent bodies as the site for mischief. Sexually aggressive behavior is constructed as a sign that characters are demonically possessed, rather than an indicator of teenage sexual experimentation.

In the novels, Caroline Forbes—Elena's friend and occasional rival—

dates the werewolf Tyler Smallwood. She is later possessed by an insect-like Malach spirit under the control of a Japanese trickster fox or *kitsune* named Masao, who is herself a shapeshifter. During this stage, Caroline is able to shift her shape in unusual ways. Rather than taking on the form of a recognizable animal, when Elena's friends Bonnie McCullogh and Meredith Sulez confront Caroline, she is "scuttling ... [l]ike a lizard. Her bronze hair, unkempt, hung down over her face. Her elbows and knees stuck out at impossible angles" (*Nightfall* 263–64). Caroline is further able to hide under a bed which only has a "five-inch clearance" (265) and grab both girls simultaneously from different sides of the bed (266).

During this time Caroline behaves very provocatively, as do the younger girls whose behavior was discussed in Chapter One. Caroline attempts to seduce Matt, succeeds in seducing Jim, and finally tells her astonished friends after their defeat of Masao: "'I don't need your help! I need a *husband!*... Or at least a fiancé,' [with] one hand on her abdomen. 'My family would accept *that*'" (*Nightfall* 573). At the time of writing, this storyline is yet to be resolved. Caroline, for her part, accuses Matt of rape as an explanation for her condition. In *Nightfall* there is a suggestion that she is carrying an infant malach (573), but by the opening pages of the next novel, *Shadow Souls*, first-person narrator Elena tells the reader that she subscribes to Damon's theory that Caroline will deliver a "werewolf litter" (12) fathered by Tyler during their relationship.

In the television series of the same name produced by Kevin Williamson and Julie Plec, the character of Caroline has itself shifted shape significantly. Caroline is a newly-transformed vampire in a relationship with Matt Donovan. Tyler Lockwood (Matt's friend, rival and football teammate) is a teen werewolf who becomes romantically interested in Caroline when she helps him through his early transitions. Tyler's romantic desires are problematic, given that a werewolf bite is fatal to a vampire. This conundrum more or less encapsulates the core problem of the paranormal romance, highlighted in the previous chapter on gender — that the mortal love interests are at risk of great physical harm, or even death, from their boyfriends' supernatural strength and unnatural desires.

In the Canadian film *Ginger Snaps*, however, it is the female who is both the lycanthrope and the sexual threat. Ginger's transition into becoming a werewolf coincidentally begins on the night of her menarche. As her younger sister Brigitte furtively tracks her cycles, Ginger reacts to her merging bloodlust by behaving in a more sexually provocative way. When Ginger leaves in a car with her new love interest Jason, Brigitte warns him that "she's ovulating!" but the usual fears about teens having unprotected sex here are shifted in supernatural ways. Rather than resulting in an unplanned pregnancy, their interlude results in Jason catching lycanthropy. Like an unplanned pregnancy, however, there are lasting repercussions: Jason has a tail, fangs and increased aggression in subsequent scenes.

Mating for Life

It is noteworthy that the books, films and television series that are aimed at a teenage market strongly reinforce heterosexual romance. The shapeshifter is a figure generally associated with fluidity, so it is remarkable that gender appears to be non-negotiable even in figures who can choose their forms, such as the shifters in *True Blood*, and that they appear to choose monogamous, lifelong, heteronormative relationships, as in *Twilight*, *The Wolves of Mercy Falls* series, *Low Red Moon* and *Once in a Full Moon*, examined in Chapter One. Noticeable exceptions are the long-term lesbian romance between non-shapeshifting but nevertheless powerful witches Willow and Tara in *Buffy, the Vampire Slayer*, and in Amelia Atwater-Rhodes's novel *Wolfcry*, the penultimate book in her five-volume *The Shapeshifters: The Kiesha'ra of the Den of Shadows*. Although the *Shapeshifters* series initially appears to follow standard romance plots, exploring fears about miscegenation via the inter-marrying of two previously warring groups of shapeshifters, the avians and the serpiente, which we discuss further in Chapter Four, the fourth volume focuses on the heir to the newly joined communities, Oliza Shardae Cobriana. Oliza is the Wyvern after whom the Wyvern's Court is named. As the heir to both kingdoms, she has inherited from her mother the ability to shift into a full hawk, from her father the ability to shift into a full cobra, access to both their demi-forms (where she remains essentially human, but retains some of the features of the animal, such as wings or fangs), or her wyvern form, wherein she is a hooded cobra with wings, capable of flight. Oliza is a truly hybridized figure in a world populated by shapeshifters.

Oliza is under pressure to name her consort and ascend the throne, and appears completely unaware of the deep-seated reasons why she is reluctant to choose a (male) mate and produce heirs. When she is lost in wolf territory, having been kidnapped and narrowly escaped being raped, she meets a feral shapeshifter; a young woman who has also narrowly escaped being taken by force by the same man who threatened Oliza, and who has retreated to her wolf form so completely that she appears to be unable to shift back into her human self. Ultimately she finds a way to shift back to human form in order to guide and nurse Oliza.

Oliza feels an immediate bond with the wolf, Betia. For the serpiente people, dance is a form of expression and particular dances are associated with passion. Suitors and friends present the object of the affection with *melos*, or woven scarves, to request dances. Oliza accedes to Betia's request for a dance, something which she has always politely declined from the many men who have courted her, for fear of it being misconstrued. She also continues to wear Betia's *melos* as a talisman, even though the thread colors are those usually reserved for bonded mates. Oliza explains this as being a cultural miscommunication, but it is apparent to a number of the people around her that it means more to her than even she realizes; as one of her rejected suitors points out, it is significant that she has never even wanted to dance like that for any male partner. Velyo, the Alpha wolf who threatened both Oliza and Betia with sexual assault, offers unsolicited advice that he does not care what her "*preferences* are," but that in order to be a leader, she needs to choose a King and produce an heir (Atwater-Rhodes 750).

Although still in denial about her sexuality and insulted by the comment, Oliza initially accepts the political wisdom behind such a sentiment, and rather than choose a hawk or a cobra and risk him being the target of violence from the other community group, she selects her consort Vere Obsidian from the outlawed white viper group. Oliza is thus hybridized both in her physical form, and in her apparent — albeit pragmatic — bisexuality. Her cousin, Hai, however, herself a hybrid and outcast as the daughter of the late Cobra heir Anjay and white falcon royalty Darien, has access to magic that she is ill able to control, and which shows her through a series of visions that the child Oliza and Vere will conceive, Aleya, will also have uncontrollable magic. This will be stronger and more destructive than Hai's magic, and in due course, fatal to Oliza.

Ultimately Oliza opts to install her purebred cousins to their respective avian and serpiente thrones rather than risk the birth of Aleya and her own death. This frees her to begin a life with Betia. When she approaches Betia to declare her love, she goes down on one knee in a gesture traditionally linked to heteronormative marriage. Betia accepts her declaration of love, but warns her, "Wolves mate for life," to which Oliza replies, "So do wyverns" (Atwater-Rhodes 780). This relationship challenges the heteronormative traditions upheld in the other four volumes, yet is still morally conservative in that it privileges lifelong monogamous relationships. Nevertheless the inclusion of a homosexual couple is enormously important for non-heteronormative readers, for, as van Roosmalen argues, sexuality and sense of self are inextricably linked. In her analysis of letters to the advice column of a teen magazine, van Roosmalen notes that only three out of 875 letters addressed the issue of homosexuality (van Roosmalen 214), which does not bring with it social benefits in the way that some heterosexual teen romances do. For such romances to also be invisible in literature and popular culture only increases the sense of social isolation and fear of "abnormality" in such readers.

Even novels such as Kathy Love's urban romance *My Sister Is a Werewolf,* which could also be classified as erotica, ultimately strongly subscribe to the notion of monogamous mating. The sequel to a trilogy of books that focuses on the protagonists' vampire brothers, *My Sister Is a Werewolf* is the story of Elizabeth Young, a research scientist seeking a cure for her own lycanthropy. Elizabeth is frustrated and restless, noting that "her family, her research, even her drink — nothing seemed to be satisfying her. Nothing reduced the feelings inside her" (15). Within the opening pages of the novel, however, she discovers a temporary cure for her restlessness, in the form of a man she desires greatly. Elizabeth's highly sexually aggressive actions throughout the novel are constructed as being aberrant, as though she were "a bitch in heat" (18). The object of her desire, a young veterinarian who has recently returned to the district, notices her in a crowded bar and is surprised by the vehemence of his physical response (26). Their first sexual encounters are again distinguished by the use of animal metaphors, such as her "wolfish grin" and raspy tongue (40) and her insistence that she just "sniffed ... out" new lover Jensen's location (66), although this book is somewhat unusual in that the werewolf protagonist is female. The trysts are also notable in their anonymity, for Jensen does not even know her name (78) until after their second encounter.

Throughout the novel, Elizabeth is stalked by her mate and maker, Brody Devlin, a rogue wolf who has been ostracized from his pack and believes that having her return with him will lead to his reacceptance. Elizabeth thus expresses enormous guilt about her liaisons with Jensen, even though it is evident that her relationship with Brody was neither functional nor satisfying. Elizabeth feels strongly drawn to Jensen and notes that when he offers her food, he

> was acting like a mate should. A male made sure his female ate before she did.
> Unless, of course, you were mated to a rogue wolf like she was. Then none of the laws, human or animal, applied.
> She didn't want to think about that. And she certainly didn't want to think about how much she'd rather be mated to Jensen [Love 81].

Brody's animal nature is constructed as being negative and unpredictable, whereas the thoroughly human Jensen is depicted as possessing the positive traits of animal mating, including sensing when she is in danger (106), and becoming even more protective of her when she is carrying his child; even when neither of them is as yet aware of the pregnancy, he "rests a hand on her belly, not sure why he needed to touch her there" (281). He is also able to track her when she is abducted by Brody (308). Even Brody at one point refers to Jensen as her "real mate" (290). In the final showdown between Brody and Jensen, Elizabeth reveals her werewolf nature and Jensen tells her to turn him so that the fight is more even. The hero is spared the ignominy of murdering her previous partner, however, by the timely arrival of a pack of werewolf enforcers, who end Brody's unconventional behavior conclusively, leaving the way open for a traditional romance novel ending in the form of a wedding between Elizabeth and the newly-turned werewolf Jensen. At the reception, a delighted Elizabeth hears from her mentor that he has analyzed the latest laboratory samples she sent, and he can confirm that it was not the experimental serum she was using that attracted her to Jensen; but rather that they an example of the "rare ... [but] reported cases of humans and werewolves being natural mates" (324).

This idea is again explored in Karen MacInerney's *Tales of an Urban Werewolf* trilogy, which features another female werewolf who is isolated from pack politics and thus has limited knowledge of werewolf behavior. The first book, *Howling at the Moon*, introduces Sophie Garou, an auditor with a top accountancy firm in Austin, Texas, who has a sports car, a luxurious loft apartment and a very desirable boyfriend. Unlike a number of other heroines in contemporary supernatural texts, then, including working class Sookie Stackhouse, and teenagers Bella Swan, Caroline Forbes and Buffy Summers, Sophie has financial independence and the agency to make independent choices; her need to morph is a factor in her life that she cannot control, but concerns about paying bills or needing parental approval are noticeable by their absence. In the opening pages of the novel, however, her independent existence is somewhat threatened by the arrival of a box of wolfsbane to Sophie's office, complete with a threat to reveal her werewolf identity to the boss, and the precarious situation is exacerbated by the rumors circulated by her personal assistant, who believes the box to contain a large quantity of marijuana.

In stark contrast to the majority of werewolf texts that explicitly link transformation with puberty, Sophie has had the ability to shift shape since birth, and has been able to limit her involuntary transformations to the equinoxes and solstices thanks to a wolfsbane tea recipe concocted by her mother, a Romany witch with psychic powers. The novel also co-opts or adapts a number of unusual traits from the vampire genre, including death by staking and increased (although not eternal) longevity.

Sophie's mother has been a single parent because of prejudice towards the then-infant half-breed, Sophie, so when Sophie meets a "guy with long blond hair," "iridescent gold" eyes (*Howling at the Moon* 10) and a scent "so intoxicating it almost brought me to my knees" (*Howling at the Moon* 92), and instantly recognizes him as a fellow were, he is ostensibly the first werewolf with whom she has had any meaningful contact. In first person narration, Sophie asks herself a number of rhetorical questions about the handsome stranger, before chiding herself for "acting like a dog in heat" (*Howling at the Moon* 10).

The novel focuses on the murder case of a local politician, Ted Brewster, in which Sophie's mother is the prime suspect. Sophie must work with her friend Lindsey to prove her mother's innocence, while juggling her work commitments, staving off transformations, maintaining a relationship with boyfriend Heath, and fighting her own attraction to the mystery werewolf, Tom Fenris, whom Lindsey begins dating. When Lindsey officially introduces Sophie and Tom, Sophie notices his physical characteristics in a very familiar way, complete with sexual innuendo: "Tom gave me a full-on view of his gleaming white teeth. *The better to eat you with, my dear*" (*Howling at the Moon* 130).

Sophie's attempt to hide her animal identity from her friends and colleagues is further tested when an important pitch is scheduled for the day of the full moon. Despite almost overdosing on wolfsbane tea, she is unable to stave off the involuntary transformation for the entire meeting. Indeed, she begins to sprout facial hair, and speaks with a lisp because her tongue feels thick. Her teeth grow longer, she is feverish and she begins to hallucinate, thinking that she can hear a cat and noticing the apparent appearance of horns on the head of the CEO of the client company, Southwest Airlines (*On The Prowl* 242–44). Yet it later appears that when she was in this state between her human and animal selves, she was actually very perceptive, as a co-worker is revealed to be a werecat and the CEO, we learn in the final book of the trilogy, is actually the demon of lust and capable of manifesting horns.

The second novel, *On the Prowl* introduces a trio of made werewolves who seek leadership from Sophie (*On The Prowl* 24), but she is unwillingly drawn into local pack politics. Although attracted to Tom, Sophie is still dating an increasingly distracted and unavailable Heath. In addition, she has drawn the attention of the CEO of her largest account, Southwest Airlines, Mark. He is a man characterized by his wealth and his smoky smell, who has the power to scare off threatening werewolves (*On The Prowl* 252) and who evades Sophie's pointed question "What are you, Mark?" by telling her that she is not the only one with a secret. In a peyote-induced hallucinatory state, she becomes involved in a showdown with Mexican werewolf-sorcerer Xochitl, from which she emerges victorious. Both Tom and Mark offer assistance and information about Xochitl, and Mark gives her a ring that he claims is protective, but is clearly mystical, because she is unable to remove it, even in werewolf form.

On Valentine's Day Sophie finds her relationships with all three men collide in one memorable, sexually-charged evening. At dinner, Heath proposes, complete with a diamond solitaire ring. Sophie, who still has not revealed to him that she carries werewolf genes which she would likely pass on to any children, tells him that her life is rather complex and she needs more time (*On The Prowl* 356). The date ends early, and Sophie is then visited in her apartment by Mark, who heals the wounds from her fight with Xochitl. She and Mark have passionate sex, and she notes that her responses are more amorous than usual: "I'd always enjoyed sex in the past, but today I was starving for it" (*On The Prowl* 358). This is despite her insistence a mere two pages earlier that she would not sleep with him again until she knew what he was, and her stated concerns about his fondness for using the archaic phrase: "[s]he's mine" (*On The Prowl* 356–67). The later revelation that Mark is actually Asmodeus, the demon of lust, explains her wanton behavior (*Leader of the Pack* 242). Finally, half an hour after Mark leaves, Tom visits, and they share a kiss so intense that Sophie fears that her legs might give way (*On The Prowl* 362). Despite the intensity of her response, and the fact that she claims that "just the smell of him had [her] body yammering to forget about everyone and everything but Tom, and how right it felt just being with him" (*On The Prowl* 363), she halts proceedings out of loyalty to Lindsey.

Sophie's attraction to Tom, is, as we have seen is typical in shapeshifting texts, linked to the animal side of her nature. She describes his scent as "Almost savage. And whatever it was made my body respond in the most primal way. A disturbingly primal way" (*Howling at the Moon* 94). In the final novel of the trilogy, the reader learns that these feelings are reciprocated. Tom claims to have been "numb to the world" since the death of his betrothed mate, Beate, some six hundred years previously, but he feels a connection with Sophie (*Leader of the Pack* 237). They also apparently share a psychic connection, with Sophie finding that she is able to alert him that she is under attack in a hotel (*Leader of the Pack* 217). When her estranged father returns and is accused of murdering another werewolf, Sophie enlists the help of Heath and Lindsey — both of whom ask to be made werewolves so that they may attend the trial — and Tom to prove his innocence. Luc Garou challenges the existing Alpha, Wolfgang, to duel and is victorious. He asserts that he will return to his role as Alpha of the pack in Paris, but that Sophie, as his biological heir, will be Alpha of the Texas pack. This claim is then challenged by the existing female Alpha, Elena, who battles Sophie in wolf form. Tom is able to psychically send Sophie instructions that assist her in the unfamiliar realm of the wolf fight (*Leader of the Pack* 313).

In the aftermath of the fight, Sophie nurses her wounds as she attempts to decide whether or not she should accept the Alpha role. Lindsey and Heath confess that they have developed feelings for each other, leaving Tom and Sophie suddenly available to pursue their attraction. When they consummate this relationship, Tom sends her another psychic message: "*I love you, Sophie Garou*" (*Leader of the Pack* 329). Sophie, for her part, finds sex with another werewolf so satisfying that she thinks she "may have howled" (*Leader of the*

Pack 330). Despite the newness of the relationship, Sophie surprises both of them by asking Tom to be her co–Alpha (*Leader of the Pack* 338), invoking the notions of wolves mating for life, and of the equality they share as two powerful werewolves.

In short, while a small number of contemporary texts aimed at primarily adult audiences (*True Blood, Wolfcry*) explore different iterations of sexuality, almost all subscribe to the romance-genre conventions of championing one lifelong, monogamous relationship between soul mates. The vast majority of those aimed at adolescents (*The Vampire Diaries, Once in a Full Moon, Low Red Moon, The Wolves of Mercy Falls* series) adhere to his pattern within the less transgressive paradigm of heterosexual partnerships; indeed, *Twilight* even goes so far as to preach abstinence outside of a marital commitment. The figure of the shapeshifter has long been used to examine fluidity of identity and subconscious sexual desires, but its scope to examine sexual difference appears to be, as yet, under-utilized, in that it is only used strategically in a small number of texts aimed at adult, rather than adolescent, audiences.

Four

The Alpha Race: Racial and Social Politics of Shapeshifting

> *Meaningless hatred: the hatred of an enemy without a face. No one knows why we fight; they only know that we will continue until we win a war it is too late to win.*
>
> —Atwater-Rhodes, *The Shapeshifters* 2

That shapeshifters can represent minority groups is not unexpected: fantasy has long called on fictional creatures to symbolize particular social and ethnic groups. Yet where shapeshifting figures have associations with race and class, it is important to pay attention to the issues because of the implications of aligning specific groups to monsters. However, these texts can also use the positive elements of shapeshifting, where shapeshifters can move outside the boundaries and restrictions. In this chapter we explore how several texts in particular engage with this area: HBO's television series *True Blood*, Amelia Atwater-Rhodes's *The Shapeshifters* novels, *The Vampire Diaries*, and Stephenie Meyer's *Twilight* series, among other works.

"A War Between Species": Shapeshifters as Racial Groups

There is a familiar scene in many paranormal texts when a human character asks the supernatural creature a series of questions about their rumored strengths and weaknesses. Are werewolves susceptible to silver? Do they only change in the full moon? Are they at war with vampires? Do vampires fear crosses, holy water, and sunlight? We can see such conversations in *Twilight*, *True Blood*, *The Vampire Diaries*, *Buffy* and numerous other texts. On one level this is simply the chance for the authors to shape and explain their own treatment of the fantasy traditions. Yet on another level it is strongly suggestive of a rhetorical strategy relevant to how people may respond to other groups in society whether the difference is racial or otherwise, by recalling and testing stereotypes against an insider. Thus the use of supernatural creatures as metaphors for minority groups is furthered by the common practice of debunking myths in many of these novels.

Critics have noted that there are potential links between werewolves and race. In her discussion of werewolves in children's literature, Chappell notes that there is a modern trend to attribute lycanthropy to genetics, a link that "demands that lycanthropy be read in these texts (at least in part) as a metaphor for racial and ethnic difference" ("Contemporary" 22). For some critics, the werewolf operates as a disruptive element to social norms. Du Coudray (*Curse of the Werewolf*) notes the "grotesque imagery" of the werewolf, suggesting that "in its monstrous lupine form, it is usually represented as an entirely alien other threatening the social collective" (4). Creed reads the werewolf as uncanny, representing instability, disorder, lack of borders, the breaking of taboo; Bernhardt-House similarly seizes on the werewolf's "hybridity and transgression of species boundaries" (159). This "transgression of species boundaries" takes on intriguing implications when we relate shapeshifting to race. If we read shapeshifters as a racial group separate to others, then there are fairly clear possibilities for texts to interrogate racial stereotypes in a similar way to how gender can be examined.

The links between race and supernatural creatures are made explicit in several texts dealing with shapeshifting. Werewolves are presented in racial terms in Barnes's *Raised by Wolves* when Bryn calls humans a "species" opposed to werewolves, and conflict between the two groups is known as "interspecies aggression" (7, 360). In the film *Underworld*, vampires and werewolves are again presented as different "species" divided by a "blood feud." Television's *The Vampire Diaries* draws on the traditional notion of an enduring lycanthrope-vampire war, and Elijah's language reinforces the sense that this divide is racial:

> Klaus is from a different bloodline. Of course when my father discovered this he hunted down and he killed my mother's lover and his entire family, not realizing of course that he was igniting a war between species that rages until this day ... vampires and the werewolves [2.19].

In *The Vampire Diaries*, there are some attempts to show the two groups are not intrinsically opposed. For instance, when werewolf Tyler says, "I thought vampires hated werewolves," vampire Stefan dismisses this as an ideology that belongs in the past: "That's some sort of leftover idea from another time. Doesn't have to be that way anymore. We go to the same school, we have the same friends, we keep the same secret. It's going to work, Tyler" (2.13). Stefan's words thus contextualize the conflict as a kind of racial enmity that has no real meaning except in history. Despite this, the show cannot mask its contradictory treatment of this theme. Damon rejected werewolf Mason's offer of peace and then tortured and murdered him, claiming natural enmity as his justification; when Mason's werewolf friends use the same premise to justify their torture of Caroline, it is treated far less favorably. Jules's friend Brady describes their conflict against vampires as a shared goal for their group: "They cross one of us, they cross all of us" (2.13).

True Blood frames vampires as a minority group with links to race. As Sookie Stackhouse notes in the short story "Vampires, Two-Natured, and Fairies, Oh My! Sookie Discusses the Creatures She's Met,"

> A few of the countries around the world went wacky and killed all the vamps they could get their hands on. But the good old U.S. of A. was always a melting pot, so we figured they were just another minority wanting a home, a dangerous minority if pressed the wrong way, but still one that wanted the same freedoms as the rest of the people in this nation [Harris 219].

Even the more sympathetic main characters are not always supportive of vampires: shifter Sam thinks vampires should have rights but ought to remain separate, and tells Sookie that Bill "belongs with his own kind" (1.07). Yet as Tara points out, focusing on the racial implications of supernatural creatures can effectively divert attention from the other racial politics in the texts around real minority groups:

> People think just 'cause we got vampires out in the open now race isn't the issue no more. But do you ever see the way folks look at mixed couples in this town? Race may not be the hot button issue it once was, but it's still a button you can push on people [1.04].

True Blood is less concerned with exploring the politics of shapeshifters than it is with vampires, but the series does work with the idea that there are hierarchies and different groups within shapeshifters. Sam is able to choose his times for shifting, but full moon times cause him to shift involuntarily. Sam makes a distinction between shifters and werewolves, the latter of which he designates as dangerous. Sam tells Sookie that he can choose the form he shifts into, but there are degrees of difficulty attached to particular forms such as birds. His form of choice is a dog, and he relies on having other animals around to give him a model, an "imprint" (1.10) but there also seems to be restrictions on his shifting abilities: he cannot transform into a different human, for instance, because "humans are too complex" (1.10), although it becomes apparent in Season Four that this ability may be triggered in extreme circumstances; namely, when a shapeshifter kills a member of his or her own family, a little-known fact within the shapeshifter community which is first introduced as a Navajo legend (4.02).

For shapeshifters in *The Vampire Diaries*, lycanthropy is very much constructed as essential to an understanding of shared identity that separates them from other groups. Their lupine identities give a sense of purpose and support. As Jules describes it, "It's our duty to help him [Tyler], it's who we are" (2.13); Tyler similarly says that "Jules has been helping me come to terms with what I am, how to deal with it" (2.20). Yet there are contradictions of stable and shifting identities between human and non-human creatures. Stefan tells Bonnie that Caroline must "hold on to her humanity" if she wants to stop harming people as a vampire; he also says that vampires find their human traits "amplified" (2.03); everything is heightened (2.20). Vampire characters speak of choosing to abandon or ignore their human aspects. If vampirism magnifies human qualities, lycanthropy minimizes them, instead emphasizing the animalism. Even Tyler becomes a vampire in Season Three, diminishing his lycanthropy as he becomes Klaus's first hybrid. This seems to constitute a loss of group identity, which in *The Vampire Diaries* has been configured as integral to lycanthropy.

In Atwater-Rhodes's *The Shapeshifters: The Kiesha'ra of the Den of Shadows*, which was discussed in the context of sexuality in Chapter Three, race becomes an important issue that divides shapeshifting groups. *Shapeshifters*—which comprises Atwater-Rhodes's five novels *Hawksong*, *Snakecharm*, *Falcondance*, *Wolfcry*, and *Wyvernhail*—adopts the point of view of a range of characters who are attempting to broker peace between warring groups. In *Hawksong*, the rulers of the eternally-warring avian and serpiente groups agree to marriage in an attempt to create peace. Shapeshifting is a genetic inheritance and even within broader groupings of shifters, hierarchies exist: falcons are seen to be superior to hawks, and hawks superior to sparrows, ravens and crows. The shapeshifters are able to control their transformations, and there is no conflict between their dual identities. As avian ruler Danica Shardae puts it, "the beautiful golden hawk's form ... is as natural to me as the legs and arms I wear normally" (1). With these divisions come racial hatred:

> Almost before a child of my kind learns to fly, she learns to hate. She learns of war. She learns of the race that calls itself the serpiente. She learns that they are untrustworthy, that they are liars and loyal to no one. She learns to fear the garnet eyes of their royal family even though she will probably never see them. What she never learns is how the fighting began. No, that has been forgotten [1–2].

Throughout the series the distinctions between groups are maintained by some characters, who talk of purity of bloodlines, which has obvious connotations of race. What the avian and serpiente groups do not realize is that their original war was begun by a third group, the falcons, who manipulated events to create conflict and fractured groups so that their own power would not be threatened. The overall message is one of unity and equality across the shapeshifting groups, with Danica marrying serpiente ruler Zane Cobriana and forging the beginnings of peace between the previously warring groups.

"I Am What I Am Because of Birth": Shapeshifting, Bloodlines and the Racial Politics of Genetics

Beyond simply situating shapeshifting groups in racial terms, often opposed to the vampire race, many texts go further to engage with notions of bloodlines and purity of racial heritage. In *Underworld*, vampire elder Viktor sees the mixing of lycan and vampire races as an "abomination," justifying killing his daughter because of the danger to vampire (racial) purity: "I did what was necessary to protect the species." In a similar way, in Atwater-Rhodes's *The Shapeshifters*, when avian Danica and serpiente Zane have a child, the hybrid potential of intermarriage is met with fear and suspicion by some groups. The falcon race is particularly against intermarriage: "A match between, say, a hawk and a falcon, two very similar creatures, is seen as disgusting; any child born of them is considered mongrol, a travesty of nature" (272). Zane wonders if both avian and serpiente groups might view the child "with disgust for the cross, and sorrow for the loss of pure-blooded cobra or hawk features," and even questions whether he himself might "look at it [the child] and regret the loss of my own bloodline" (273). There are political considerations in this as well, in that if a half-avian child married an avian shifter, the two dominions would be governed by the avian race by default. Danica's language reduces the shapeshifting species differences to that of skin only: "I thought maybe we were past feathers and scales. We are not talking about two *falcons*, we're talking about two *people*" (376). Lupine shifters are also focused on genetics, because Alphas choose their mates based on "who will add worthy qualities to the bloodline" (665).

Teen Wolf makes a similar distinction between different types of shapeshifters based on their bloodline. In the television series, lycanthropy is both genetic and infectious (a combination also found in Davis's *Never Cry Werewolf*, and Jennifer Lynn Barnes's series). As Derek tells Scott, "I am what I am because of birth. You were bitten. Teaching someone who is bitten takes time. I don't even know if I can teach you" (1.06). The implication is that Derek's skills are natural, inherent, and superior to anyone not born into lycanthropy. Barnes's series also explores some of these ideas of lupine purity of bloodline:

> He was a purebred werewolf, one of a relatively small number in the country who'd been born to two werewolf parents instead of just one. Purebreds were larger,

stronger, and faster and had fewer weaknesses than werewolves with human blood flowing in their veins [*Trial by Fire* 43].

We find the same concept in Millar's *Lonely Werewolf Girl* but here we can see that inheriting lycanthropy is not only superior to catching it but that the latter is seen as an insult:

> "How long have you been a werewolf?"
> Kalix looked insulted.
> "What do you mean?"
> "When were you turned into a werewolf?"
> Kalix emitted a small snarl, enough to make Moonglow draw back.
> "Did I say something wrong?"
> "I was not *turned into a werewolf*. I was born a werewolf, fourth child of the Thane, a pure-blooded wolf of the Royal Family of Clan MacRinnalch."
> "Sorry," said Moonglow. "I thought you had to be bitten."
> "A werewolf can be created that way," conceded Kalix. "But it's an insult to a pure-blooded wolf to accuse them of being bitten" [45].

When Kalix sleeps with someone who is less than pure-blooded, however, she suffers the social consequences of her actions, triggering a chain of events that see her banished from the castle:

> Gawain was the great-great grandson of the renowned warrior Gerrant Gawain MacRinnalch. His family had always been welcome guests. Their status had only been slightly diminished by Gawain's grandfather marrying a human. Gawain's one quarter human blood would not have precluded him from much though it meant he could never ascend to a position on the Great Council. Apart from that, he was free to do anything he liked, except sleep with the Thane's adolescent daughter [158].

Cliff Diving and Campfires, or Cars and Credit Cards: Social Divisions

It is clear from this that the racial implications of inherited shapeshifting carry over to social hierarchies, where there are distinct social groupings operating within tightly defined boundaries. For some groups, as in the works of Atwater-Rhodes, Barnes and Millar, pure blood has social status, prestige, or simply superior qualities that are not available to the other groups. Shapeshifters as a group are often at war with other groups, most usually vampires, renewing racial enmity over centuries. When we consider the class implications of these supernatural creatures, these racial undertones take on more troubling aspects given that vampires are often associated with the upper class and werewolves with lower classes. Thus, beyond bloodlines, vampires are more usually aligned with higher status social groups than are werewolves. As Billson notes, in general there is a popular hierarchy of supernatural creatures based on class distinctions: "If vampires are the aristocrats of the monster world and zombies the unwashed masses, werewolves are somewhere in between — honest manual workers who get the killing done without recourse to fancy manners, or even clothes" (14). This is certainly evident in many shapeshifting texts discussed here. In *The Vampire Diaries*, Jules and her werewolf friends travel in a trailer but the Salvatores occupy an enormous boarding house. Although Tyler and Mason Lockwood are werewolves with a wealthy, privileged lifestyle, Mason leaves town to adopt a surfer lifestyle while Tyler later becomes a vampire. In *True Blood*, vampire Bill occupies the (admittedly rundown) Compton mansion while shapeshifter Sam Merlotte lives in a trailer outside his diner bar. He wears check shirts and jeans; Bill is more likely to be seen in suits. The lycans live underground in a dirty environment in contrast to the vampires' inhabitation of a luxurious, ornate, neo–Gothic mansion in *Underworld*. In some ways this makes their uprising rather symbolic, especially in light of Du Coudray's comment more generally that "lycanthropy was often presented as a threat emanating from the underclasses" (*Curse of the Werewolf* 45). Du Coudray notes an "aristocratic lycanthropy" version, about the downfall of the aristocracy compared to "bourgeois vitality" (*Curse of the Werewolf* 45), but the lower class associations of werewolves are more common.

Stephenie Meyer's *Twilight* series offers a particularly stark representation of these racial and social divisions, where shapeshifting and vampire groups are divided by particular hierarchies. Although gender and sexuality in *Twilight* are perhaps the most popular topics under analysis to date (for example, Seifert; Silver; Summers), the series' use of ethnicity and class has also gained traction in academia (for example, Chappell "Contemporary"; Jensen; Wilson). The chief focus in the novels is the highly romanticized vampire heroes of *Twilight*, yet the series also glamorizes the werewolf characters, who appear in a sympathetic depiction similar to other werewolf heroes in current YA literature, such as in the works by Stiefvater and Barnes. While in one sense the series simply reflects and in turn reinforces the current popularity of these particular fantasy creatures, Meyer's werewolves warrant closer attention. Readers of the *Twilight* series quickly become aware that there is a hierarchy of the vampires and werewolves and that their relationship is essentially one of hostility and conflict. More than this, however, Meyer has aligned the two groups with particular racial and class backgrounds: in short, the vampires are generally wealthy white European Americans superior in almost every way to the werewolves, who are framed as poor Native Americans from the Quileute tribe. Yet although the wolves appear to be marginalized, they nonetheless gradually move beyond the margins as shapeshifting figures of postcolonial power and freedom, as we discuss later. Given the apparently unplanned nature of the wolf storyline, it seems prudent to discard any idea that the hierarchies and connections between ethnicity, class and creatures are intentional. Yet the links are there, even if unintended, and it is important to assess some of their implications and consequences.

The basic plot of *Twilight* and its three sequels —*New Moon, Eclipse,* and *Breaking Dawn*—is a romance between the human Bella and vampire Edward. When Bella arrives in the small town of Forks, Washington, for an extended stay with her father, she meets and falls in love with Edward. Upon discovering that Edward and his family are "vegetarian" (non-human–eating) vampires, Bella decides to become a vampire so she and Edward can live, quite literally, happily ever after. In this respect the series offers a fairytale as the awkward and ordinary Bella is elevated to the status of a beautiful and desirable princess by means of a powerful and rich male figure. Although this is the central focus of the narrative, other plots include attacks on the Cullens by malicious vampires, and also conflicts between the Cullens and a local werewolf pack from the Native American Quileute tribe. In particular, shapeshifter and eventual wolf pack leader Jacob Black has an important role as the alternative potential love interest for Bella, and *Eclipse* and *Breaking Dawn* include sections from Jacob's perspective.

We are not concerned here with the adherence of Meyer's work to shapeshifting or Quileute traditions (see Jensen for a discussion of the latter). And although authorial intention is not the focus here, it is nonetheless worth noting that Meyer has claimed that Jacob's emergence from the margins to become a major figure in the series was seemingly serendipitous, for she has said that she wrote Jacob as a plot "device" rather than a character in his own right ("The Story"). Given the narrative focus on vampires and Meyer's late addition of the werewolves, it is perhaps unexpected that the character of Jacob takes any significance in the plot. Yet the shapeshifting Jacob moves from the margins of the first novel as a plot device to become a key character along with other wolf characters in the subsequent novels. Added to this, the narrative sections from Jacob's perspective in later novels further promote him as a protagonist.

In the novels, lupine shapeshifting is a manifestation of ethnicity: all shifters are members of the Native American Quileute tribe, thus creating an intimate link between the werewolf and race. Unlike most literary werewolves, the shapeshifters of *Twilight* cannot spread their monstrosity in any way, with the exception of reproduction. Meyer's werewolves are homogenous in ethnicity because their lupine status is derived from genetic inheritance rather than infection. Becoming a werewolf is a transformation ritual that seems to coincide with the adolescent coming of age process in Meyer's series: "Taha Aki fathered many sons, and some of these found that, after they had reached the age of manhood, they, too, could transform into wolves" (*Eclipse* 222).

In comparison, the creation of vampires — infectious biting with its connotations of viruses and uncontrollable disease — is traditionally part of the threat of the vampire, as others have noted of Dracula's potential to colonize the world into a vampire race (Gelder 12–13). In the *Twilight* and *The Vampire Diaries* series, however, the contagious possibility of these vampires is unthreatening precisely because what they offer — eternal youth, beauty, and material riches — is so tantalizing for the human characters. Thus, in *Twilight*, vampiric infection has become a mark of favor. Cullen uses it to choose members of his "family" by saving them from the sick and dying of the human race, while Bella actively seeks vampiric contamination so that she can become one of the Cullens and remain at Edward's side. Yet despite the infectious possibilities of vampirism, Meyer's characters are remarkably homogenous in racial terms. There are some minor vampires from other ethnicities, but the Cullens are all white Americans or Europeans with a "chalky pale" appearance (*Twilight* 16). The distinction here is thus ethnicity: werewolves are Native Americans and vampires are predominantly white. The novels further enforce a color divide in that Jacob's surname is Black, another color difference between his Indigenous family and the pale Cullens.

As others have noted, literary monsters have been increasingly cast as outsider figures in sympathetic depictions. Gordon and Hollinger note this shift in vampires from "grisly nightmare" to sympathetic "outsider" (1–2), and Carter makes a similar argument. We can see a similar movement in literary werewolves, who often now represent marginalized groups rather than evil. Yet although Meyer's wolves are linked to a minority group (Native American peoples), this association does not seem intended to highlight injustice or inequality, and certainly Meyer's vampires are not outsiders, instead more closely resembling Hollywood celebrities than minority figures, and this representation is, of course, literalized in the film adaptations. That is, Bella describes the vampires in celebrity terms and there is no attempt on Meyer's part to engender sympathy for these "outsiders" beyond noting that the vampires cannot live long in particular locations or socialize more freely, for fear of their supernatural identity becoming known.

What we have instead is a clear hierarchy between the two groups, where the wolves are frequently drawn as inferior to the vampires. For example, their introduction in *Twilight* marginalizes the Quileute wolves. Bella is initially patronizing and manipulative of the younger, unsophisticated Jacob, flirting with him solely for the purpose of gaining information about Edward. Despite Bella confessing her flirting is "idiotic" and "sure-to-be-pitiful" (105–06),

Jacob is instead "elated by my inept flirting" (110). When the subplot of the wolf pack is introduced in *New Moon*, the Quileute characters are portrayed as a human gang, and Natalie Wilson suggests that they are depicted as "dangerous ... gang-like outsiders who others suspect of being drug users or dealers" ("It's a Wolf Thing" 198). However, the characters' comments suggest that this is more a schoolboy gang than anything sinister: Jacob, at that stage unaware of their real identity as shapeshifters, calls them "hall monitors gone bad" (152) and Bella interprets the group as "annoyingly goody-two-shoes for a gang" (153). In contrast, readers are told repeatedly that the vampires are mysterious and special: "their faces, so different, so similar, were all devastatingly, inhumanly beautiful" (*Twilight* 16–17), a relentless refrain throughout the series. Thus, when Bella discovers their supernatural status, there is little surprise that Edward and his family are "something more" than human (*Twilight* 120).

A key point of inferiority relates to the wolves' lifestyles, relative power, and economic status. Bella's perception of Jacob's world draws on a patchwork of simplicity and naturalism: "[a] thousand memories spun in my head, tangling together — a rocky beach strewn with driftwood trees, a garage made of plastic sheds, warm sodas in a paper bag, a tiny room with one too-small shabby loveseat" (*Eclipse* 63). The difference between this humble setting and the vampires' glamorous mansion, parties and designer clothes is stark.

In *Twilight*, the Quileute wolves live in relative poverty in the La Push area. The modest vehicles of the Black clan — Jacob rebuilds a Volkswagen "out of scraps" (*Eclipse* 209), and they have a "black car, a weathered Ford" (*Twilight* 304) — contrast with Edward's silver Volvo in the color and class divide, and with the other European cars of the Cullens (Audi, Mercedes, Porsche). Jacob's motorcycle for Bella is "shabby-looking" compared to the "big and sleek and silver" bike Edward provides for Bella (*Eclipse* 206). Jacob and his friends more often enjoy cliff diving and campfires; the vampires live a privileged life with medical degrees and music. Bella watches the Quileute boys drink root beer and eat hot dogs on wire hangers (*Eclipse* 212); Edward takes Bella to an Italian restaurant (*Twilight* 143). None of this matters except how Bella reacts to it: she wants the vampire life because it is Edward's life, and thus it is privileged to the reader over any alternative. Bella is the protagonist and the first-person narrator of most of the novels, although the text does allow for some resistance of her viewpoint by giving Jacob the narration of some of the series, which may potentially undermine Bella's status as the dominant voice.

This simplicity of lifestyle for the werewolves is starkly different to the Cullens, who operate within the richest and most privileged spheres. Gordon and Hollinger point out that vampires have usually been painted as "well-groomed horror[s]" (1) even in more threatening guises, and certainly the Cullens are positioned in aristocratic terms, fulfilling many of the points of aristocracy that Moretti argues are lacking in Dracula:

> Dracula is an aristocrat only in manner of speaking.... Dracula lacks precisely what makes a man "noble": servants.... Dracula also lacks the aristocrat's conspicuous consumption: he does not eat, he does not drink, he does not make love, he does not like showy clothes, he does not go to the theatre and he does not go hunting, he does not hold receptions and does not build stately homes. Not even his violence has pleasure as its goal [Moretti 90–91].

The Cullens have accumulated wealth over centuries, host grand parties at their stately home, and their possessions (luxury cars, designer clothes, private islands) and lifestyle (music, traveling, hunting) reinforce a picture of hedonistic affluence without the necessity of earning incomes or contributing to society. Most of Meyer's Quileute group seem to spend their time entirely outside employment and education, which only reinforces the extraordinarily privileged world of the vampires. Jacob does attend school, but it is a different, segregated school on the La Push reservation, and because we never see him in this setting he essentially remains outside the educational system for the purposes of the narrative. In contrast, in *Breaking Dawn*, when Bella becomes engaged to Edward the markers of her new life in the vampire world are primarily superficial and financial "perks"— even if she insists otherwise (7)— "did it really matter what people were saying about my engagement? About my new car? About my mysterious acceptance into an Ivy League college? About the shiny black credit card that felt red-hot in my back pocket right now?" (4). For Bella, however, "the best parts about being a Cullen were not expensive cars and impressive credit cards" (*Breaking Dawn* 7) but rather the superhuman abilities that will supersede her human weakness.

Perhaps there is some unintended irony in positioning the Cullens — and the Salvatores of *The Vampire Diaries*—so resolutely in material and consumer terms. As Moretti reminds us in his discussion of Dracula, Marx has framed capitalism as a vampiric pursuit of material riches: "[l]ike capital, Dracula is impelled towards a continuous growth, an unlimited expansion of his domain: accumulation is inherent in his nature.... His curse compels him to make ever more victims, just as the capitalist is compelled to accumulate" (Moretti 91–92). Readers' ravenous consumption of these novels and the associated films, television series, ancillary texts, and merchandise is hardly unprecedented, but there is perhaps a special aptness in the wholehearted consumption of these *Twilight* characters, who are themselves the ultimate consumers: wealthy vampires. Perhaps we could also argue that vampires are also linked with capitalism in somewhat nebulous ways in *The Vampire Diaries* given Katerina's story occurs in 1492, the same year as Columbus "discovered"

America — binding the story of vampirism with that of capitalist America. Indeed, many vampires from *Twilight* and *The Vampire Diaries* seem to have migrated from Europe to America (Carlisle Cullen, Katerina Petrova, Klaus and Elijah), perhaps echoing the Eastern European origins of Dracula and his intentions to travel the world and create more like him.

Not just vampires but werewolves are linked to consumption in critical thought. As Denis Duclos points out, the figure of the werewolf offers a fitting metaphor for American culture:

> The werewolf culture is America's signature culture. It is the collective expression of a people that lends no credence to the idea that its suppressed urges have been sublimated, perhaps because objects command a greater fascination in this society, which is still based on conquest, an enthusiastic use of physical force, competition, and takeovers.... On the other hand, Americans have not renounced their human nature, and so they may spend their lives wavering between two alternatives: the fetish and the need for love, the things that they can possess and consume and the never acknowledged things they are missing [119].

Duclos links the influence of the werewolf model of duality to violence in American culture, but if we take the point here that supernatural creatures can have class and capitalist overtones, not to mention accumulation and conquest, it is easier to see the vampires as representative of this in today's popular fictions rather than werewolves.

Thus, in all these features, the shapeshifting wolves occupy a lower status in the schema of Meyer's *Twilight* world, lacking the education, employment, wealth and lifestyle that Bella prizes in the vampires. The werewolves of *The Vampire Diaries* also seem inferior in many ways to vampires: Tyler is characterized as hot tempered, naive and ignorant; Jules and her werewolves are helpless to inflict any kind of damage on vampires; and all seem surprisingly weak physically against vampires. None of these points suggest any equality between werewolves and shapeshifters, although this is unsurprising in a text primarily focused on its male vampire leads. As is the case in so many examples, shapeshifting characters are used more to raise the specter of danger for other characters and then leave town (*Buffy*, *The Vampire Diaries*, *Harry Potter*), unable to forge any lasting social connections, although Ward at least suggests *Harry Potter*'s Lupin moves towards some social communities (*Cultural Contexts* 343).

Postcolonial Politics of the Werewolf-Vampire Conflict

If we acknowledge that shapeshifters and particularly werewolves are very often linked to Indigenous groups, and that the vampires often represent white, privileged groups, there are several disquieting elements of their relationship and conflict that become apparent. In several texts, vampires have hunted werewolves near to "extinction" (*The Vampire Diaries* 2.03; *Underworld*). Attempts to "exterminate [the werewolf] species" (*Underworld*) might provoke comparisons with racist colonial expectations that Indigenous groups would "die out," or bring to mind policies of forced assimilation. Despite the apparent superiority of vampires in *The Vampire Diaries* series, the werewolves are an older group that existed before the European vampires settled in their area, again suggesting a link between werewolves and Indigenous groups. If Klaus and Elijah are telling the truth about being the Original vampires (and have not simply watched too many *Buffy* episodes about The First), then werewolves predate vampires because their family were the first vampires and they lived among werewolves when they were still human. That these European vampires then settled in the American lands of the werewolves does perhaps reflect the colonization of "new" lands. The werewolves of *Underworld* were slaves and servants to the vampires before rising up against them, again invoking ideas about race and class structures.

In *Twilight*, the Native American werewolves seem entirely dependent on the white vampires for their existence. As Jacob says, "It's the reason we exist — because they [the vampires] do" (*New Moon* 272), and as the vampires increase, so do the werewolves (*Eclipse* 229–30). Vampires can exist without werewolves; werewolves seemingly cannot exist without vampires. Since shapeshifting is a unique mark of tribal inheritance, the fact that the Quileute members entirely miss their heritage without the presence of these European vampires has disturbing implications of the colonial gaze. Wilson has identified similar problems in her analysis of the *Twilight* novels, arguing that the series "renders the oppression colonialism relies on and the white privileges it fosters invisible" ("It's a Wolf Thing" 204). What might concern readers is that these European vampires possess superior knowledge about the Quileutes' very existence. One of the reigning vampires of the Volturi family informs them: "[t]hough the creatures think of themselves as werewolves, they are not. The more accurate name for them would be shape-shifters. The choice of a wolf form was purely chance. It could have been a bear or a hawk or a panther when the first change was made. These creatures truly have nothing to do with the Children of the Moon" (*Breaking Dawn* 654). This is unknown to the wolves. Irrespective of the Volturi vampire's superior age and experience, it does seem rather extraordinary that somehow the Quileute tribe members are all ignorant of this important part of their cultural and racial history and require the European vampires to explain their very existence to them.

As Said and Ryan remind us more generally, European imperial acts of mapping and assigning English names to Indigenous territories operated as modes of control and power that attempted to dispossess Indigenous peoples of their land throughout the colonial world. Dodson highlights a similar point: "Since their first intrusive gaze, colonising cultures have had a preoccupation with observing, analysing, studying, classifying and labeling Aborigines and Aboriginality" (3). For Dodson and others, such as Anderson, one of the problems of writing about Australian Indigenous groups is the lack of self-representation. Instead, non–Indigenous writers (and, indeed, critics in postcolonial theory) may be seen to be speaking on behalf of Indigenous groups, which has obvious implications of silencing their voices. We can see this in all colonized groups, including Native American peoples. Here, it is not difficult to question whether the Volturi's rewriting of Quileute history might also be an act of neo-colonization, particularly when they are effectively redefining the essential identity of the Quileute group.

It is in this postcolonial context, therefore, that readers might find aspects of this characterization troubling. For instance, regardless of how frequently the vampires call themselves monsters, they always maintain their human shape, their human form; they do not transgress their human physical boundaries. The shapeshifters, however, constantly change into animals, into wolves. Bella even describes Jacob as akin to a pet (*Eclipse* 383; *Breaking Dawn* 564), an attitude that we can also find in *The Vampire Diaries* when Damon makes a crack about Mason and "obedience school" (2.04). In *Teen Wolf*, Chris Argent speaks meaningfully about rabid dogs as he looks at Scott, who also works for a veterinarian (1.04); *Being Human* (U.S.) has vampires insulting werewolves repeatedly by comparisons to dogs, and they even organize a caged werewolf fight (1.10). In *Twilight*, both groups insult each other and the insults about pets may seem to be humorous, but this nonetheless has the potential to invoke unpleasant associations, particularly when one considers some of the early colonial racist ideas that held Indigenous groups as less than human, or alternatively the ideologies of eugenics and the desire for a super race, which may be seen in these novels in the aestheticization of the powerful, enlightened and beautiful vampires. Indeed, Jensen points to the "evolutionary ladder" in the series promoted by textual references to chromosomal differences between vampire, wolf and human (101).

The connection between the wolves and the physical world in the *Twilight* novels is a common association that other commentators have noted about werewolves generally, and which again suggests stereotypical images of Indigenous groups. Du Coudray writes that "the wolf has long been associated with nature in Western thought" (*Curse of the Werewolf* 3), while Billson suggests that "[v]ampires and zombies are essentially walking corpses, which means there is something intrinsically unhealthy about them. Vampires and zombies are against nature; werewolves are nature, red in tooth and claw" (Billson 14).

Jacob tells Bella that the vampires are unnatural because their "existence goes against nature," whereas the wolves' status is natural (*Eclipse* 99). Choosing Jacob over Edward would have been Bella's "natural path," an organic state that would be as "easy as breathing" (*Eclipse* 530). Edward is compared to an artificial element, "like a drug," while Jacob calls himself "healthier ... the air, the sun" (*Eclipse* 531).

The wolves' naturalness is not necessarily a positive feature in *Twilight*, however, for the implication is that they lack the civilized maturity and self-discipline of the vampires. That the Cullens represent civilization against the wolves' savagery is a sufficiently obvious point that others have noted (Chappell "Contemporary"; Jensen; Wilson). Chappell in particular makes several cogent points about the binaries in the series between the vampires and wolves, including the maturity of the two groups where the wolves are seen as undisciplined adolescents ("Contemporary"). Certainly the *Twilight* novels position the werewolves as uncontrollable and immature compared with the vampires. The very essence of shapeshifting seems negatively characterized here, because werewolves stop transforming once they attain "enough control ... restraint" (*Eclipse* 107). Bella and the vampires dismiss the werewolves as young: Bella calls them "children" (*Eclipse* 341), and Edward describes them as "immature, volatile" (*New Moon* 446). Given that Native Americans are werewolves and Europeans/white Americans are vampires, this again approaches neo-colonization, where the vampires assert themselves as the native inhabitants while the Indigenous characters are young and new, who must accept their subservient position. In other words, werewolves are children: once the characters mature into disciplined adults, they grow out of their shapeshifting (their cultural heritage); vampires, meanwhile, remain vampires even as they attain self-control (see also Wilson).

A similar theme of shapeshifters as immature is present in television's *The Vampire Diaries* when Mason, a werewolf, mocks vampire Damon and other human friends for being too much like "a bunch of adults" in refusing to join him for drinking more (2.04). In the *Twilight* novels, both groups attempt to keep their supernatural identities secret, but for the vampires this is by choice and the werewolves by force, compelled to maintain pack secrets and their Alpha wolf. We could read this as implying that vampires choose not to reveal their true identity to humans because they recognize it is better for humans not to know, and that they have the restraint and discipline to maintain this silence (with the exception of newly infected vampires). The werewolves, however, seem unable to exercise this same self-discipline or recognize the necessity of silence and secrecy of their own volition.

These ideas recur across shapeshifting texts, where notions of control and discipline take on added significance. Werewolves in *Harry Potter* are despised for their lack of reason and control. This becomes an even more sharply defined hierarchy when we consider that the Animagi are admired because they have achieved their shapeshifting by intellect and self-discipline, by the study of human transfiguration. Thus there are connotations of discipline, will, and self-control rather than the loss of control from contamination, an issue we discuss further in Chapter Five. More than this, however, these characters are validated because they sought shapeshifting powers and attained it by study; shapeshifters such as Lupin do not wish to be werewolves and exercise no control over their shapeshifting except by means provided by those who have studied and applied themselves to intellectual endeavor, such as Snape who can create a potion to control Lupin's shifting (see also Ward).

Stefan teaches newly-turned vampire Caroline Forbes in television's *The Vampire Diaries* to control her vampirism and stop hurting people by using her willpower. He also tells Caroline to eat more food to stave off her blood thirst, and while neither Stefan's nor Caroline's efforts are entirely successful, it is still very much configured as self-discipline using the mind in contrast to Mason Lockwood, who can only rely on chains and manacles to limit the danger of lupine shapeshifting. This seems closer to the model of lupine shapeshifting in *Harry Potter* that retains the human/animal divide where the animal is in full control during the shift, but the human is in control at all other times. In *The Vampire Diaries* Caroline compares this to vampirism at one point, saying that when she first changed she had no control either.

Divisions of intellect, reason, folklore and mysticism are evident in many texts that link particular groups with race. In the television series *The Vampire Diaries*, the black American witches chant meaningless words with their eyes closed, and they sense vampires by touch and feeling; Elena's brother, Jeremy turns to the internet to research vampires and Elena uses the scientific means of a compass to identify vampires. However, this is rather neatly undermined by the fact that the Jonathan Gilbert was never able to make the compass invention work; instead, Emily (an African American witch) used magic to enable the compass to function. In the television program *Teen Wolf*, Stiles uses the internet to find out information on Scott's lycanthropy; he also uses technology in the form of a heart rate monitor to assess Scott's triggers for shifting. In addition, we have both technology and a more folkloric approach from the wolf-hunting Argent family, with Allison searching for family history online and in a rather ancient book. In *Twilight*, accounts of Quileute heritage begin as "scary stories" (*Twilight* 106) and become mystical and mythical campfire entertainment for Bella (*Eclipse* 212–30) in contrast with her research of "academic-looking" vampiric information through the (implicitly) objective-scientific-educational medium of internet technology (*Twilight* 116).

Reading this in a postcolonial context, such distinctions are fraught with potential cultural violence against Indigenous groups. It is important to consider these postcolonial issues in shapeshifting works, particularly in the context of the enormous international popularity of the *Twilight* novels. Meyer's work moves the vampire figure away from that of the outsider or Other, instead recasting vampires as white, wealthy and privileged members of society. Meyer positions the wolf characters as a poor minority group, Native Americans, but not for the purposes of highlighting social injustice. Adolescent readers consuming the series uncritically might potentially see such hierarchies of ethnicity and class as naturalized, implicit as they are within the narrative.

The Possibilities of Shapeshifting

Yet shapeshifting offers many possibilities for going beyond and outside racial and class divisions. Shapeshifting, after all, can destabilize the notions of boundaries and fixed identities. Previous research has noted that the werewolf has the potential to interrogate identity and open up spaces of power and transformation (Ward), and that shapeshifters offer the opportunity to "negotiate borders" particularly in postcolonial contexts (McMahon-Coleman, *Indigenous Diasporic* 46). The shapeshifting figure has positive implications for its ability to move beyond fixed boundaries, to move from the margins toward becoming postcolonial figures of freedom and change.

In Atwater-Rhodes's *The Shapeshifters*, the avian and serpiente groups eventually decide to form a new utopian space in an attempt to move outside the racial politics that govern their lives. They name the new location Wyvern's Court, after the winged dragon-like wyvern creature, in recognition and appreciation of both avian and serpiente qualities. Thus Wyvern's Court becomes both metonym and metaphor for the dissolution of racial, sociopolitical and also physical boundaries between the two groups. Zane and Danica's daughter, Oliza, embodies this shift as she becomes a wyvern herself: the body of a serpent with wings. Oliza, in fact, is something of a chimera; in addition to her wyvern form she has four other shapes: human, avian, serpiente and a mix of all her characteristics. Oliza, however, dislikes the nickname of Wyvern, and feels "out of place" because she belongs to neither avian nor serpiente people (422), which suggests that the goal of multiracial unity is perhaps unachievable, although the concluding section of the five-book series suggests some optimism.

In *Underworld*, Michael is a human who has been bitten by a lycan and a vampire, and he transforms into a powerful hybrid of both groups: "half-vampire, half-lycan, but stronger than both," and the possibilities of hybrid bodies are further explored in the sequel *Underworld: Evolution*. There is a freedom and strength attached to those figures who move outside boundaries. This is also evident in television's *The Vampire Diaries*. Klaus is a werewolf-vampire hybrid, who is from the first generation of vampires and the oldest of them. His father was a werewolf, which gives him the gene, but this potential is contained by a cursed moonstone and cannot be unlocked unless a Petrova *Doppelgänger* is sacrificed. The Curse of the Sun and the Moon is faked by Klaus and Elijah to ensure the vampire and wolf populations will search for the moonstone. Klaus's mixed heritage is a source of special power: "A hybrid would be deadlier than any werewolf or vampire. Nature would not stand for such an imbalance of power" (2.19). Thus Klaus's werewolf potential lies "dormant" and bound by the curse of the moonstone. Klaus's interest in breaking the curse is not simply to experience this power but to extend it to a race: "If allowed, Klaus would sire his own bloodline, he'd build his own race, endangering not just vampires but everyone" (2.19). Despite this power, Klaus is most vulnerable during the full moon when he is transitioning: shapeshifting is his weakness. Once he attains his new powers, he is able to shift at will rather than only during a full moon. And unlike Mason and Tyler who speak of losing self to the animal, Klaus is able to recall each wolf kill as a human (2.22). A werewolf bite is fatal to vampires and can only be healed by Klaus's blood as a hybrid. Of course, Klaus operates as the chief villain for some of the series, which suggests that there are no positive associations from his hybrid identity, yet he still exercises a power that is not available to those with a more "pure" heritage.

What is perhaps most interesting for its potential to shift boundaries in *The Vampire Diaries* is the attention paid to history. The television series alternates between past and present times, and characters (and viewers) are continually revising their understanding of the history of Mystic Falls. Alaric Saltzman — his own name suggestive of foreign influence — is the history teacher who plays an important role in the series to date; his wife was a researcher in mythology and lore, which also has connotations of discoveries. There is much made of the founding families and the maintenance of town traditions, with parades and festivals and celebrations of the founding of Mystic Falls. We see caves with drawings on them illustrating the past, historical artifacts, books, libraries, journals, computers, all repositories of knowledge that shift the characters' knowledge about the true history of the town. The rupturing to the prevailing idea about the white founding families of the town comes in several ways. One is the presence of the witches. Unlike vampires and werewolves, witches and warlocks seem to be rather more bound by ethnicity in Seasons One and Two: primarily African Americans (Bonnie, Lucy, Luka, Jonas, Greta). Luka tells Bonnie all witches are "family" (2.11). Elijah calls witches "servants of nature" (2.19); Elena echoes this when she says "witches are supposed to maintain the balance in nature. It's your duty to them, to keep this curse sealed" (2.21). Greta replies: "My duty is to Klaus. New order" (2.21). And indeed it is a new order: servants not to nature but to other groups, for these witches and warlocks appear to exist only to do the bidding of the (white) main characters: Emily and Lucy served Katherine, Bonnie assists Elena, Greta serves Klaus, and Luka and Jonas Martin worked for Elijah. In many cases the witches attempt resistance or revenge on the ones they serve but these seem rather limited statements of freedom. Yet Elijah tells Jenna that the original founders of Mystic Falls were the witches of Salem rather than the self-proclaimed founding families who are the current white, wealthy leaders of the town, which seems to suggest a postcolonial rupture to the power dynamic of the town and its ruling (white) members and their fervent interest in the town's (white) colonial history. It is their shared power in the form of dead witches that allows Bonnie to attack Klaus (Season Two). The historical revisions become even more complex when we are told in Season Three that Mystic Falls was originally inhabited by werewolves before Klaus and his family came from Europe. Klaus's mother, Esther, is a witch — "the Original witch" (3.08) — and is white, which undercuts the earlier characterization of witches as linked to African American ethnicity, although Ayana is another black witch in the same episode. Their emigration to the United States was provoked by plague and the rumor of a "mystical land where everyone was healthy, blessed by the gifts of speed and strength" (3.08). This is itself rather utopian and reflective of the colonial discourse around the United States (and other nations) as new worlds of promise and plenty. Elena argues that the American land had not been "discovered" at that time, to which Rebekah (Klaus's sister) retorts "not by anyone in *your* history books" (3.08), in another undermining of historical accuracy. Once there, the superior beings are discovered to be werewolves, and after a wolf kills one of Klaus's brothers, Esther makes her children and husband vampires so they will be able to defend themselves against and defeat the wolves: they will now be superior to the wolves in speed, strength, agility, and senses (3.08). That these white settlers arrive in the Americas and proceed to conquer all around them has obvious overtones of colonization. In many cases in this series, what viewers are told about the mythology or history of this world is later shown to be false; regardless of whether these revisions are intentional or simply due to retroactive continuity to accommodate new ideas, it is an interesting approach where history is challenged continually over the series in an ongoing rewriting, revising, and revealing of the origins of the vampire, werewolf, and witch groups.

Racial politics and the potential in shifting boundaries can be seen in Anderson-Dargatz's *The Cure for Death by Lightning*. Although of British stock, Beth clearly has strong connections with the local Indigenous community. Indeed, she has flirtations with Nora, Billy and Dennis, all three of whom are the grandchildren of the local Indigenous matriarch, Bertha Moses. Bertha's family is one wherein she claims that the mark of the trickster, Coyote, is physically present, manifesting in a range of birth defects and minor deformities. Yet elsewhere, Bertha argues that the white settler-invaders are truly Coyote's children, for they, like the trickster figures from Indigenous mythologies, create chaos and disorder. Beth draws these two worlds together when she becomes the focus of Coyote's attention.

Beth operates in but is never quite at home in any of the spaces she inhabits or visits, be that her home, school, or the nearby Indian Reserve. Many of the narrator's experiences within the novel only make sense because she is open to Indigenous belief systems; she becomes more empowered as she engages with the Reserve and its inhabitants. *The Cure for Death by Lightning* is thus a maban realist text, using both the transformative powers of the mission or reserve space and chaos — the adolescence of the narrator, her dysfunctional household and the broader sociohistorical context of World War Two — to explore postcolonial race relations in Canada. She is a first generation Canadian daughter of an antisocial immigrant war veteran father, and something of a pariah in the town; yet it is her flirtations with people of another race which are deemed to be problematic by the people of her township.

She finds comfort and companionship among the local Native population, demonstrating that she is a conduit between the two ideations of "Coyote's children" as represented in the novel — Whites, and the children and grandchildren of First Nations' matriarch Bertha Moses. Whilst Bertha warns Beth to beware of Coyote, she also encourages Beth's habit of walking in the bush, noting that that was how boys and girls meet their guardian spirits. She notes that now "young girls don't get their power from anywhere. They're afraid to go out searching for it" (168). She encourages the girls to find their own power by being cautious but never afraid.

When Fox Is a Thousand by Larissa Lai is a novel that brings together sexuality, gender and race issues with Taoist spirituality in a novel that is told by three different and interwoven voices: those of the ninth-century poetess, Yu Hsuan-Chi, an unnamed contemporary narrator, and a thousand-year old shapeshifting fox. The fox has the ability to not only shift shape, but also to reanimate and reincarnate. Through her explanations of her exploits, it becomes apparent that the fox is a trickster-figure. The trickster is defined by Penny Petrone as being anti-social, a hero and a fool (Petrone 16); at once every man and no one. Lai's fox is as cunning as one might expect, but is sometimes rendered a fool by love, or is thwarted by the minutiae of life (such as reading modern calendars). The shapeshifter is something of a prankster, as we see here when the fox influences the narrator's relationships in order to locate a suitable body for her to use when she gains immortality on her thousandth birthday. Yet the fox uses her influence to bring together the narrator, Artemis, Rachel and Diane, who have been romantically involved in various permutations and many of whom are no longer to speaking to one another, to farewell another of their number, Mercy Lee, who has been recently murdered. They do so using a sacrifice of chicken, joss sticks and paper money, as described in the sections set in ninth century China, deeming this to be culturally appropriate. With the exception of Rachel, the women are all of Asian descent — Artemis Wong has been adopted by Euro-Canadian parents; Mercy Lee has family in China, and her father still has business dealings there; and Diane is a statuesque Asian woman who appears to loathe her family, yet conversely plans to steal valuable Chinese artifacts in order to take her mother back to China for a visit. Fox, for her part, is using the body of an Asian woman with dyed-blond hair prior to reaching immortality, at which point she animates Mercy's body.

Turning back to the *Twilight* novels we can see some themes that partly undermine the negative connotations of the Indigenous werewolves and the simple rendering of the poor Native American werewolves as inferior compared to the aristocratic white European vampires. Several elements point to a validation of the werewolf over the vampire, where their key traits — shapeshifting and stasis, respectively — favor the werewolf. Change is the natural state for the *Twilight* shapeshifters. The act of imprinting, which is akin to forming a permanent, unchanging emotional attachment to a soul mate, is virtually the only constant in a werewolf's life, and even this state is (initially) thought to be rare among wolves (*Breaking Dawn* 135). Jacob and his friends are humans and wolves, both and neither at once. They can be "rooted in place, and yet not completely still" (*Eclipse* 336). The tremors and ripples that cascade through their bodies prior to the transformation are recurring themes: "[m]idstride, a long tremor shivered down Jacob's spine. He leaped forward, diving headfirst into the empty air. With another sharp tearing sound, Jacob exploded, too. He burst out of his skin — shreds of black and white cloth blasted up into the air" (*New Moon* 286). It is tempting to read this shredding of "black and white cloth" as (unintentionally) symbolizing the breakdown of defined racial identity, but regardless, it is clear that identity is fluid in these shifts. Identities fray at transformation — "Sometimes I'm afraid that I'm losing myself" (*New Moon* 304) — and Jacob narrates this experience as a collapse of identity, the self fragmenting and re-forming each time:

> I started shifting. The fire trembled down my spine, throwing tight spasms out along my arms and legs. It only took a second. The heat flooded through me, and I felt the silent shimmer that made me something else. I threw my heavy paws

against the matted earth and stretched my back in one long, rolling extension ... closing my eyes and pulling myself together again. It felt like the air was trembling around me, shaking out from me in small waves. I lifted myself up on my hind legs, catching the moment just right so that I was fully upright as I shimmered down into my human self [*Breaking Dawn* 143, 239].

Jacob retains his moral identity, able to act in accordance with his conscience regardless of form. But these descriptions emphasize the disjunction between forms for a shapeshifter. Jacob's "shifting" transforms him into "something else," and we are stopped in our attempts to draw clear lines of identity here. These slippery boundaries remind us that shapeshifters cannot be contained so easily, they elude our efforts to fix particular identity on them.

To reinforce this theme in the *Twilight* series, Bella repeatedly (and unconsciously) highlights Edward's limitations and boundaries by comparing him with stone, statues, marble, rock, carvings, and other immovable objects. Vampires cannot change physically, a state that is reflected in their general inability to change emotionally or alter their temperament (*Breaking Dawn* 85): "[y]ou think of me as a ... living stone — hard and cold. That's true. We are set the way we are, and it is very rare for us to experience a real change. When that happens, as when Bella entered my life, it is a permanent change. There's no going back..." (*Eclipse* 444). Given that the romantic premise of the series relies on just such a "real change," Edward's inability to change seems a limitation. His inflexibility is in stark contrast to Jacob's mutability. Meyer does not canvass these issues, but the suggestion that the Cullens are inflexible in contrast to the wolves provokes questions about the future, where any notions of progress and moving towards greater intergroup cooperation must surely rely on precisely such a shift. In a practical sense, the Quileute shapeshifters can envisage and plan a future life open to change as they later age, whereas the vampires are frozen in a moment in time. Of course, this is perhaps a negative in the schema of these novels where eternal youth is the ultimate goal. Despite this, there is certainly a limitation to growth and development for vampires whereas the wolves possess all the opportunities and possibilities of age.

A further point is the wolves' ability to evade the vampires in ways that others cannot. Alice Cullen's future visions allow the vampires some measure of control over other people in the power of foreknowledge. Yet the werewolves' mercurial nature renders them invisible to this psychic gift, and thus free from outside authority: "Carlisle theorizes that it's because their lives are so ruled by their transformations. It's more an involuntary reaction than a decision. Utterly unpredictable, and it changes everything about them. In that instant when they shift from one form to the other, they don't really even exist. The future can't hold them" (*Eclipse* 56). This ability to confound predetermined destiny and evade vampiric (white) control has positive implications for moving beyond the margins. It is worth emphasizing the notion that the future cannot "hold" the werewolves. Whereas colonial representations of Indigenous groups may have attempted to fix and devalue their racial identity and control their future, Jacob and his Quileute peers cannot be controlled by white outsiders, and their future is theirs to decide alone.

Shapeshifting therefore brims with opportunities and potential for positive changes. Caroline Walker Bynum has noted that early texts evidenced anxieties about unnatural change:

> writers [are] returning again and again to worry, as one might a sore tooth, the possibility of species crossing, body hopping, metamorphosis. Surely the tremendous intellectual effort devoted to categorizing types of change, to ferreting out its rules, to limiting while not denying species crossing, to preventing contact with animals and angels from changing the human body suggests the importance of understanding person as psychosomatic unity ["Metamorphosis" 1013].

Such anxieties are absent from Meyer's contemporary work, and indeed the Quileute wolves are far less tormented about self-identity than the vampires, despite the fragmented nature of the changing self inherent in shapeshifting. While Rosalie yearns for the human ability to have a child and Edward worries that vampires might be damned without a human soul, the werewolves are stable in their purpose. Their destiny is to protect humans, whereas vampires are inherently monstrous, naturally desiring to kill humans. As Jacob says, "What I am was born in me. It's a part of who I am, who my family is, who we all are as a tribe — it's the reason why we're still here" (*Eclipse* 99), and this shared identity is a source of power for the wolves. Du Coudray writes more generally of a shift in werewolf fiction that we can apply to the context of *Twilight*, as well as Barnes's *Raised by Wolves* and the like:

> The werewolves in such fiction are (or become) competent, self-assured, and organised, integrating their lupine and human needs.... Indeed, this breed of werewolf often finds love, happiness, stability and spiritual growth ... they are more strongly characterized by a focus on circularity, a willing acceptance of embodiment, a recognition of the inevitable cycles of birth and death, a sense of connection with the natural world, and an emphasis on spirituality ["The Cycle of the Werewolf" 58].

We can see these points in the Quileute wolves, who generally suffer less of the angst and yearning for humanity than do the vampires. The La Push community may seem a limited space; yet in one way it represents belonging and a grounded connection to home that the vampires lack, for vampires are unable to exist in any human community for long periods because their inability to age rouses suspicion. For Bella, with her unstable family life, there is an attraction for a life with Jacob. Therefore, the werewolves are, contrarily, in many ways more grounded than the vampires in important areas. Sam Merlotte's comments in *True Blood* continue this theme; as he tells Sookie, "I may be a shapeshifter but I want what every man wants ... a good life, a good woman" (1.11). It is stability, security, and family that are associated with shapeshifting in these texts.

Physical change, therefore, is one important way that the narrative favors the wolves over the vampires. The second way that the series undercuts neat hierarchies of vampires and werewolves is seen in the emerging social connections between the two groups, which are all initiated by change. In *Breaking Dawn*, Jacob's decision to break his lupine covenant as pack member and leave Sam's wolf pack to form his own brings him "freedom" (193). Another wolf, Seth Clearwater, calls this "a pretty significant move. A change" (*Breaking Dawn* 197), and this shift allows Jacob to move away from old laws enforcing wolf-vampire conflict to instead forge a new alliance with the Cullens to protect Bella and her unborn child. Breaking the ancient rules enforcing wolf-vampire enmity signals a positive move towards unity and shared power.

Significantly, the catalyst for Jacob to break away from the pack is the desire to protect Bella and her child, Renesmee. Renesmee is herself a hybrid character of both human and vampire blood, and the connection of these two hybrid figures — human-vampire and human-wolf— is important. Jacob imprints with Renesmee at the conclusion of the series, and although this notion of romantic imprinting between adult males and child females rightly warrants further critique, we might nonetheless read this as symbolizing a breakdown in the boundaries, a unity between werewolves, vampires, and humans that collapses the idea of fixed and separate identity. Renesmee's love for Jacob encourages the Cullen clan to move towards Jacob, and friendships between characters such as Edward and Seth also bring the two groups closer. Both groups, therefore, move towards each other. Perhaps this reflects in some way Du Coudray's remark that werewolves can represent a bridge, "as Slavoj Žižek argued of monsters more generally, the werewolf also appears as a *bridge* between nature and culture, by exceeding both categories and representing slippages between them" (*The Curse of the Werewolf* 3).

Jacob's social integration into the vampire clan is perhaps symbolic of a growing unity of class and race, collapsing the borders and traditional markers of identity and difference. Ward offers a similar analysis of Lupin's move away from the margins in *Harry Potter* to form social connections (*Cultural Contexts*). It seems significant, however, that although both groups draw closer in the *Twilight* series, Jacob moves the most. Indeed, Jacob's move to the Cullen cause might almost be read as an elevation to their exalted status as he abandons his people, his land, his tribal law, and thus, by implication, his Quileute identity. This has serious implications for reconfirming the negative ethnic and class features in the series. Despite these problems, Renesmee's connection with Jacob suggests a special status accorded to fluid figures that are not contained by one particular racial or social identity. By no means does this negate the troubling aspects of the series, yet there is certainly evidence that the shapeshifting abilities available from Jacob's tribal connections allow him to move beyond the margins both physically and socially in ways that the white vampires cannot.

While we may be rightly wary of hierarchies as embodied in the shapeshifting and vampire groups in many texts, some works do offer several themes that complicate the issues. The shapeshifting figure can provide scope and imagination for postcolonial issues of identity and ethnicity, allowing freedom by refusing fixed borders and imposed structures, shifting shape, and creating a space to challenge simple constructions of power and difference. Their ability to shapeshift and to move beyond simple and marginalizing boundaries of identity and position suggests an additional potency and power that is not available to vampires. While this is certainly a muted possibility in many texts, it is also evident that the possibility remains for texts to seize the opportunities afforded to the shapeshifting figure and move beyond former understandings of racial and social differences in our culture.

Five

Shapeshifting and the Body: Disability, Illness and Mental Health

> LUPIN: *You don't know how most of the wizarding world sees creatures like me! When they know of my affliction, they can barely talk to me!*
>
> — Rowling, *Deathly Hallows* 175

In the previous chapter we discussed how shapeshifting can be used to explore issues around race and class. Shapeshifting figures can operate on the margins of society, and may be excluded in ways that remind us how dominant groups in society can treat racial minorities. Yet shapeshifters can provide possibilities to rethink boundaries and identities.

There is another side to this, however, when we extend this potential beyond ethnicity to a more general conception of difference in society. Indeed, several writers have seized this potential to use shapeshifters as metaphors or representatives of disability, illness, and mental health disorders. Shapeshifting figures increasingly represent difference in recent popular fiction, and particularly in werewolf narratives, where authors have specifically drawn links between their werewolf characters and disability.

This chapter explores works where werewolves and other shapeshifters are either implicitly or explicitly aligned with disability, illness, exclusion and isolation. These metaphors bear closer analysis because of the problematic implications of conceptualizing disability and difference as monstrous. Yet in this chapter we also argue that the shapeshifting figure nonetheless offers powerful potential for rewriting disability, illness and difference as social constructions.

"The Bite Is a Gift": Shapeshifting and Enhanced Abilities

Before discussing how shapeshifting may be used to reflect the experience of difference and disability, however, it is important to note that this may be compromised by another aspect of this paranormal genre. In the genres of fantasy and science fiction, plots of superhumans and enhanced abilities problematize and implicitly attack the concept of disability. Such plots can invoke the specter of eugenic philosophies, and as much as texts may warn of the dangers of scientific pursuits of a superhuman race, there remains an estheticization of superhuman, more-than-able-bodied characters. While eugenic plots may seem either unreal or restricted to one time in real-life history in Nazi Germany, Pernick's work reminds us that there has been one strand in American medicine that has long argued for similar eugenic goals, proposing the termination of deformed or weak babies. Current health care debates about aborting babies with particular conditions or about reproductive rights of people with disabilities are not, therefore, modern concerns only.

For all the possibilities that shapeshifters can in some ways reflect the experience of isolation and exclusion from dominant groups in societies, in another way these shapeshifters are often the antithesis of disability. In many of the modern iterations of lupine shapeshifting, they are portrayed in very romanticized, idealized ways — as we mentioned of the Alpha male underwear models adorning Meyer's *Twilight* world — with superhuman strength and abilities. As we noted in Chapter Two, contemporary texts tend to characterize werewolves in glamorized ways more akin to male models than monsters: they are frequently depicted on screen shirtless with defined jaws and abs. This is not unusual on television and in film given the conventions of Hollywood casting, but it is certainly far from the monstrous appearances of earlier (and some current) lycanthropes. Scott and Derek regularly wander around onscreen without their shirts in the *Teen Wolf* television series, as Mason and Tyler did in *The Vampire Diaries*, much as those vampire heroes Stefan and Damon do. Being a shapeshifter in these iterations is no different to being the lead male on any television teen drama, except with even more physical strength.

Conveniently, these shapeshifters can often be neatly fitted into that same celebrity world that vampires occupy with their attainment of that holy grail of eternal youth and beauty by their non-ageing. Barnes's wolves stop aging in their thirties (*Trial by Fire* 217); Millar's wolves appear to be in their late twenties (*Lonely Werewolf* 4); MacInerney's Sophie Garou, herself in her twenties, meets her long-estranged father and is mortified that he only looks about ten years older than her (*Leader of the Pack* 7, 8, 28); and Atwater-Rhodes's falcon shifters stop aging after turning twenty (*Shapeshifters* 523). Latham's discussion of vampirism, consumption, and *The Lost Boys* offers much of relevance here, and particularly his points relating to "the pervasive juvenilization of adults" (139) and "Contemporary capitalism's fetishism of youth" (147). They are particularly apt in the context of *Twilight*, given Bella's determination to end her youth by seeking a permanent union with a century-old man and his ageless friends who are, contrarily, frozen in their own youth.

In some versions of the shapeshifting narrative, the side effects of lycanthropy lead to increased popularity and social status. Werewolf Ginger rejects the notion of returning to her non-lupine self when she asks "You think I want to go back to being nobody?" (*Ginger Snaps*). In the *Teen Wolf* film and series, Scott becomes faster, stronger, and more popular following his transformation. The same theme is in *Teen Wolf Too* when Todd excels at boxing and becomes more popular after his lycanthropy manifests itself. Although the films differ from the television series in that Scott's lycanthropy is open knowledge rather than hidden as it is on television, it nonetheless has positive outcomes socially and physically. In the television series, Scott's medical condition of asthma is solved, not caused, by shapeshifting. As Derek asks in the television series, "Is it really so bad, Scott, that you can see better, hear more clearly, move faster than any human could ever hope? You've been given something that most people would kill for. The bite is a gift" (*Teen Wolf* 1.02). A similar line is found in *Being Human* (U.S.), where werewolf Ray insists that despite his loneliness, "the wolf is a gift" because it makes them faster, stronger, "more than alive. We're the best of human and animal" (1.05). In television's *Teen Wolf*, Scott's enhanced abilities prove to be his entree to popularity, and when his rival and captain of the lacrosse team, Jackson, realizes that Scott is a werewolf, he decides he has to become one too in order to maintain his social prestige by becoming more powerful physically. He threatens to reveal the secret and destroy Scott's chances to reunite with Allison if Scott does not turn him into a werewolf. Scott continues to complain that "it ruins your life," but Jackson insists that the fault is with him for mishandling lycanthropy: "you had all the power in the world and you didn't know what to do with it" (1.10). Power is again a side effect of lycanthropy that Alpha Peter uses to tempt Stiles into becoming a werewolf: "That first night in the woods I took Scott because I needed a new pack. It could've easily been you. You'd be every bit as powerful as him. No more standing by his side, watching him become stronger and quicker, more popular, watching him get the girl. You'd be equals. Maybe more" (1.12). Stiles refuses and says that he has no desire to be like Peter, but his hesitation and Peter's insistence that Stiles is lying suggests that there is an appeal to lycanthropy.

Similarly, Bryn wants to become a werewolf to escape human weakness and frailty (Barnes's *Trial by Fire*). At times her humanity helps her to thrive outside the strict boundaries of werewolf politics, but she blames her humanity for causing pack member Lucas's death, when he challenges her as Alpha believing he would win because she was human: "If I'd been stronger, if I'd been faster, if I'd been the type of opponent that other people feared, Lucas would still be alive. He'd challenged me because I was human. I'd won because I wasn't — not really, not anymore" (*Trial by Fire* 350–51). Bryn's growing connections with her pack give her more psychic abilities to channel their powers through herself, and after her confrontation and domination of Lucas, she then seems to ask Callum to change her into a werewolf, although this is not explicitly said, thus concluding the second book of the series. Bryn's apparent decision to abandon her humanity is tied to her feelings of responsibility to her pack: "the stronger the alpha, the stronger the pack. I wanted my pack to be safe. I wanted to be able to protect them. I didn't want a giant target forever drawn on my very human head" (357). Callum agrees, but tells her she must wait until she has had more "human time" (355).

Of course, this is not the message of every shapeshifting text: *Twilight* privileges human blood over animal or vampire blood because the blood from humans makes newborn vampires stronger. Again, in *The Vampire Diaries*, Damon is physically stronger than Stefan because he drinks human rather than animal blood. However, just like vampires, shapeshifters are often physically superior to humans precisely because they are something more than human. Shapeshifting and hybridity are such prized assets in some versions that they are useful in the attempt to create a super race, as in *The Vampire Diaries* television series, Meyer's *Twilight* series, and *Underworld*.

Thus, in many ways, shapeshifting might actually be seen to be a superior, desirable state, and many contemporary texts play with this concept. Hence, any recognition of the possibilities of shapeshifting to represent disability or illness must acknowledge the counter narrative that promotes shapeshifting as an enhanced ability.

"Unimaginable Pain": Shapeshifting and the Body

In this reading of disability and difference, the body becomes the key point of interest: the body is the site of transformation and we find issues of control and discipline at work. Many shapeshifting texts emphasize the physicality and the pain of the transformation, such as the television programs *Being Human* and *The Vampire Diaries*, and Kevin Hearne's novel *Hammered* (177). Josh's transformation in the United States version of *Being Human* is presented as painful, with his body changing and expanding in unnatural ways, as is George's in the British original. In Jennifer Lynn Barnes's *Raised by Wolves*, lupine shapeshifting can be a form of punishment if an Alpha forces a wolf to change:

Change. The word was a whisper, but also a command.... This was domination. And punishment. It was cruel.... I heard Chase's bones breaking, felt his skin give way as he lost his human form. The Rabid laughed. *Change back.* Shifting took energy. It was painful. Chase needed to recover. *Change. Change back.* The Rabid didn't let Chase settle fully into one form before forcing him into another [311].

The Vampire Diaries television series highlights this pain in a visual way by showing the transformation of Mason Lockwood as a lengthy, excruciating experience. Mason's last appearance in Season Two is post mortem in the form of a video diary of his first transformation that his nephew Tyler watches to learn about his condition. Tyler and Caroline Forbes read his journal and watch the video diary:

> I chose the garage. I could deadbolt the door; it was far from the street so no-one could hear. I bolted hooks to the floor for the carabiners.... I diluted wolfsbane with water to weaken myself but I could barely get it down without puking. It felt like I was drinking battery acid. Over an hour passed. Nothing happened. It got so quiet I could hear my own blood pumping. That's when ... [Caroline covers her mouth as she watches the screen]. I kept thinking I'd black out and not feel it but I did, I — I felt all of it. [Cut to Tyler, looking upset. Cut to Mason, on video, lying on floor and face to screen, covered in sweat, screaming Help — won't somebody help!] ... Unimaginable pain. I thought it would never end. It was the worst night of my life [2.10].

Tyler and Caroline's distressed reaction to the video emphasizes the sympathetic portrayal of physical pain as they contemplate what Tyler's future holds. The scene focuses on Mason's lengthy attempts to harness his violence and the agony of shapeshifting, shown in close ups of him lying on the floor and screaming for help, accompanied by music in a minor key. Thus, for Mason at least, shapeshifting seems to result only in a rather tragic and short life — even if his storyline is sidelined by the usual focus on the romantic plots of the series — and the inference is that Tyler's life is similarly doomed.

Tyler's first transformation in *The Vampire Diaries* is accompanied by the show's familiar horror music motif used to signify danger; sound effects include bones crunching; visual effects show his eyes changing, his spine shifting, his arms bending in unnatural ways. Tyler insists Caroline must leave before he changes, because once he has shifted he cannot call on his human side to keep her safe from him. As Mason remarks several times, he has no control over himself: "On every full moon, I lose control. If I don't sedate myself and chain myself down, I'll kill anything in my path" (2.05). Given that werewolves are the eternal enemy of vampires in *The Vampire Diaries*, it seems odd that their violence is random rather than targeted at vampires, as in *Twilight*. Every element reminds viewers that he is losing his humanity and cannot exercise any control over it. Mason's journal reveals the experience of shapeshifting is a loss of self: "My body is changing, edgy, angry, impatient,

I get so mad I black out and forget what I say or do. I'm not myself, not since Jimmy's death" (2.10). Yet there is some complexity — if not contradiction — in that Mason stops attacking Stefan and Caroline in his wolf form when Tyler intervenes and shouts at him, after which he runs away (2.03), while Jules runs straight to Damon's house in lupine shape to attack him (2.11); it is clearly not the case that werewolves have no control or no sense of self in their lupine form. Like Sam Merlotte in *True Blood*, whose identity remains stable even as a dog (see, for instance, his turning away in canine form as Sookie undresses, 1.09), there appears to be some exercise of human-control in *The Vampire Diaries* during shifting.

These texts emphasize the physical pain of shapeshifting. Others, however, depict changing bodies as a natural, even pleasurable experience. Mason's traumatic shift is unlike the more integrated shapeshifters in Atwater-Rhodes's *The Shapeshifters*, where avian shifter Danica Shardae has feathers growing within her hair or where serpentine shifter Zane Cobriana wears snakeskin clothing as a human, or can partially transform by changing the skin on his forearm, actions that collapse the differences and serve as an ever-present physical reminder of the two forms. Despite this, there is a naturalness, a "smoothness" (361) to their transformations and a sense that the animal form is actually the preferred one; as Danica describes it: "Taking a deep breath to gather my thoughts, I changed shape, luxuriating in the wonderful feeling of sliding from the awkwardly shaped human form into the beautifully streamlined, graceful one of a golden hawk" (90). Erica, a falcon shifter, refers to shifting as instinctive, and integrated to the point that if an injured human changes into their other form, they take with them that injury (325). Yet there is an emphasis on balance between the shifted forms.

Like Atwater-Rhodes's shapeshifters, the werewolf of Pat McIntosh's short story "Cry Wolf" has a physical reminder of his dual identity present on his body at all times: "Everyone knows the marks of the werewolf: hair on the back and none on the chest, different teeth, the extra nipples down the belly like a wolf" (174). Others, like Ginger Fitzgerald of the film *Ginger Snaps*, are shown to have a gradual physical transformation from human to animal, compared to the more usual practice of authors keeping the two bodies entirely separate: most werewolves of *Teen Wolf*, *Twilight*, and Barnes's work are fully human when not in wolf form.

Werewolves Are People Too: The Shapeshifting "Condition" as Illness

Many shapeshifting texts create a sense of instability around the body, where the body is unreliable, uncontrollable, and subject to pain that cannot be stopped, which has obvious connections to the experience of illness. Shapeshifting is often associated with extreme pain and physical discomfort, yet many texts take this further and use medical language and allusions to frame it as a medical condition or illness. For example, dialog in *Buffy, the Vampire Slayer* calls on the notion of shapeshifting and illness when it refers to lupine shapeshifting as a "condition" experienced by a human:

> XANDER: So then I'm guessing your standard silver bullets are in order here?
> GILES: No. No bullets. No matter who this werewolf is, it's still a human being, who may be completely unaware of his or her condition.
> ...
> BUFFY: He's still a human being. Most of the time.
> ...
> CAIN: First they tell me I can't hunt an elephant for its ivory.... Now I've gotta deal with People for the Ethical Treatment of Werewolves.
> ...
> GILES: You hunt werewolves for sport?
> CAIN: No, no, I'm in it purely for the money.
> BUFFY: And it doesn't bother you that a werewolf is a person twenty-eight days out of the month? [2.15].

If we turn to other texts, we find in Barnes's *Trial by Fire* similar themes: when a coven of psychics call werewolves "not natural ... Not animals. Worse," Bryn rejects this link to monstrosity: "We weren't — my family and friends, *they* weren't monsters. Werewolves were people, too" (174).

Ginger Snaps emphasizes the contagious aspects of lycanthropy when characters are infected with the condition after biting and scratching. When Brigitte realizes her sister Ginger has been infected, she seeks the help of Sam, who manufactures and deals drugs, to find a solution. Sam suggests that there must be a "cure," and Brigitte then frames this as "like an infection, works from the inside out, like a virus." Sam proceeds to look up folklore and homeopathic remedies and uses monkshood, which he calls a "super oxidant, radical detox. It promotes white blood cell growth, which fight infection." He creates a cure using monkshood, which works, but he dies while attempting to inject Ginger with the drug.

Thus there are linguistic links to medical *conditions* and *infections*, and many texts do conceptualize shapeshifting as something external to the body, a foreign agent that has entered the body. This may even be unknown to the human, as a kind of latent shapeshifting ability, which we can see in texts when characters (usually werewolves) wake after a shapeshifting event not knowing what has happened. This disrupts a coherent identity between human and animal identities given that the latter is imposed. In *Buffy*, this unconscious aspect is reinforced by Willow's comment that sees shapeshifting as an external, involuntary element to a human being: "Yeah, he's a werewolf, but he doesn't mean to be" (2.15). *True Blood* again uses this theme but in the vampire context, when Bill Compton explains that "heightened senses are a common side effect of our condition" (1.6). The use of these words *side effect* and *condition* encourage us to see the connections between these fictional creatures and disease. In Charlaine Harris's novels on which the series is based, the original public service announcement that became known as the moment when vampires "came out of the coffin" untruthfully explained that vampires were humans who had been infected by an illness which left them vulnerable to garlic and sunlight.

Jenny Hale's *Jatta* links the language of illness with the experience of shapeshifting. Jatta's brother Arthmael tells her that "people are terrified of some epidemic" (59), and Jatta wonders about the castle being "infected" and "plague-ridden" (31). In particular, the idea of cancer is evident in Jatta's werewolf:

> Eventually this tumour of hatred would prove lethal, would invade each human hour to murder her love for him.... This cancer of bloodlust was invading her soul. She felt it lurking silently inside to spread with the next wolf-moon. She was sinking, drowning, in dull, deadening hopelessness. She curled into a tighter ball.... Eventually she would be alone. Alone with her malignant, murderous wolf [365].

Here we see a metaphor of illness and cancer, but there is a second metaphor employed in that the cancer is a war. Words such as *invade, invading, cancer of bloodlust, tumour of hatred* frame the illness (and the werewolf) as an invading enemy, attacking and destroying what it finds. This reflects common medical discourse where medical practice often draws on the language of war as patients and doctors "fight" disease, where cancer cells "attack" (Hodgkin; Reisfield and Wilson). Incidentally, the reverse is also true, where the language of war returns the favor by borrowing medical language such as clinical strikes and surgical bombings (De Leonardis). Like Lupin in *Harry Potter*, Jatta is able to 'pass' as human much of the time, or at least until others learn of her condition. As with the traditional concept of the split self in relation to the werewolf figure, cancer is often seen as a diminishing of the self (Sontag 98), and even in science fictional terms as a malicious external force, "an invasion of 'alien' or 'mutant' cells" (Sontag 69). Jatta similarly feels like she is losing her "self": "It was only a matter of time, though. Her personality would decay.... A black hole in Jatta's heart was expanding, swallowing her up. She would start to dissolve after next wolf-moon" (365, 388).

The United States television series *Being Human* also shows this idea when werewolf Josh insists that the werewolf is something separate to him: "It isn't me! It's an infection, a disease!" (1.05). Josh's medical framing of his state is reinforced by his employment in a hospital; his friend, coworker and vampire, Aidan, also calls lycanthropy a "condition" (1.02). Josh has nightmares about his girlfriend giving birth to a baby with lycanthropy, explaining to her that he has "deep genetic level problems" (1.11). This language frames the shapeshifting as a medical condition and closer to science than the supernatural. When Michael transforms in *Underworld*, the show includes images inside his body, akin to *CSI*'s graphics showing the effect of physical trauma and injuries inside the body. The first immortal of *Underworld*, Alexander Corvinus, survives a plague because "his body was able to change the disease, mould it to his benefit," and this is understood in medical terms as a virus, the "Corvinus strain" which lies "dormant" in his descendants. In Rowling's *Harry Potter* series, there are similar references to the werewolf's condition as an infection or "contamination" (*Half-Blood Prince* 580), terms that invoke the idea of an uncontrollable spread. As we discuss later in this chapter, Rowling has linked her werewolf character Lupin to the experience of illness and AIDS. Susan Sontag has pointed out there is the "potential of AIDS as a metaphor for contamination and mutation" because it is invasive, infectious, and associated with "the specific imagery that surrounds viruses" (153).

As others have noted, medical metaphors can be problematic. In Sontag's view, assigning too much meaning to illness can victimize those with the condition, robbing them of agency. The cultural meaning attributed to diseases may in fact deter patients from actively seeking and assessing treatment options:

> The metaphoric trappings that deform the experience of having cancer have very real consequences: they inhibit people from seeking treatment early enough, or from making a greater effort to get competent treatment. The metaphors and myths, I was convinced, kill.... To regard cancer as if it were just a disease — a very serious one, but just a disease. Not a curse, not a punishment, not an embarrassment. Without "meaning" [Sontag 99–100].

Likewise, Hodgkin points out that another metaphor of disease, "diseases are objects," where the cancer is seen as an alien entity in the body, positions the doctors as active and the patients "as mere vessels for disease ... passive and less important than the disease itself" (Hodgkin 1820–21). The metaphor of war, meanwhile, can be counterproductive when it comes to treating sick children, who "associate war and battles with dying and death, so I think that is a pretty scary way to frame it for a child" (Penson et al. 710). We might wonder if framing the werewolf as a metaphor for disability, illness, cancer or AIDS is an equally difficult association for children to grasp.

Shapeshifting and Mental Health

As others have noted (Noll; Otten), lycanthropy itself has a particular meaning as a real-life medical condition. According to Noll, "The essential feature of this disorder is the notion of a human taking the form of a wolf and then literally behaving like one (transforming into other animals such as dogs and cats is also not uncommon)" (84). Clinical lycanthropy has links with mental illness (Du Coudray, *Curse of the Werewolf* 56–57) as well as dissociative disorder, because they share elements such as disturbances to identity, consciousness, memory, and a shift in personality (Noll 91). Nor is this clinical lycanthropy a thing of the past. As Poulakou-Rebelakou et al. note, earlier beliefs that werewolves have links to Satan and witchcraft (477) have metamorphosed into clinical diagnoses: "Psychiatrists and psychologists are still seeing patients with the strong belief that they have taken the form of a wolf (or other animal, frequently a dog or a cat). Earlier supernatural or religious descriptions of werewolf manifestations are now explained in terms of mental disorder, organic brain syndrome or abuse of hallucinogenic drugs" (Poulakou-Rebelakou et al. 469). Thus, as Du Coudray discusses, the scientific interpretation of lycanthropy increased over time (*Curse of the Werewolf* 38), which is reflected in today's contemporary works that often use medical and psychological terminology in their treatment of fictional werewolves.

Although we are concerned with fictional imaginings of shapeshifters and not with the medical condition of lycanthropy or its variants, some texts do explore shapeshifting in the context of mental health. Josh's father in *Being Human* suspects that his son has clinical lycanthropy (1.07), and his sister assumes his sudden, unexplained departure was due to madness, like their mother's, not realizing his real condition (1.02). In Glen Duncan's *The Last Werewolf*, narrator and werewolf Jacob Marlowe points to the link between *luna* and *lunatic*, describing his lycanthropy as a kind of madness (50).

As we noted in the previous chapter, many texts use concepts of race and bloodlines to frame shapeshifting. The fear of multiracial children was a theme in Atwater-Rhodes's *The Shapeshifters* because of the loss of purity in bloodlines. Yet another reason for this fear in *The Shapeshifters* is the psychological effects on the child of mixed race. In the eyes of the falcon race, "children are infinitely precious.... Pure-blooded children, that is. Mixed blood children are more easily conceived, but far more dangerous. The magic gets warped in them, and it drives them mad. They usually die by their own hands, but only after they destroy everything around them" (351). The chief example of this is Hai, whose mother was of the falcon race and father of the serpiente group. Hai's experience is linked to mental illness as she is essentially catatonic to the outside world, accessible only by dreams: "Their magic grows too quickly, too wildly. As a young child, Hai would become lost in illusions no one else could see. One day she stopped speaking. Finally, a few years ago, she fell while dancing. She lost control of her magic, and you can see what it did to her. Even if she regains her mind, her wings are broken; she will never fly again" (480). Hai exists in a "nightmare landscape" (494), trapped in her mind in a "void world" (889), and she has no desire to escape because to do so would mean returning to the real world and its "pain" (536).

In some respects this state might be seen as linked to depression. As the reader learns, those characters trapped in their minds "are the ones who have fled from a world that holds too much, into a world where they can rest. Sometimes they do so intentionally — it only takes an instant, a single thought that perhaps nothingness would be easier — and sometimes they do so unintentionally ... caught by illusions, which are created by their minds to protect them from oblivion" (533). Beyond these illusions lies "nothingness" with "no desire to return" (533). Fear is another motivation for avoiding real life by going into the "darkness" of the void world (538).

Hai is helped by Nicias, a falcon raised in Wyvern's Court, and Nicias becomes seen as "the prince who brought you back to life" (844), but Hai's decision to escape is a shared effort and as much to save Nicias as herself. Hai is able to return from the madness to the real world, but she still has difficulty understanding temporal space and is often confused by seeing visions and returning to the void world at times. She is also unable to function in healthy relationships for some time after returning to the real world, with Nicias accusing her of seeking dysfunctional relationships to avoid pain, to find "oblivion" (870) to escape her unhappiness.

Being tied to one's identity is a key part of escaping the madness, and this means balancing the two (or more) identities. Nicias is able to navigate the nightmare world because of his strong sense of self-identity and his lack of fear: "You have a lifetime of bonds holding you to this world, vows you've made and connections you've forged. Even more important, you are old enough to have a strong image of who you are" (539). Nicias is most at risk when he is in the dream world and is "forgetting everything I was and had ever known.... There was no *I*" (537). Nicias cannot return to reality until he recalls the physical world, with its pain, and five senses (hearing, vision, taste, touch, smell), his responsibilities to others, and his own sense of self ("hearing my name, I remembered *I*"), all elements of his identity (537). Similarly, Hai is called back from her visions by Nicias calling her name (889). Social connections and self-identity become part of what eventually grounds Hai more closely to the real world as she chooses to take responsibility and seeks a relationship with Nicias.

Without this link to identity and humanity, shapeshifting can become dangerous. As Oliza, daughter of Danica and Zane, points out, "[w]hen a shapeshifter went feral, it meant that she had spent too much time in animal form. Eventually the human characteristics eroded, along with the memory of her original form. Usually a feral shapeshifter was volatile, without an animal's sense of balance or a human's sense of morals, prone to attack those who had been closest to her" (655). Hai's gradual healing culminates in her confidence in her identity, and this transcends her forms: "I am more than my animal form.... I am more than feathers or scales" (964). Hai's eventual acceptance of her multiple forms and identities is embodied in her serpentine scale-colored wings, a literal representation of her now-coherent sense of self as she has moved from the void world into reality. If we read fictional shapeshifting as dealing with some of the same issues as the real-life mental disorder of lycanthropy, perhaps Hai's fictional journey reflects the resolution to the disturbances to "the normally integrative functions of identity and consciousness" (91) that Noll identifies in his description of clinical lycanthropy.

Shapeshifting as Disability

Some texts explicitly reference the notion of shapeshifting as disability. For instance, in Diana Wynne Jones's *Howl's Moving Castle*, Percival has been cursed by the Witch of the Waste into canine form, and this is directly linked to the experience of disability:

"But someone told me Lettie was fond of someone else," she said.
"Sorry for him, you mean," said Mrs Fairfax. She lowered her voice. "There's a terrible disability there," she whispered suggestively, "and it's asking too much of any girl. I told him so. I'm sorry for him myself—"
Sophie managed a mystified "Oh?"
"—but it's a fearsomely strong spell. It's very sad," Mrs Fairfax wound on. "I had to tell him that there's no way someone of my abilities can break anything that's put on by the Witch of the Waste" [119–120].

Percival is able to shift back into human form at times and with great difficulty, but his abilities are limited. In this case, Percival's canine form is due to a curse by a witch, which can only be removed by someone as powerful as the wizard Howl. When Howl returns Percival to his human shape, Percival cannot remember who he really is, and he is "incomplete, and he has parts from some other man too" (253). Percival, as it turns out, is actually made up of different parts of Wizard Suliman and Prince Justin, scattered around in a scarecrow, dog and skull, in a kind of grotesque dissection, until they are restored to their own bodies.

Catherine Hardwicke's film version of *Red Riding Hood* offers another connection between difference, disability and monstrosity in a boy who exhibits symptoms of an unnamed disability: he rarely speaks, laughs inappropriately, and is treated as a simpleton by those around him. The villagers suspect he is the werewolf, or has knowledge of who is, and lock him away and eventually kill him, and the only apparent motivation for their suspicion is his disability.

Anderson-Dargatz's *The Cure for Death by Lightning* links Tourette's Syndrome to Coyote possession. As was noted in Chapter One, Beth's relationships with three of Bertha Moses' grandchildren are complex. Her flirtation with bad boy farmhand Dennis is short-lived, and her main relationship throughout the novel is with Nora, a girl whose "difference" and mixed race are evident in her eyes, which are two different colors; in her skin tone; in her apparent allegiance with Coyote, who is often present or nearby; and in her bisexuality, as Beth discovers to her surprise when she walks in on Nora and Dennis. Yet when Beth refuses to join Nora in Vancouver, she cites her attachment to place and family, rather than any of these aspects of Nora's personality. In rejecting Nora's offer of a new life in another place, Beth is also subliminally signaling her allegiance to Nora's cousin, Billy. Known to all as Filthy Billy, he appears to suffer from Tourette's Syndrome, but this is again explained in terms of Coyote possession. In the beginning of the novel, Billy seems eccentric, and adheres to a number of superstitions, including jumping over fires and tying together the legs of his pants to stop lizards from eating his heart while he sleeps. Beth, perhaps because of her affection for his grandmother, Bertha Moses, is accepting of Billy's eccentricities and indeed, his incessant swearing and equally frequent apologies. Ultimately Billy is depicted as the most stable romantic option, and one with whom Beth is happy.

Shapeshifting, Disability and Monstrosity

Between shapeshifting, mental health, illness and disability, readers might assume the authors are creating these associations with worthy intentions, but might also question if a werewolf, a monster, is indeed an appropriate metaphor for these experiences. In our discussion here, we understand metaphor in line with Fogelin's definition where "both similes and metaphors express figurative comparisons: similes explicitly, metaphors implicitly" (23).

To contextualize our analysis of these works, some points relating to disability and illness are worth highlighting. One term that has been used to mean the study of disability and abnormal development, especially congenital defects, is teratology. While the word can also relate to animals and plants, the Teratology Society states that "[t]eratology is the study of abnormal development. More particularly, it is the study of the causes, mechanisms, and manifestations of abnormal development, whether genetically, gestationally, or postnatally induced; and whether expressed as a lethality, malformation, growth retardation, or functional aberration." The word teratology is made up of two elements: terato, meaning monster (from the Greek, teras), and logy, meaning the knowledge, science or study of. Hence, teratology, the study of abnormality or disability, can literally mean the study of monstrosity (Costello). This unsettling background seems to compound the problematic aspects of the trend of authors connecting disability and werewolves. *Being Human* (U.S.) series makes these links perhaps unwittingly, when werewolf Josh worries that his unborn baby will be like "monsters or deformed" (1.12), and as it turns out, his girlfriend Nora does miscarry the baby on the full moon (1.13).

According to Lennard J. Davis, disability is the single greatest minority group within the United States, at 15 percent, a number greater than any ethnic or racial minority ("Preface/Introduction" xv, xviii). Despite this prevalence, in humanities studies "disabilities are still often forgotten when the litany of race, class, gender, sexual orientation, and so on are articulated" ("Preface/Introduction" xiii). In terms of popular depictions of disability, Tressider writes that films limit their engagement with disability to three main stereotypes: "Those which treat disability as grotesquerie, for whatever purpose.... Those which use disability as a cynosure for pity or redemption.... Those which use disability as a hook for a distinct 'issue,' usually war or a social cause" (6). We can see these tropes in literature as well. As Davis ("Constructing Normalcy") notes, few main characters in literature have a disability; disabled characters are often villains, or sometimes objects of pity, such as Tiny Tim in Charles Dickens's *A Christmas Carol*.

There are serious limitations in reading the werewolf itself as a direct metaphor for disability. Certainly there are difficult aspects of linking disability and illness with the werewolf, a traditionally monstrous creature. Given Fogelin's distinction between similes and metaphors where metaphors provide implicit rather than explicit comparisons, it is more productive to dismiss literal attempts to read the werewolf as a metaphor for any of these conditions. Shapeshifting works cannot sustain a literal reading because the werewolf figure remains dangerous, a malevolent force of contamination and monstrosity.

In her categories of werewolves in "Contemporary Werewolf Schemata," Chappell classifies Rowling's Lupin, whom we discuss later in this chapter, as a "sympathetic werewolf" (26), distinct from other classes of werewolves (monstrous, benevolent, non-essentialist, and incommensurable). The sympathetic werewolf is characterized by a split identity where "their wolf form [is] an undesired outbreak of monstrosity abhorrent to their human selves"

(24). Chappell argues that Lupin's representation is "problematic" (26): "The sympathetic werewolf can only be tolerated and is understandably socially excluded because the wolf remains objectively dangerous and distasteful. The schema thus maintains a negative representation of biological difference" (26). Chappell reads Lupin's wolf in racial terms, but her point is applicable to disability and illness. Chappell also contends that the infectious nature of the werewolf state can suggest the threat of other races and recall eugenic and racial ideologies where the problem (the werewolf/race) must be eliminated (26). The issue remains that a direct equivalence of werewolf and race (or, in this context, disability and illness) is an inherently flawed metaphor that cannot be sustained without serious objection, for the wolves in Rowling's world are not misunderstood people but are very real monsters who threaten the safety of humans. That is, there is some justification for fearing werewolves. For this reason, the werewolf will always fail as an effective metaphor for minority groups.

The Social Model of Shapeshifting: Disability and Shapeshifting

One of the developments in disability studies has been the critique of conceptions of normality. Davis argues against the concept of *normal*, writing that "the 'problem' is not the person with disabilities; the problem is the way that normalcy is constructed to create the 'problem' of the disabled person" ("Constructing Normalcy" 3). In particular, critics have targeted the understanding of disability solely as a medical condition. As Tremain notes, "people classified as 'handicapped' or 'disabled' have developed sociopolitical conceptions of disability in order to counter medicalized approaches" (1–2). Davidson explains this development as moving from understanding disability from a medical to a social perspective:

> The medical definition of disability locates impairment in the individual as someone who lacks the full complement of physical and cognitive elements of true personhood and who must be cured or rehabilitated. The social model locates disability not in the individual's impairment but in the environment — in social attitudes, institutional structures, and physical or communicational barriers that prevent full participation as citizen subject [119].

The social model of disability has its critics, such as Shakespeare who claims it implies that people are only disabled by society and not by their body. He suggests that this potentially means "rejecting medical prevention, rehabilitation or cure of impairment" (200). A better view, Shakespeare proposes, takes into account that people are disabled by both their body and society.

These perspectives from disability studies can offer us a useful way to approach shapeshifting. If we look at the social model of werewolves, so to speak, we can explore fictional societies' reaction to shapeshifters, to see how authors use werewolves as metaphors for society's reaction to aspects such as disability, illness, difference, and mental health disorders.

As Ward notes, the werewolf figure offers many possibilities, seen in Rowling's *Harry Potter*, where they are "characters of ingenuity, of difference; they upset readers' expectations and force them to question their assumptions and beliefs, especially those about identity and difference" (*Cultural Contexts* 3). This concept of instability, in the context of difference in society, proves to be a useful way of understanding the potential of shapeshifting.

One of the minor recurring characters in Rowling's *Harry Potter* series is Professor Remus Lupin. Theoretical and popular readings of Lupin have included linking the werewolf figure to Rowling's mother's multiple sclerosis (Kirk), complexities of good and evil (Natov), queer theory (Bernhardt-House; Pugh and Wallace), and the Other (Green). Ward studies Lupin in detail in her *Cultural Contexts* in relation to how he is able to challenge notions of difference. Here, however, we are discussing lupine shapeshifting as it relates to disability and illness, not simply because Rowling herself refers to this, but also because of the growing trend to relate the werewolf to a range of minority figures.

Lupin is a werewolf who appears initially in Book Three, *Harry Potter and the Prisoner of Azkaban*, where readers learn that he was bitten as a young child and could not be cured (258). Like the classic werewolf, he transforms during the full moon and is a danger to any human around him and cannot retain his human mind; he calls himself "a fully fledged monster once a month" (258). Lupin describes the transformations as "terrible. It is very painful to turn into a werewolf" (259). As teenagers, Lupin's friends learned how to transform themselves into animals to keep him company during the werewolf time, and this helped him retain some of his human mind (260). As adults, Lupin's former enemy Snape gives him a potion that allows Lupin to retain his mind during the full moon, which keeps him "safe": "I keep my mind when I transform.... I am able to curl up in my office, a harmless wolf" (258). Readers may assume that werewolves are normal or ordinary in this world of fantastical creatures, but Lupin has difficulty finding employment and he is isolated and feared by those around him.

In interviews, Rowling has identified disability and illness as the meaning behind Lupin: "Professor Lupin, who appears in the third book, is one of my favorite characters. He's a damaged person, literally and metaphorically. I think it's important for children to know that adults, too, have their problems, that they struggle. His being a werewolf is a metaphor for people's reactions to illness and disability" (Rowling "Harry Potter—Harry and Me"). As we noted in passing earlier, Rowling has elsewhere stipulated AIDS as the meaning, where Lupin operates as

> the H.I.V. metaphor. It was someone who had been infected young, who suffered stigma, who had a fear of infecting others, who was terrified he would pass on his condition to his son. And it was a way of examining prejudice, unwarranted prejudice towards a group of people. And also, examining why people might become embittered when they're treated that unfairly ["Warner Bros. Entertainment and J. K. Rowling V. RDR Books" 73].

Here, Rowling deflects literal readings of werewolves as disability or illness and instead highlights the distinction raised by the social model of disability: she talks about Lupin as a metaphor not for disability or illness, but for people's reactions to disability and illness.

Reading Lupin in this approach draws out the ways in which disability resonates with the werewolf figure in Rowling's interpretation. One of these intersections is the concept of passing. Because the shapeshifting occurs only once a month, Lupin is able to hide his condition most of the time. At one point he tells Harry he is "off-colour" (*Prisoner of Azkaban* 118) when he is actually suffering the full moon effects, and this is highly suggestive of the concept of passing. While passing is often related to race, Linton notes that it is also a common concept amongst other minority groups, including people with disabilities, where "passing may be a deliberate attempt to avoid discrimination or ostracism" (166). Lupin's fears prove justified when his condition is discovered: "the owls will start arriving from parents—they will not want a werewolf teaching their children" (*Prisoner of Azkaban* 309). He is neither fully human nor fully animal, at once both and neither. Lupin's attempts to pass as either human or werewolf are unsuccessful: once humans discover his identity they reject him, and the werewolf population do not trust him because of his "unmistakeable signs of having tried to live among wizards" (*Half-Blood Prince* 313).

Lupin internalizes this rejection and attempts to cut himself off from the human world by rejecting another character, Tonks, whom he loves. He tells Tonks that his lycanthropy makes him "too old ... too poor ... too dangerous" for her (*Half-Blood Prince* 582), although the first and third of these elements need not trouble Tonks if she views older dangerous men as appealing, as most contemporary female protagonists in paranormal fiction apparently do. Although they do marry, at one stage he regrets it because he has made her an "outcast":

> Don't you see what I've done? Even her own family is disgusted by our marriage, what parents want their only daughter to marry a werewolf? And the child—the

child.... My kind don't usually breed! ... how can I forgive myself, when I knowingly risked passing on my own condition to an innocent child? And if, by some miracle, it is not like me, then it will be better off, a hundred times so, without a father of whom it must always be ashamed! [*Deathly Hallows* 175–76].

Lupin's problem can be managed, with potion or otherwise, but society does not want to manage it. Instead, it wants to isolate, control and oppress it. The Ministry of Magic requires that all werewolves be listed on a registry. Lupin is restricted by society: society's reaction to his werewolf status, his so-called disability, is one of fear, persecution, and control.

This is precisely what some disability studies scholars insist lies at the heart of oppression in disability in real life. McWhorter argues that our real world is governed by legislation, registration, and control, and we can apply her comments to Lupin's situation in *Harry Potter*: "power-knowledge networks that produce and regulate disability also produce and regulate ability, ableness, normality. The practices and institutions that divide, for example, the 'able-bodied,' 'sane,' and 'whole' from the 'impaired,' 'mentally ill,' and 'deficient' create the conditions under which all of us live" (McWhorter xv). Yet despite the restrictions placed on werewolves in this society, the werewolf figure resists control. Creed argues that the transformation from human to wolf frees the werewolf "from the dictates of the law for the period of the transformation" (133). Ward points out that in Lupin's case it is no use regulating werewolves because "Lupin's inability to retain his conscious and rational self when transformed places him outside of the control of the systems that regulate society" ("Shape-shifting" 5).

As Ward points out in some detail in her analysis (*Cultural Contexts*), control is a central concern. Given this, we should not overlook Tonks's own shapeshifting abilities, for she is a Metamorphmagus, able to change her physical appearance "at will" (*Order of the Phoenix* 52). Yet the issue appears to be just this choice and "will": Tonks's ability is valued and represents control (and is the result of innate ability) while Lupin's werewolf is feared and signifies the loss of control (the result of external infection). There is some suggestion that Metamorphmagi may owe their abilities to genetics (Lupin and Tonks's child inherits the ability). They are also rare, which further enhances their value. As Tonks tells Harry, her ability cannot be learned: "Metamorphmagi are really rare, they're born, not made. Most wizards need to use a wand, or potions, to change their appearance" (*Order of the Phoenix* 52).

Animagi are able to shapeshift as well, but unlike Metamorphmagi they are limited to one animal form, and their abilities are attained by education, not birth. It is also described as a very difficult skill to learn (*Tales* 80); only seven Animagi are listed on the official register, though more exist (*Prisoner of Azkaban* 257). The Marauders — Sirius, James, Lupin, and Peter — each shift into an animal: Lupin's is a wolf and due to lycanthropy, not magic, but Sirius, James, and Peter become Animagi to accompany their friend, in the forms of a dog, stag and rat, respectively. Their abilities are only attained by years of difficult study (*Prisoner* 259) and their nicknames for each other are based on their animal identities: Moony, Padfoot, Prongs, and Wormtail. Thus their identities carry over to some extent. More than this, their appearance as humans bears some faint resemblance to their animal identities, as with Rita Skeeter and her beetle (*Goblet of Fire* 631) and Professor Minerva McGonagall and her cat form (*Philosopher's Stone* 13), both of whom wear glasses that are reflected in markings on their animal selves.

In interview, Rowling has stated that the Animagi can only transform into an animal close to their personality: "you can't choose. You become the animal that suits you best. Imagine the humiliation when you finally transform after years of study and find that you most closely resemble a warthog" ("World Book Day Web Chat"). This concept certainly appears in the novels where the Animagi characters' personalities do resemble their animal forms. Transfiguration, meanwhile, is a more generic term meaning the shifting of a person or object into another, but this is also "some of the most complex and dangerous magic you will learn" (*Philosopher's Stone* 100). Transfiguration can include transforming oneself into an animal, but this appears to be permanent because it involves the loss of the human identity and consciousness (*Tales* 83).

Perhaps we can see this as a hierarchy of shapeshifters in the *Harry Potter* series. At the top are Metamorphmagi: extremely rare, having an innate ability, and able to take on any appearance at will. Next is Animagi: rare, having learned the ability, and able to change into one animal at will. Transfiguration into an animal appears to be rather pointless since it relies on someone else reversing the spell, but still relies on ability and choice. And finally, lycanthropy: contagious, uncontrollable except by potion, and dangerous to other people. Lupin is, then, firmly at the bottom of the hierarchy of shapeshifters within the series, and in broader terms he is unlike the more recent lycanthropes in other fictions who are usually more glamorously displayed. Ward points out that even his physical human body and health seem to be decaying over the years because of his lycanthropy (*Cultural Contexts* 274).

As critics such as Ward, and Green have noted, Lupin's werewolf opens up intriguing possibilities about resistance to fixed identity and borders, which we can relate here to disability. Lupin's character can challenge our ideas about normality and difference, a theme that has been highlighted in disability studies more generally: "Normality has a history, a set of investments, an entire array of supports and assumptions that bring it into being, sustain it, and alter it when conditions so demand. To look at our world as it is seen by disability activists and scholars ... is to open ourselves to the possibility of imagining something new" (McWhorter xv–xvi). This possibility of imagining something new is akin to fantasy's ability to open our eyes to new ideas, and this is perhaps Rowling's achievement in that she has placed the popular Lupin character as the symbol of society's ills. Lupin's compassion and mercy are in stark contrast to the bigoted and ignorant hatred that he receives, and this does suggest that the problem is perhaps society's reactions rather than Lupin's condition alone.

Where literature produces sympathetic representations of disability intended to inspire, some have argued that such depictions are patronizing and recall offensive and racist ideas. For instance, Linton suggests that "the popular phrase *overcoming a disability* is used most often to describe someone with a disability who seems competent and successful in some way" (165):

> The expression is similar in tone to the phrase that was once commonly used to describe an African American who was considered exceptional in some way: "He/she is a credit to his/her race." The implication of this phrase is that the "race" is somehow discredited and needs people with extraordinary talent to give the group the credibility that it otherwise lacks ... the implication [is] that the group is inferior and that the individual is unlike others in that group [Linton 165].

This can be applied to Rowling's work, where Lupin is very much portrayed as being exceptional for a werewolf, unlike the other wolves in his goodness and humanity. Lest Lupin be reduced to an inspirational stereotype in the tradition that Linton labels offensive, however, Rowling gives Lupin faults that undermine his status as a role model. He is morbidly aware of his own state and isolates himself because of it. At one point he abandons his pregnant wife because of his fear and self-loathing, although his actions are implicitly redeemed when he returns to his wife and they die as heroes in the final battle of the series. Nor is Lupin proactive in fighting for werewolf rights; instead he accepts rejection and remains silent, a passive reaction that Horne has pointed out is evident in other "oppressed racial group[s]" in the novels (93). Readers are thus unlikely to pity or sympathize with Lupin so much as admire those specific traits that make him far more human than all around him, including, at times, Harry himself.

While direct metaphors of werewolves and disability or illness offer little of value beyond objectionable inferences, returning to the concept of the social model of werewolves offers far more scope. The persecution and exclusion of Lupin can remind readers that society's treatment of those who are different is often ignorant and malicious. Sontag suggests that AIDS replaced cancer as a highly stigmatized disease, an "illness which becomes identified with evil, and attaches blame to its 'victims'" (101). In this sense, using metaphors of (sympathetic) monstrosity may effectively highlight the unjustified stigma faced by those with particular conditions. Rowling's reference to

Lupin's werewolf as disability or illness thus interrogates constructions of normality and difference, creating a space where our own ideas and assumptions are subject to transformation, as is the werewolf. Rowling's work suggests that the problem of the werewolf—the disability, the illness—is indeed rather a problem of society's norms and attitudes. Although this challenge remains unresolved in the books, and despite the negative implications, the werewolf in many ways nevertheless proves a powerful metaphor for Rowling to address her themes of difference and identity.

Adapting to Difference

Jatta, by Australian author Jenny Hale, describes the experience of female werewolf Jatta, a princess who has to come to terms with her shapeshifting. Jatta learns that the wolves were formed out of hatred:

> In our tenth century A.M. the great Sorcerer Andro Mogon created a final punishment for our Isle's traitors: the wolf curse. Of all his curses, this be most terrible. His wolf continues in human form except on the three nights of the full moon. With the setting sun he transforms, having a wolf's instinct to hunt and a madman's passion. He kills throughout the night, first devouring his family and all who once loved him. All men detest him and drive him, if they can, from their midst. Even so, many fear a wolf's bite more than being devoured for, if King Brackensith commands it, the victim might also be cursed ... taking inspiration from the monsters of his people's nightmares ... the Dark Sorcerer's own contribution was deadliest, for the hatred that consumed his wolves was his own [31, 61–62].

Although Jatta becomes a werewolf as she enters puberty, in the novel the werewolf functions less as a symbol of adolescence than a metaphor for disability and illness. On her website for the novel, Hale has linked the werewolf figure to the idea of disability: "I wanted to write a story about a princess with a disability, something that made her unpopular, something she had absolutely no control over. The afflictions that Jatta and Noriglade endure arouse my sympathy, even if most strangers would find them horrific and dangerous" ("The Author"). As in *Harry Potter*, Jatta's werewolf is dangerous to others, and therefore society's fears are in fact justified. Again, this makes a direct metaphor of werewolf as disability or illness problematic. However, Hale's reference to the negative reactions of others to Jatta's condition aligns her work with a social model of disability. This suggests that the problem is partly society's fault, for its treatment of those who are disabled, or, in this case, werewolves. As with Lupin, the discovery of Jatta's status as werewolf isolates her from society, alienating her from family and friends. Wolves in Alteeda are feared and hated, and Jatta's condition excludes her from other people, despite being their princess. This is a blow to Jatta, who, even before the wolf, is shy and stammers, two features that again invoke disability in that shyness and anxiety are frequently described as crippling or paralyzing experiences while stuttering is a speech disorder, an impediment.

In many of these texts, shapeshifting is aligned with monstrosity in terms that recall previous attitudes to people with disabilities. Jatta's brother, Arthmael, calls her a "freak" (*Jatta* 25), even though he is the only person who supports her. Jackson calls Scott a "freak" in the *Teen Wolf* television series (1.03); Ginger calls herself the same thing in *Ginger Snaps*.

In the earlier quotation, Hale links the character of Jatta with Noriglade, a vampire, for their shared "afflictions." Noriglade is a vampire, one of the Undead, and Jatta's brother refers to Noriglade as having a "handicap" (344). Like the Hollywood vampires of other juvenile and adolescent texts that have saturated the market, Noriglade's beauty dazzles ordinary people; unlike such glamorous vampires, Noriglade hides her mouth full of black teeth and speaks of herself as a "rotting, animated" corpse (331). The reader's view of Noriglade is filtered through the eyes of Arthmael, who tells Noriglade: "Listen, this is all new to me. Give me a chance. If I can adapt to Jay, I can adapt to you" (328). It is clear that this is a problem of perceptions — it is Arthmael who must adapt and change his perceptions, not Noriglade.

The characters of Jatta and Noriglade thus reinforce the novel's interest in challenging perceptions. When Jatta meets Noriglade, she reacts with fear and horror in just the same way as those who have scorned Noriglade. However, Jatta's perceptions quickly shift as she attempts to accept Noriglade with the understanding she herself desires. Moreover, Jatta meets Noriglade in a different kingdom, Dartith, where werewolves and vampires are accepted by the ruling family: "What lesser men dread, we royals embrace" (334). In other words, a different social context provides a different social response to the same condition, although this theme is somewhat weakened by the fact that Dartith is a decidedly brutal place with little else to recommend it. While other themes may invoke the concept of overcoming disability — Noriglade is seen as unusually good for a vampire; she is "nothing like other Undead" (306) — in the sense that Linton argues against, it seems more useful to read the werewolf in *Jatta* as a challenge to ideas of normality and difference. The characters' shifting perceptions and contrasting experiences in Alteeda and Dartith are devices that add a layer of complexity by focusing on the concepts of difference and normality as subjective and cultural notions that can change over time and place.

The werewolf concept in *Jatta* differs to *Harry Potter* because the focus is more on the werewolf's battle with its condition and attempts to overcome it, rather than a passive resignation to the condition. There are also positive aspects to Jatta's journey. As she flees Alteeda and seeks a cure, she finds confidence and discovers the true extent of her creative and imaginative powers. In the conclusion of the novel, Jatta transforms into a Sorceress and discovers her werewolf has disappeared. While it is difficult to interpret this, suggesting as it does that disability or illness can simply disappear, the close of *Jatta* leaves the protagonist with a new disability, one that Hale describes as an "extreme sensitivity to touch" that makes physical contact painful (Hale Re: Jatta). Despite this, *Jatta* challenges perceptions and focuses attention on society's treatment of those who are different.

The social model of shapeshifters shows that society's reaction to disability and illness can be ignorant and misplaced, and that the real monstrosity might just be located in particular social norms and concepts of difference that negatively exclude people with disabilities or mental illness. While the works discussed here do not always attempt to solve this problem, the shapeshifting figure nonetheless provides an intriguing way to conceptualize disability and illness in the social context.

We cannot forget that shapeshifting in many modern texts is a gift of superhero proportions that involves eternal youth and increased power, social status, and physical abilities. In such texts, there is limited potential to use shapeshifting as a metaphor for the experience of illness, disability, or mental health disorders.

Despite this, and despite the negative implications of rendering disability and illness as fantastical creatures, the shapeshifter as metaphor reminds readers that society's treatment of those it deems outside the norm (the disabled, the chronically ill) is not always justified, morally right, or even helpful. Indeed, such a metaphor of monstrosity suggests that society itself can become the monster, rather than those who wear the label.

Six
Coping, Masking and Addiction: A Little Drinking Problem

> *"Kalix needs help!" protested Vex.*
> *"She needs to stop filling herself with cheap wine and laudanum," retorted the Fire Queen, "which, I perceive, is more the cause of her current state of collapse than a minor wound."*
> *Moonglow rose to her feet, a bewildered look on her face. She couldn't understand the Queen's hostility. "She probably needed some laudanum to dull the pain," suggested Moonglow. "I think a silver bullet would be agony for her."*
> — Millar, *Curse of the Wolf Girl* 100

Masking strategies and the ability to "pass" as human have long been part of vampire and werewolf narratives. Characters such as Rowling's Lupin and the United Kingdom *Being Human*'s George go to extraordinary lengths to mask their lycanthrope identities and protect the humans around them when they change once a month. Others, however, self-medicate, such as the werewolf cousins Kalix and Dominil in Martin Millar's *Lonely Werewolf Girl* and *Curse of the Wolf Girl*, who differ from the rest of their whiskey-drinking clan in that they choose to use laudanum in order to cope with their complicated double lives. A variation on this theme is explored in television's *The Vampire Diaries*, where Stefan chooses to drink animal blood because he is a "problem drinker" on "the human stuff"; ironically, in the novels on which the program is based the ability to shapeshift is directly related to the amount of human blood consumed and Stefan's non-human diet precludes him from this ability. A werewolf-vampire hybrid becomes the arch-nemesis character in Seasons Two and Three of the series. Similarly in *True Blood*, vampire blood known by the street name of "V" is a powerful aphrodisiac and provides extraordinary strength, creating super-villains when used by a gang of werewolves. In *Ginger Snaps*, Ginger's "hunger" for power and control is linked to blood and her own bodily changes, both menarchal and supernatural. What, then, do we make of powerful characters who are not limited to one physical persona, who are still somehow haunted by their supernatural abilities? Is the power provided by being other-than-human, in itself, something of an addiction? This chapter examines the notions of masking, passing and hiding difference through the use of artificial stimulants, and in particular, in individuals who experience loss of agency in the process.

The idea of "passing," in relation to ethnicity and disability is one that has already received much critical attention. The figure of the shapeshifter, who is able to "pass" as human most of the time, has already been discussed in this book in Chapter Five. In some instances, arguably, the attempt to pass is tantamount to hiding or removing oneself from mainstream company, as with werewolves George and Josh in the United Kingdom and United States versions of *Being Human*, Oz in *Buffy, the Vampire Slayer*, and Mason and Tyler in television's *The Vampire Diaries*. Rowling's Lupin and Millar's werewolf enchantress Thrix take this idea to a supernatural level, using magical abilities and potions to minimize shifts or the impact of shifts. In both of these examples, the characters are further marginalized even among their own kind because of these decisions; as Ward argues in her thesis *Cultural Contexts and Cultural Change: The Werewolf in Classical, Medieval, and Modern Texts*, Lupin is ostracized among both wizards and werewolves because of his dual nature (Ward 269, 288, 320, 323, 332, 336); in Millar's *Lonely Werewolf Girl* and *Curse of the Wolf Girl*, werewolf enchantress and fashion designer Thrix MacRinnalch has removed herself from Scotland and werewolf politics, noting that "[o]thers of her kind always meant problems" (*Lonely Werewolf* 3). Thrix is one of many of the MacRinnalch women who finds herself attempting to avoid the intrigue and machinations of her kind, however; also living in London, away from the castle and family in Scotland are her fugitive younger sister Kalix and her cousins Dominil, Butix and Delix. Kalix and Dominil are both laudanum addicts, and twins Butix and Delix, known as Beauty and Delicious, are so far removed from their werewolf heritage because of their life of alcohol-fueled debauchery that they have forgotten how to change shape voluntarily (*Lonely Werewolf* 32).

Family Failings and Mental (un)Health

These characters belong to a further subset of supernatural characters that has appeared in recent years: those who are psychologically incapable of coping with their difference and complex family circumstances and who self-medicate through the use of addictive substances. Michael Millar's *Lonely Werewolf Girl* signals these concerns as early as the second paragraph of the novel, when the protagonist, Kalix MacRinnalch, is described as being skinny, thin like a reed, not an ounce of fat to show for her seventeen years of existence: a werewolf without an appetite. How her family had hated that. Her mother used to plead with her, beg her to eat. Until last year when Kalix attacked her father, lord of the werewolves. Now her mother had more to worry about than her daughter's poor appetite, or her violent temper, or her addictions, or her madness [*Lonely Werewolf* 1].

Kalix MacRinnalch is the youngest daughter of the Thane of the werewolves, born a century and half after her siblings. Kalix is further isolated from her family members by the nature of her birth, which was on the night of the full moon, while both she and her mother were in werewolf form (Millar, *Curse of the Wolf* 186, 187, 387). Her cousin Dominil suggests that this is the reason why Kalix is less impacted by "events that affect other werewolves" (Millar, *Curse of the Wolf* 507). Certainly Kalix believes that this is the reason why she is affected by the "unparalleled savagery that had been both a gift and a curse to the lonely werewolf girl" (*Lonely Werewolf* 7). Kalix is expected, as both a female and an heir to the MacRinnalch Thaneship, to behave in certain, civilized ways; indeed, a number of the characters throughout the novels go to great pains to point out just how civilized the MacRinnalch werewolves are (*Curse of the Wolf* 518). Yet Kalix's memories of her childhood with her family seem to suggest that she was largely ignored by her family, making it difficult for her to internalize expected behaviors. Indeed, many of her choices bemuse and confound her mother, Verasa. Verasa characterizes Kalix's behaviors as "foolish." This Kalix does internalize, as seen through free indirect discourse:

> Kalix was always doing foolish things. It had been foolish to attack her father. It had been foolish to crawl into Gawain's bed when she was fourteen. It had been foolish to drink the entire contents of her family's malt whiskey cabinet when she was thirteen, though Kalix had protested that as a Scottish werewolf, she was merely exploring her heritage. And it had been foolish to eat the contents of her mother's medicine cabinet just to see what would happen, an escapade that led to her being the only teenage MacRinnalch werewolf ever taken to hospital for an emergency stomach pump [*Lonely Werewolf* 20].

Kalix's difference is thus only exacerbated over time. As she becomes aware of others' responses to what is known as her "battle madness"—a complete loss of control when under physical threat—and difference, she develops an anxiety disorder. In addition to seeing a psychiatrist (whom she doesn't like) and taking prescribed Diazepam (which she does), she self-medicates with the narcotic laudanum.

Although there are several contemporary theories with regard to the causes of addiction, it is now generally recognized that many people with diagnoses of mental illness subsequently develop addictions (Hirschman 538–

39). Hirschman cites studies conducted in the 1990s that demonstrate strong correlations between not only mental disorders and addictive disorders, but also hereditary abnormalities in brain chemistry (538). Thus the behavior of the MacRinnalchs as depicted in these novels follows psychological studies that indicate that individuals may turn to what Hirschman terms "folk remedies" such as alcohol or illicit drugs as a means of dealing with "emotional symptoms such as anxiety, depression and manic behavior" (538).

Kalix's behavior is more than simply self-destructive, however; her mental disorders and addictions also impact on her family and broader werewolf society as depicted in Millar's world. Nycole Prowse notes that "the addict makes trouble because of his/her non-compliance with the patriarchal symbolic order" (1) and this is certainly true of Kalix, who fatally injures her father, the patriarch of the family and ruler of the Scottish werewolves, during an altercation over her affair with Gawain. In her book *Using Women: Gender, Drug Policy, and Social Justice*, Nancy Campbell argues that non-addicted women are already "othered," so when "women violate gender norms by using illicit drugs, they are represented as spectacular failures — callously abandoning babies or becoming bad mothers, worse wives or delinquent daughters" (20), and Kalix is certainly depicted as the latter. Kalix's "wild" affair with Gawain (*Lonely Werewolf* 79) is viewed by her parents as delinquency; partially because of her youth, and partially because Gawain is not deemed a suitable partner because he has a human grandfather, and is therefore not a pure-blood werewolf. In an altercation with her father, Kalix (in her human form) manages to seriously injure her father, even though he is in his superior werewolf form, again suggesting that the unusual circumstance of her birth has afforded her innate superhuman strength. The punishment for such a transgression against the monarch is death, and so Kalix flees the castle, moving to London where she lives on the streets, begging and stealing in order to survive and feed her laudanum habit.

Predictably, Kalix becomes even more vulnerable under these circumstances. As her anxiety and depressive episodes become deeper and more frequent, she becomes even more reliant on self-medication. Prowse argues that addiction positions addicts in a liminal space where they are both viewed as victims, because their behaviors are beyond their control, and demonized because of their socially irresponsible choices (1). Prowse further argues that representations of female addicts (and mothers, in particular) are often constructed as though they were destabilizing to the very foundations of civilization, because women "are traditionally viewed as gatekeepers between good and evil, chaos and constraint" (1). For the double-natured werewolf Kalix, these lines are mutable. Her self-loathing means that she is ill-able to differentiate between good and evil, and her chaotic life makes constraint unlikely.

Kalix's werewolf form is depicted as her "true" or stronger form. When a human, Kalix refuses to eat and largely survives on laudanum, alcohol and Diazepam, so that her strength is progressively depleted over the course of the lunar month (*Lonely Werewolf* 39). When she changes involuntarily at the full moon, however, her werewolf self must eat. Millar notes rather ironically that when "full of meat and transformed into a werewolf, she seemed like a whole new person" (*Lonely Werewolf* 126). Rather than "passing" or trying to behave as a human, then, Kalix stumbles her way through a subsistence existence when in human form, but is whole — stronger, healthier and more vital — when she is a werewolf. In the beginning of the novel, this prompts her to behave like a human teenage girl with an eating disorder: she experiences nausea after having eaten, attempts to regurgitate the food consumed the night before when she transforms back into her human form (*Lonely Werewolf* 39), and uses food as a means of self-punishment. For example, when she learns that Gawain has taken a new lover, she refuses to turn into a werewolf "because then she would eat," convinced that "Gawain having a new lover was final proof that she was a worthless creature who didn't deserve to live. Her left arm was a mass of new cuts. She sipped laudanum, and slipped in and out of bad dreams" (*Lonely Werewolf* 447).

After being attacked by werewolf bounty hunters on the streets of London, Kalix meets Daniel, a young and largely unmotivated college student who invites her back to his flat to recover. Kalix inadvertently leaves her journal in his car, necessitating a return visit to the flat in which Daniel and his roommate, Moonglow, reside. Kalix's journal reveals not only her loneliness and her other identity, but also that she is not functionally literate. This is again linked to her family life and resultant anxiety. Verasa had decided that her children should be sent to "normal schools to complete their education.... As soon as the family felt confident that one of their young werewolves was responsible enough not to give their true nature away they would be enrolled. This had never happened with Kalix" (*Lonely Werewolf* 167). Kalix's "true" form is not one that she is capable of hiding, and nor does she want to. Interestingly, the pure-blood royal MacRinnalchs are able to transform at will, as well as into full wolf form; abilities which are not shared, in Millar's mythology, by the rest of the werewolf population. If Kalix appears to be, as Moonglow attests, "acting for the first time something like a normal human being, but not being in human form" (*Lonely Werewolf* 134), she is even more amenable when even further removed from her human form and its frailties: "Wolf-Kalix seemed far more enthusiastically friendly than werewolf-Kalix ever had ... [Moonglow] thought she'd never seen anything as beautiful as Kalix in her full wolf form" (*Lonely Werewolf* 381). The anxiety-ridden and violent Kalix does, however, feel every bit as uneasy in her full-wolf form as she does in her wholly human one, noting that it is "not so good for fighting,' said Kalix. 'And you just can't do anything with your paws. It's hard to even open a door. You can't talk. And you don't think so clearly'" (*Lonely Werewolf* 136). Kalix is most at home in the most liminal and uncanny of her shapes — the half-human, half-werewolf monster.

Kalix truly believes that she is abnormal and a monster, although it is not her werewolf heritage but, rather, family disapproval, which convinces her of this. When asked to go downstairs to meet Moonglow's boyfriend, Kalix becomes anxious that she will do something socially unacceptable and thus upset Moonglow. She associates this situation with social occasions in the castle where she found the disapproval of her mother. Her anxiety prompts her to take laudanum, so that by the time she is introduced to Jay, she is high and incapable of remaining upright (*Lonely Werewolf* 269–70). Her drug-addled state is mirrored in the sudden and unannounced arrival of her sister Thrix and the Fire Elemental Malveria, two magical creatures who are in such a state from indulging in the MacRinnalch whiskey that they are holding each other up. In this vignette, the young humans are shown as more responsible than all of the magical entities, who have chosen to hide from their issues through imbibing addictive substances. Even Kalix is aware that using laudanum is not a particularly efficient strategy for dealing with the complexities of her life. After one instance of using the drug and self-harming, Kalix ends up "curled on the floor, her hands over her head, shivering, and crying, and quite certain that this was the time when she was finally going to go insane" (*Lonely Werewolf* 312). This is perhaps ironic, given that Kalix clearly already has significant mental health issues, but it is clear to the reader that, in her mind, things could still be worse.

Prowse notes that: "[l]ikeable or not, relatable or not, sympathetic or not, the characters of vice are centre stage in drug literature, illuminated, and the world is perceived via them," a perception that she characterizes as inherently subversive (3). When Kalix agrees to join the students' household, Moonglow, as the more responsible house member, becomes, in Kalix's eyes, the *de facto* mother figure. It is true that Moonglow appears more responsible than many adults within Kalix's family, as noted above; she is observant enough to notice that Kalix cuts herself (*Lonely Werewolf* 242), to realize that Kalix's ill-health has caused menstruation to cease (*Curse of the Wolf* 188), and to check on Kalix when she is depressed and therefore at greater risk of "cutting herself ... or descending into the grip of an anxiety attack, or dying of a laudanum overdose" (Millar, *Curse of the Wolf* 19). Harder to accept, however, are Kalix's perceptions that Moonglow is being unreasonable in "always ordering her about and telling her to eat," or that Daniel likes Moonglow more than herself (Millar, *Lonely Werewolf* 329). These appear to be a function of her low self-esteem and anxiety, both of which are further obscured by her continued use of a perception-altering narcotic.

Through their interactions with Kalix, Daniel and Moonglow are also introduced to the machinations of the greater MacRinnalch clan, including the other of Kalix's unlikely substitute-mothers, Dominil. Dominil is described as the "only living MacRinnalch to have white fur when she transformed into her werewolf form. If she changed into her full-wolf form, as many of the MacRinnalchs could do, she appeared as a great arctic wolf. It was commonly held that the icy-white coat reflected her character, and Dominil did nothing to dispel the notion" (*Curse of the Wolf* 23). Like Kalix, then, Dominil is noticeably different from birth. Again, this correlates with Hirschman's findings that the biopsychosocial model indicates that addiction springs from underlying emotional abnormalities, with the "roots of the inauthentic self extend[ing] to early childhood (and even to conception)" (545). Dominil confesses to Kalix that she used to hide in the snow when she was a child in the castle; later, her disappearance is complete when she moves to Oxford for her education, rarely returning to the castle, and losing her Scottish accent. Interestingly, the continued and arguably worsening addictions of both young women support an alternative addiction model, that of social dislocation, articulated by Bruce Alexander in 2001 (qtd. in Luntz). This suggests that individuals adopt compulsions when "dislocated from myriad intimate ties between people and groups — from family to the spiritual community — that are essential for every person in every type of society" (Luntz 7). Both Kalix and Dominal develop their habits as a result of feeling dislocated within the insular society of the Scottish werewolf fiefdom, and both are further dislocated from that community when exiled, whether voluntarily, as in Dominil's case, or involuntarily, as in Kalix's.

Dominil has the ability to truthfully articulate her thoughts, even when it is perhaps socially questionable to do so, as when she tells Kalix that she should eat, because she is more useful to Dominil when she is healthy. She further compounds this extraordinarily pragmatic advice by telling Kalix, "You may be better off dead. Which I presume is your ultimate aim in starving and cutting yourself. As you are so determinedly unhappy all the time, you may be right. There is little point in hanging around just to be miserable" (*Lonely Werewolf* 480).

Even though Dominil's assessments are harsh, however, Kalix reflects that she finds her easier to talk to than most people (*Lonely Werewolf* 460). Dominil, like Kalix, uses laudanum as a means of dealing with uniqueness within the family. Unlike Kalix, however, who has been living as a fugitive, Dominil is still able to operate within the family. Her bluntness has earned her some respect, and the widow of the Thane, Verasa, assigns her the task of supervising rogue cousins Butix and Delix, who have been living in London for several years. Verasa's motives are pragmatic and political; to gain the numbers for her younger son to inherit the Thaneship, she needs the twins' support.

Known in London as Beauty and Delicious, these young MacRinnalchs had been orphaned when they were teenagers, and had "coped with this bravely ... some years later [they] arrived in London a pair of cheerful, drunken, drug-taking degenerates who had started abusing their bodies when they were young and carried on happily ever since.... Now twenty-two, the twins spent most of their time in an alcohol-induced haze in their house in Camden in North London" (*Lonely Werewolf* 32).

Dominil is tasked to resuscitate the twins' music career, which was aborted when they were banned from playing in all local venues because their gigs were characterized by alcohol-induced violence, disorder, damage, and poor playing. Dominil manages to convince the twins to listen to her by delivering cases of MacRinnalch Scotch to their door as a bribe. They are unimpressed with her efforts to clean their house, writing her such odes as "Evil Werewolf Slut," but she nevertheless hires backing musicians and convinces a local publican to allow them to perform. Although their gig is chaotic—largely because the MacRinnalch clan use it as an opportunity to battle for succession to the throne—their guitarist Pete sagely notes that Dominil's efforts to curtail the twins' alcohol intake have worked in that "They can still walk. That's better than last time" (*Lonely Werewolf* 538).

The second novel sees Dominil again trying to ready Beauty and Delicious for a gig, this time in Edinburgh. Kalix, having been briefly reunited with Gawain at the end of the first novel, only to learn that her sister Thrix had been his recent lover, receives a letter from him seeking a reconciliation. Kalix goes to meet him, but finds his dead body. Her attempts to find his killer distract her from her literacy and numeracy studies, prompting Dominil to ask with her trademark candor:

> Do you really think this is the best way to spend your time? ... Only a few months ago your life started taking on some order. You moved in with Daniel and Moonglow. You started taking care of yourself. You started college. All of it was a great improvement from sleeping rough. Now look at you. You've stopped eating, you're cutting yourself again and you're in a worse mental state than ever. Hunting for Gawain's killer is destroying you. Is it worth it? [*Curse of the Wolf* 239].

Soon after, Kalix begins to be haunted by dreams from childhood werewolf tales about Robber Wolf, Poor Wolf and Baby Wolf (Millar, *Curse of the Wolf* 240), which puzzle her. She wonders why she feels "oddly reassured to have remembered the children's tale. Normally she couldn't remember anything good about growing up at Castle MacRinnalch" (*Curse of the Wolf* 240).

Later, Kalix learns that it was Dominil who killed Gawain, and she attacks her cousin. Dominil is thrown out of her werewolf form, however, by a magically-induced lunar eclipse, used by a group of werewolf hunters in an attempt to eradicate the world of the MacRinnalch clan. Kalix, however, because of her unique nature, is not affected as the others are, and is able to maintain her werewolf shape (*Curse of the Wolf* 479). Despite her werewolf form and outsider status, Kalix clearly retains rational thought and some sense of propriety, for she "howled in anger and frustration. She couldn't kill Dominil like this. No werewolf could take on their werewolf shape and kill another werewolf who was human. It would be dishonourable beyond measure. Dominil struggled to rise, Kalix struggled to control herself" (Millar, *Curse of the Wolf* 480). At this moment, the symbiosis between Dominil and Kalix is finally explained. Kalix remembers "sitting next to the teenage Dominil, listening raptly while Dominil told her stories about Robber Wolf, Poor Wolf and Baby Wolf. She had a brief urge to sit there again. To Dominil's surprise, Kalix changed back into human" (*Curse of the Wolf* 481). Dominil, as a teenager, had recognized that Kalix was being neglected by her immediate family, and, as another outsider within the clan, had sought to build a relationship with her. Kalix had felt she was better able to talk with Dominil, not realizing that it was because she provided the only isolated nurturing she experienced as a child. As we have seen, both cousins, because of their oddness within the family, had escaped the castle and its environs, attempting to rebuild their lives while still using an addictive substance in order to repress their emotional responses to that earlier time.

Heredity, Addiction and Mental Illness

Families with a predisposition to mental illness and addiction who are influenced by the supernatural are also to be found in *True Blood*. Lafayette Reynolds, the short-order cook at Merlotte's Bar and Grill, often offers support to his cousin Tara, herself a heavy emotional drinker, and the self-professed "adult child of an alcoholic" (1.03). Lafayette believes that the only way he will improve his life in Bon Temps is to have money; in addition to working at Merlotte's and on the Renard County road crew, he is a gay prostitute and drug dealer. In several episodes Lafayette is shown using drugs, or even supplying them to his cousin in order to make her feel better (3.01). Despite his illegal money-making activities, however, Lafayette is constructed as a person who has a strong sense of family loyalty and his morals with regard to family are never brought into question. It is he who realizes that Tara, who has locked herself in the bathroom, is at immediate risk of overdose. He pulls the pills she has taken from her mouth and promptly attempts to take her to the hospital. Her mother, who is mentally unstable, an alcoholic and who exhibits a religious fervor that borders on the addictive, stands behind him screaming, "Praise Jesus!" as Lafayette saves Tara. He retorts: "You're too busy praisin' Jesus to realize yo' daughter trying to move in with him permanently.... You failed this girl for the last time, you hear me?" (3.02). Like Dominil and Kalix, the cousins are drawn closer because of their difference. Lafayette and Tara are African Americans in a predominantly white Southern town; the children of mentally ill and addicted women, and Lafayette is further othered by his homosexuality. He tells Tara that life is about dealing with the problems you are given, and that she does not "get to checkout early and leave [him t]here" (3.02).

Lafayette is a drug user, but is primarily depicted as someone who uses drugs, and the drug business specifically, as a means to escape his circumstances. Although "V"— vampire blood — is an addictive substance, as are marijuana and the other pills that he takes, it would be difficult to argue that Lafayette is an addict; he appears to partake only when he is at home; he does not appear to crave drugs whilst in either of his two places of employment; it does not appear to be impacting negatively on his social relationships or jobs.

Lafayette's life is both enriched and complicated with the introduction of a love interest in Season Three. Lafayette becomes romantically involved with Jesus Velasquez, a nurse in the mental institution wherein his mother is housed. As is often the case in the world of Alan Ball's *True Blood*, the seemingly conservative Jesus is more than he appears. On his first visit to Lafayette's house, he notices the multicultural religious icons with which Lafayette has decorated, and asks what Lafayette does to appease them. Before the conversation can develop, however, Lafayette's car is attacked by thugs in a dispute over dealing V. When Lafayette hesitates to answer Jesus's direct question: "Are you a drug dealer?" Jesus demands to be taken back to his car at Merlotte's, ending the date (3.06).

A few episodes later, however, Jesus takes V with Lafayette (3.10). Jesus sniffs the vial and declares it to be magic, prompting Lafayette to ask if he is more like a shaman in a Sunday hat, an allusion to the folk wisdom of his mother, who advised him to be aware of Satan in a Sunday hat; that is, someone who appears pious but is actually evil. Jesus's reply is cryptic: "It's in you, too," foreshadowing the events of Season Four, wherein his identity as a *brujo* or witch is more fully developed. Lafayette also kisses his lover's tattoo of a leopard, foreshadowing that Jesus may have supernatural shapeshifting abilities (3.09).

Lafayette warns that the drug can be very unpredictable and the audience gains insight into this when their shared hallucination is screened. It features the activities of the couple's shaman ancestors on both sides. Shamans are shapeshifters who seek to restore balance within their communities, and the position is usually hereditary (for a further examination of this, see McMahon-Coleman *Indigenous Diasporic*). Whilst in some cultures, such as among the Inuit and Indigenous Australia, this is done through chanting or a séance, in others, notably in South America, a hallucinogenic drug such as peyote is used to prompt the mystical state. Thus the hallucinations of Jesus and Lafayette are linked specifically to their Mexican and African cultures, respectively, and thus to their family histories. Their responses are quite different, however. Jesus is exhilarated by the experience, but Lafayette is horrified when he turns to his lover and sees a monstrous face. Lafayette laughs this off as "a little aftershock" (3.10), but nevertheless asks Jesus to leave.

After this V-invoked shamanic experience, Lafayette begins to demonstrate changes in sleep patterns, increased irritability and decreased concentration, which are often identified as key indicators of addiction (Rudski, Segal and Kallen). In subsequent weeks, Lafayette experiences a number of hallucinatory "aftershocks," prompting him to ring Jesus and articulate his greatest fear: "Am I schizophrenic like my Momma?" (3.12). There is, of course, significant evidence to suggest links between schizophrenia and drug use, particularly cannabinoids (D'Souza, Sewell and Ranganathan; Hinton et al.; Williams and Farrell). Jesus reassures Lafayette that he is not mentally unwell, nor addicted to V; what the drug has done, he argues, is place Lafayette in touch with his magical heritage. Lafayette remains resistant to this for more than a year, despite Jesus's assertions that he is himself a *brujo* and a member of a coven wherein he can learn his craft. Jesus argues that Lafayette's latent abilities are a "gift.... I care about you. And I hate to see you run away from the thing that makes you special" (4.01).

Social Addictions

There is an argument to be made that, just as certain excessive behaviors such as shopping, eating, sex and gambling are now examined in terms of addiction (Rudski, Segal and Kallen), so too is Jesus's fascination with magic addictive. Despite Lafayette's protestations that he is not interested in pursuing the matter, Jesus takes him to a coven, where he participates, reluctantly, in a short-lived resurrection spell on the coven leader's familiar. Over the course of Season Four Lafayette's concerns about dabbling in magic are shown to be legitimate, as he is targeted first by Pam, who is seeking the return of Eric's memory and faculties which were removed by the coven leader, Marnie Stonebrook, possessed by a long-dead witch; and later by Stonebrook herself, when she possesses Lafayette's body (4.11). Jesus trades his magic for Lafayette's life, and Lafayette, possessed by Marnie, murders Jesus.

Here, as elsewhere in these contemporary texts, the use of addictive substances, regardless of whether or not the individual actually has an addiction, is treated negatively. Jason Stackhouse in the Sookie Stackhouse novels and *True Blood*, for instance, clearly has an addictive personality and, arguably, a sex addiction. He craves women, and has developed a regime of working out and studying pornography in order to continue to attract them. When he learns that a number of his lovers have slept with vampires, he uses V, a powerful aphrodisiac, with comically disastrous results, eventually leading to an embarrassing penis lancing incident. Despite this, and despite his romantic involvement with Crystal, whose only skill is cooking the drug for which she is named, Jason remains scathing of other drug users.

Blood as an Illicit Substance

Blood may well be the life force, but it is also associated with numerous taboos. The figure of the vampire draining blood from the throat is one of the cornerstones of the horror genre, as is the image of the werewolf scratching and biting its victim. Addiction is generally encoded as abhorrent, and addiction to the abject blood even more so. In *True Blood*, Jason Stackhouse, who has himself used V to enhance his bedroom performance, is hypercritical of high school football quarterback, Kitch Maynard, who has used it on the field to beat Jason's own football records. After observing Kitch's often aggressive and overly competitive behavior, Jason fronts Kitch at a late-night training session. In response to Kitch's sarcastic opening line "Grandpa Stackhouse, come to wish me luck?" Jason responds:

> You don't need luck, Kitch. You're on V. [Kitch stops.] It's an illegal substance. That makes you a criminal, a drug abuser and a cheater. On top of which you're an idiot cocky bull**** mother****er. I'm taking you down, boy. I'm gonna tell your coach, your momma and daddy and your principal.
>
> KITCH: My coach? Is the one who gave me the V. My parents are paying for it. My principal uses it for his sex life. They won't care what you say. And you can't prove it. There are no tests that can trace it.
>
> JASON: That's not fair. I was an athlete out there. I didn't get help from nobody or nothing but my team. That's the way it's s'posed to be.... My record stands [3.09].

Here Jason, and through him, the text, questions the validity of artificially enhanced results, and critiques the acceptance of performance-enhancing drugs within society. Kitch's behavior has changed on the drug, and he has become dependent on it, yet this addiction is sanctioned by his family and school because of the reflected glory it brings. Kitch is presented, however, as one of the villains of the season, leading the viewer to view his drug use negatively.

In Season Four, the use of V is again depicted negatively as recovering alcoholic Detective Andy Bellefleur's behavior becomes increasingly erratic because of his drug use. This is presented as an addiction over which he has little control; he uses Jason as a *de facto* sponsor, phoning him to say that he is feeling like using again (4.03), and he briefly attempts to mutter the serenity prayer before giving in to temptation. Even though V is most obviously associated with vampires, Andy's V use leads him to target Sam Merlotte on numerous occasions. He accuses Sam of violating fire codes both at Merlotte's and in a house he owns; he pulls a gun on Sam on at least two occasions, and pulls his van over to be searched. Andy focuses his generalized fury at the shapeshifter, articulating his fears about the supernatural world, "[y]ou think that gives you the right to flout my authority?" (4.03).

The suggestion that illegal and addictive drugs are also evil — particularly when used by or around shapeshifters — is also explored in the form of the villains of Season Three; the King of the Mississippi vampires, Russell Edgington, and his henchmen, pack werewolves who are addicted to his blood and the power it affords them. The idea of werewolves on V, according to Alcide Herveaux of the Shreveport wolf pack, "[g]oes against everything we stand for" (3.09). That the idea of werewolves on vampire blood goes against nature is further demonstrated when Sookie reads wolf packmaster Colonel Flood's thoughts and learns that, far from being able to lead, he is rendered catatonic with fear by the V-fueled werewolves. Eric later reveals that Edgington has "had a pack of weres serving him for centuries" (3.05), and that he has come across similar figures in Nazi Germany. Edgington's pack of werewolves has been present at the fall of civilizations (3.07).

Edgington's reason for such an unusual combination of supernatural powers is ideological; his aim is to conquer humankind and slow what he terms its "race to oblivion," citing environmental reasons, asking rhetorically, "What other creatures actively destroys his own habitat? Do you remember how the air used to smell?" (3.06). This arguably positive motivation is immediately undercut, however, when he links himself with Hitler, remarking that "Adolf was right about one thing; there is a master race. It's just not the human race" (3.06).

Illicit drugs of addiction are linked elsewhere in the texts with shapeshifters through the community of Hot Shot, on the outskirts of Bon Temps, a community that is supported by drug manufacturing. Unlike Edgington, however, who believes the supernaturals should band together and take over the world, the werepanthers of Hot Shot are purists. When community leader Calvin Norris is fatally injured and Lafayette cures him with a shot of V, his first response is to demand of his daughter, "You let the faggots put vampire juice in me?" (3.10). The extreme level of revulsion Calvin and his family feel for the impure vampires and so-called "faggots" is still superseded by that which is traditionally reserved for the practice of incest which they engage in for the sake of the "purity" of their werepanther bloodline.

Blood is configured as a drug elsewhere in the series, too. Humans can develop an uncontrollable compulsion for vampire blood; for vampires, the need for human blood is innate. Harris and Ball establish that there are "grades" of blood, too; the older a vampire is, the stronger his or her blood and the more of a "hit" a human will receive when they drink it, increasing the likelihood of addiction. Conversely, the longer it has been stored away from its source, the greater the risk of a user having an adverse reaction or psychosis (1.08). Similarly, real blood is prized over the ironically named synthetic TruBlood, and particular types of human blood are more desirable again, as seen when Harris's characters discuss "Royal Blend," an expensive and exclusive blend of synthetic blood and that of royalty. Finally, the blood of Sookie Stackhouse, who is revealed to be part-fairy, is very highly prized indeed. Fairy blood is intoxicating to vampires, and the inability of vampires to resist the urge to drink it has led to the fairies being all but eradicated from the mortal realm, as evidenced by the scene wherein Eric drains Sookie's fairy godmother, Claudine, before demanding more. Sookie replies: "You can't have more! There isn't any more! You drank the whole fairy!" before rather comically adding, "And you're going to your room" (4.04). Eric's subsequent staggering and lack of interest in his own safety lead her to realize that he is inebriated. The language she uses when explaining the situation to Alcide further exemplifies this: "Eric can daywalk from the fairy blood, but it makes him as drunk as a skunk. He's hammered" (4.04). Eric also experiences depression after the high of drinking, becoming maudlin at the thought of being once again restricted by sunlight.

Bill refers to his superior "control" in being able to drink Sookie's blood and not drain her. In one particularly disturbing incident, however, we learn what can happen when the vampire is not in control; he rapes and almost drains her after the pair is locked in a confined space by Lorena while Bill is critically injured (*Club Dead* 217, 223; 3.07). This suggests that Bill, like any recovering addict, is capable of losing power over his urges under extreme circumstances. Sookie ultimately chooses to protect herself and rescinds her invitation to all of the vampires, once she learns that she is, in her words, "basically vampire crack" (3.12).

Interestingly, while Sookie appears to believe that humans, such as her brother Jason, and vampires, such as Bill and Eric, are capable of overcoming their demons, surpassing addictions, and being better people for it, she does not extend the same belief to shapeshifters. Specifically, she refuses to believe that Alcide's ex-fiancée and former V-user Debbie Pelt can change. She can forgive Bill for raping her, and Eric for murdering her fairy godmother in front of her, but despite Debbie's clear assertion to Sookie that her addiction is being treated: "Now I got the program, and I got Jesus on my side, and Alcide, and I'm hoping you'll give me a chance to win back your trust," Sookie tells Alcide: "She's an addict and an attempted murderer and she lives in your house" (4.03).

The unnatural fusion of werewolf and vampire examined in the world of Sookie Stackhouse has also developed into a central concern in *The Vampire Diaries* television series. As noted in Chapter Four, the arch villain of Seasons Two and Three is a wolf-vampire hybrid named Klaus. Klaus is one the Original vampires, and borrowing from mythology which is common in contemporary texts, with age comes power. In a complex storyline about the breaking of a curse to which the protagonist, Elena Gilbert, is central, it is revealed that Klaus was the result of an affair his mother had with a werewolf, making him part wolf on his father's side, yet still a vampire like his siblings. Because this is represented as too great a concentration of power, witches bound his werewolf abilities so that for centuries he was only able to access the vampiric side of his nature. After breaking the curse through a ritual sacrifice, however, he becomes able to shift. Indeed, he is beyond even the usual constraints of the werewolf, being able to transform at will, rather than being beholden to the lunar cycle. Klaus is aided in his transition by his sole remaining brother, fellow Original vampire Elijah. Elijah initially works with the Salvatore brothers to bring about Klaus's downfall, but ultimately allows Klaus to escape when he promises to tell Elijah where their siblings are buried. Klaus doublecrosses his brother; however, reuniting Elijah with the bodies of their siblings by staking him and interring him alongside them in the Season Two finale.

The complex rivalry between the brothers is established as a foil to the relationship between the central two brothers, vampires Damon and Stefan Salvatore. Their current competition for the affections of Elena keeps the tension between them simmering, even as they work together to save Elena from being sacrificed. Although Damon's drawled *brother* is usually used sarcastically and pejoratively when addressing Stefan, the notion of family ties surviving above all else is regularly implied. Indeed, in the Season Two finale Stefan sacrifices everything, including his freedom and his relationship with Elena, to procure treatment for the apparently fatally-ill Damon, who has been bitten by werewolf Tyler Lockwood.

The sacrifice precipitates the moment of relapse for Stefan. Stefan configures himself as a recovering addict, claiming that his entire personality changes when he drinks human blood. Flashbacks to the brothers soon after their death and transformation into vampires show Damon as the conservative brother, while Stefan is what his friend Lexi deems "a ripper" (2.15), a vampire who causes unnecessary carnage for his own pleasure.

Stefan's slide back into addiction is depicted as being similar to that of a recovering drug addict or alcoholic who begins to use again. Although not a shapeshifter himself, he is lured into using again by a werewolf-vampire hybrid. Klaus actively tempts Stefan, lying beside him on the floor and holding blood in front of him, while reminiscing about Stefan's "magnificent" exploits during his problem drinking days, noting that he was famous for going to "Monterey and wip[ing] out an entire migrant village ... that is the kind of talent I can use when I leave this town" (2.22). Klaus proceeds to call Katherine over and his eyes take on their wolfish shape and color before he bites her arm. Katherine, who knows that a werewolf bite is fatal to vampires and that this is what is currently killing Damon, is unable to resist as Klaus, one of the oldest and most powerful vampires, has her under compulsion. Katherine whimpers for a moment, convinced of her imminent final death, before Klaus force-feeds her his blood and the wound heals. He flippantly tells Stefan: "You want your cure? There it is," but he demands a high price, insisting that first the addicted Stefan must share a drink with him (2.22).

Like a drug dealer, Klaus acts in a manner calculated to "hook" Stefan once more, resorting to blackmail, as he first offers the cure and then withholds it. Klaus's methods are calculating and manipulative, all aimed towards his personal goal of siring a new race of vampire-werewolf hybrids, which would, in the words of his brother Elijah, "endanger ... not just vampires, but everyone" (2.19). In the world of the novels, Klaus's motives are not so clear; nor is he a vampire-werewolf hybrid, but an Original who merely uses shapeshifting werewolf Tyler Smallwood as his pawn.

In the books, in particular, shapeshifting characters including the *kitsune*, the malach, and even Caroline, are encoded as evil, as discussed in Chapters One and Three. The ability of some vampires to shift shape when others cannot is explained in L. J. Smith's version of the narrative. According to her mythology, the more human blood vampires drink, the more powers they develop, including, in some instances, the ability to transform themselves into one or perhaps two animal forms. Damon, as a regular drinker of human blood, is far more powerful than his brother and thus is capable of morphing into a crow. The crow conceit is used in the television series, although — perhaps because of the budgetary and logistical issues involved in having characters regularly change form on screen — Damon does not appear to be capable of shifting himself in that version. Rather, the crow is something of a familiar in the early episodes of the television series, which he later drains when he requires strength.

Damon's ability to become a formidable yet beautiful black crow in the novels aligns him with the other shapeshifting characters and reinforces that he is the more evil of the brothers. As the storyline develops, however, and Damon begins to show some affection for not only Elena, but also her friend, Bonnie, his crow-self appears less frequently, and in the recent novel *The Hunters—Phantom*, released in November 2011, it appears as a protective figure when Damon is believed to be dead. Damon, with his crow-formed alter ego, is further aligned with Bonnie through his affectionate name for her, "little redbird." Bonnie's red hair is one of her most notable characteristics within the books, and, along with her fair skin, is explicitly linked to her Scottish heritage and familial witchcraft back to the time of Stonehenge. This is remarkably different to her depiction in the television series, where her witchcraft and African American race are linked in significantly different ways, as noted in Chapter Four.

Damon is able to control his drinking, but Stefan adheres to the abstinence model, opting to drink only the less-potent option of animal blood in order to survive. This echoes the use of substitution treatment methods (such as using methadone as part of treatment for heroin addiction, for example). Others, such as Lexi, practice harm minimization strategies, specifically, using donor blood from blood banks. Damon is introduced at the start of the series as something of a party boy who embraces his vampiric nature and uses his powers of compulsion to coerce young women, in particular, to "donate" their blood and time for his amusement, and he is certainly not above taking blood by force. Over time, however, he moves toward the more socially responsible model of using blood bank bags. Through different attitudes to blood drinking, contemporary debates about addiction treatment are rehearsed.

This is not the first time that viewers have seen Stefan struggle with his addiction demons, however. When Stefan is attacked and injured in Season One, Elena offers him some of her blood to increase his strength and thus their chances of escaping, but he is resistant, knowing of his previous weakness. As is often the case in blood-drinking scenes within the series, this vignette is encoded as a very intimate act, with the shots, facial expressions and gasps of the two protagonists being reminiscent of love scenes. That Stefan's fears were well-founded is made explicit in the decidedly less-romantic closing scene, when Damon discovers his brother hiding behind the furniture in the living room, among empty blood bags, with a crazed expression on his face. Even the generally hedonistic Damon looks horrified by this turn of

Six. Coping, Masking and Addiction

events, which foreshadows the catastrophic consequences that would be seen as a result of a complete relapse.

By Episode Eighteen of Season One, Stefan is attempting a rapid detoxification process, using exercise and loud music as distractions. Damon argues that Stefan should attempt to control his drinking, rather than abstain, recommending a "healthy diet of human blood from a blood bank" (1.18). Despite protestations that he "ha[s] it under complete control," Stefan is clearly tempted when Damon leaves blood within his reach, suggesting that in fact, the addiction is controlling him. He begins to use a range of strategies which one might normally associate with drug addiction; using alcohol "to take the edge off" (1.18) and lying and stealing to fuel his habit. His personality changes and he becomes more outgoing at parties, turning into aggression with another party-goer at one point, which disturbs Elena and prompts Damon to express concern: "He has a fridge full of stolen blood bank contraband in the house.... He has no idea what normal is. His entire existence isn't normal. Normal to a vampire is drinking human blood. But he's spent all his time fighting it when he should have been learning how to control it. And now it's controlling him instead" (1.19).

Elena has previously had to support a loved one with drug use issues. When the series begins, her younger brother Jeremy is introduced as "the doper" (1.01). Throughout the first half of the season Jeremy is generally seen using or dealing drugs, to the point where he feels confident that he can have fellow user and part-time girlfriend Vicki Donovan stay overnight, pointing out to Elena: "I'm a drug-using delinquent. Girl in my bed doesn't really rate" (1.02). When Jeremy suggests to Vicki that they do not have to be high all the time, she accuses him of being "one of those guys" who tries to change her (1.05). Her short-lived time with Damon, however, demonstrates that he is not "one of those guys"; rather, he makes her a vampire so that he can have a companion with whom to party (1.06). Vicki rejects Stefan's recommendations that she adopt an animal-based diet, telling him she is not good with twelve-step programs, arguing that her guidance counselor had tried that with her during her mortal life (1.07). Her previously addictive personality causes problems for her in her short vampire life, too; as Stefan explains: "She's a very volatile and impulsive personality, she's a drug user. All that's gonna play a part in how she responds to this" (1.07).

Similarly, the Canadian film *Ginger Snaps* and its sequel and prequel *Ginger Snaps Unleashed* and *Ginger Snaps Back: The Beginning* also develop the notion of an individual becoming a more intense version or her or himself when under supernatural influence. Family dysfunction is explored and tied to blood and shapeshifting in remarkable and visceral ways. Pamela feels that daughters Ginger and Brigitte are "not normal" because they have not begun menstruating at ages sixteen and fifteen, respectively. Blood and lycanthropy are linked in myriad ways, from Ginger announcing that she has "the curse" when she reaches menarche whilst standing over the body of a dog, the victim of a local werewolf. Thus Ginger is linked explicitly to the werewolf, the curse of the Bailey Downs township. Shortly thereafter Ginger is bitten and infected by the same werewolf, and Brigitte notes that animals such as bears are often attracted to menstruating women by the smell of the blood. The film is swathed in gore as one might expect from a horror film, but taboos about showing blood are broken, particularly in the scene where Pamela holds up Ginger's blood-stained underwear for closer inspection. The abject is highly visible in this film, as when Brigitte begins to drink the blood of her dying love interest, Sam, and then vomits it back up, being unable — literally or figuratively — to stomach it.

As noted in Chapter Five, Sam is enlisted to help Brigitte find a cure for her sister because of his knowledge of the drug culture. Sam grows and sells marijuana, and also has the skills to make monkshood into an injectable substance. He warns Brigitte of the dangers of injecting an unfamiliar and untested drug: "Understand, you might kill her, trying to save her.... Just as long as you're prepared for that." The links between drug use and lycanthropy are made even more explicit in the sequel, *Ginger Snaps Unleashed,* when Brigitte is admitted to a rehabilitation facility after taking a large dose of monkshood to stave off her own imminent transformation, having been infected by Ginger before her death.

Kristopher Reisz's *Unleashed* makes an explicit link between drugs and shapeshifting, when a group of teenagers discover that ingesting hallucinogenic mushrooms will enable them to change shape into werewolves. Their shapeshifting abilities last only as long as the drug remains in their system; once it passes out they can no longer change into a wolf. At first the teenagers are not sure if they have actually transformed into werewolves or if they have simply hallucinated their adventures, but the physical evidence indicates that they have in fact become wolves during their drug-taking. The hallucinogenic mushroom is *Amanita muscaria,* which they learn was used by warriors to unleash their animal aggression, and used by Vikings and Druids to transform into bears and werewolves, "offering seekers a chance to tear loose of every civilized impulse" (38).

For protagonists Misty and Daniel, the mushrooms are a way of escaping the demands of other people on their lives: the bi-racial Misty is constrained by her working-class background and the racism of other teenagers towards her; Daniel carries the weight of expectations from family and friends that he will fulfill his destiny as a "shooting star" by studying at an Ivy League college and escaping the city of Birmingham, Alabama. For both, then, becoming a wolf means a kind of freedom and release that is only enabled by taking the drug. Misty finds that her drug-induced shapeshifting experiences give her more confidence and self-assurance: she is able to break up with her patronizing boyfriend and become more assertive. Similarly, Daniel discovers that he can break free from his controlling environment and explore his own identity.

Yet for Misty, Daniel, and the other wolves, the mushroom-fueled shapeshifting events soon begin to take on sinister overtones. Their graffiti tagging leads to increasingly more bold experiments, including trashing their high school and harassing and frightening strangers, and culminates in an attempt to attack and potentially kill some popular teenagers who had been in conflict with their human selves. This final confrontation is fueled by a double dose of their usual quantity of mushrooms. Prior to this Misty had expressed concern that their activities were getting out of control, but her fears were dismissed under group pressure and she agrees to continue. The need to keep returning to the drug, to find new highs when the early experiences no longer satisfy, and to increase drug quantities to do this, all speak to themes of drug addiction and dependency.

In part, the teenagers' desire to escape their world is due to boredom and dysfunctional family and peer group environments. Yet it is also configured as a search for identity, and despite the initial freedom of rebellion enabled by the shapeshifting, the wolf identity causes too many difficulties. Daniel's early attempts to maintain his perfect facade at school living up to everyone's expectations become increasingly hard to maintain as he goes about his illicit second life with Misty and her friends, taking drugs, rebelling against authority, and causing trouble. He tries to hide his life as "the other Daniel" (104) as best he can, but his experimentation with the mushroom-shapeshifting only serves to highlight his "double life" (158) and provoke an identity crisis when he can no longer reconcile his dual lives: "The wolf or the shooting star. It was getting harder to remember which one was his real shape and which was only a disguise" (163). Daniel, in fact, finds that the longer he continues his shapeshifting, the less of his humanity he retains, a problem that all the group experience. His crisis in identity is encapsulated in his confusion over his double identity and guilt for mistreating those around him: "He was a wolf. He was the shooting star. He was a natural charmer hiding a snarling animal hiding a miserable coward" (227). Misty, too, struggles with the realization that the mushrooms do not offer the true freedom and empowerment she desires: "I want to be brave even when I'm not in wolf shape. Even if I quit doing the ritual altogether" (182). This "ritual" involves eating the mushrooms, listening to music, chanting, and letting one's self disappear in the transformation into a werewolf.

Thus the initial sense of freedom and rebellion that so attracts Misty and Daniel to shapeshifting, and the loss of self they experience when they ingest the drug, prove a false promise. Both lie to each other throughout their relationship, pretending to be the person they believe the other one wants to see, and when Misty discovers one of Daniel's deceptions — hiding his plans to leave her to go to college elsewhere — she withdraws from him. This event causes Daniel to be excluded from the pack, but it is also the catalyst for his — and the pack's — salvation. When the other members decide to renounce their human selves to take revenge on their enemies, Daniel attempts to stop them. Although he is unsuccessful in saving all the pack, and he himself is injured in the process, he is able to find a new identity outside his drug-induced shapeshifting self and assist the others in doing so too. He accepts responsibility for his earlier deceptions, and finds that just as his "shooting star" persona did not satisfy, neither did escaping his humanity via his shapeshifting wolf. Misty, similarly, learns that she does not need the mushrooms or her wolf identity to overcome her feelings of boredom and misery and insecurity. The novel concludes with Misty and Daniel traveling overseas as a kind of symbolic and literal rejection of the restrictions they had experienced due to other people's expectations: that Misty would never amount to anything and that Daniel would attend college as planned. There is some irony, perhaps, in any notion that this rather privileged outcome of holidaying overseas is a rebellious solution to their struggle to defy the conventions around them, but it is nonetheless presented somewhat as an alternative path to finding their own way in life rather than subscribing to the expectations that they see as binding them.

In each of these texts, the complexities of addiction formation and treatment are explored within the supernatural realm. Addictive personalities are repeatedly constructed as being established as a result of familial neglect, and are often linked to mental ill health. The use of blood as the drug of choice in many of these texts reinforces the idea that addiction is abhorrent and aberrant. The perceived "shiftiness" of drug addicts or problem drinkers is, in these texts, transposed onto shapeshifters, either explicitly or implicitly. This is one of the areas wherein the enhanced abilities of the shapeshifter are routinely encoded negatively.

Seven

What to Do with Eternity? Shapeshifting and Spirituality

> SLATER: *I have eighteen degrees, three masters and four Ph.D.s.*
> DAMON: *The point?*
> SLATER: *Exactly. I mean, what is the point? What should I be doing with my eternity? If you have an answer, please enlighten me.*
> —*The Vampire Diaries*, 2.09
>
> ALCIDE: *Ain't there anything else we can do?*
> BILL: *Pray.*
> ALCIDE: *Werewolf and vampire. Who's gonna listen?*
> —*True Blood*, 4.09

Beyond the aspects of adolescence, gender, sexuality, disability, race and mental health discussed so far lie one final area that warrants analysis: spirituality. Readings of spirituality and faith are rather overlooked in many approaches to the genre, despite the fact that these supernatural texts are usually founded on larger issues of life and death and the prospect of eternity. Here we explore how shapeshifting texts intersect with questions of faith and immortality, and how the fantasy genre can provide a compelling template for authors to wrestle with these questions.

Shapeshifting and Existential Angst

As the opening quotation reminds us, the supernatural creatures stalking the pages and screens of much contemporary literature are usually long lived, even immortal. *The Vampire Diaries'* Slater is a vampire, but shapeshifters and werewolves are also often configured as immortal, or at least having extended longevity. In Jennifer Lynn Barnes's *Raised by Wolves*, Callum has lived for centuries, with Bryn saying that "he predated Women's Lib by a couple of centuries — at least" (9). Carlisle Cullen is 362 years old in Stephanie Meyer's *Twilight* (289). Of a similar age at "slightly more than three centuries" (*Hammered* 171) is Hal Hauck in Kevin Hearne's *Iron Druid* chronicles. All three are mere youths, however, against Hearne's shapeshifter druid and protagonist, Atticus O'Sullivan, who is more than twenty-one centuries of age (*Hounded* 1).

Despite attaining the holy grail of immortality, many of the contemporary vampires and shapeshifters are represented as bored and unhappy, searching for more purpose than simply living forever. This seems to reflect an underlying existential angst as to whether or not this is all there is to life. In the film *Underworld*, the vampire Selene finds meaning and purpose in her Death Dealer duty as a lycan assassin, but as another vampire asks her, "What's the point of being immortal if you deny yourself the simple pleasures in life?" The immortal vampires of Meyer's *Twilight* series appear to do little; at first glance it is tempting to dismiss the Cullens as the idle rich: ruled by Carlisle, the dilettante doctor who dabbles in medicine, and the rest of his family spend their eternities repeatedly educating themselves for centuries, admiring their collection of expensive cars in their sprawling mansion, or, in the case of Esme, home-making for her adult brood. Yet Carlisle, who appears to be the sole (working) financial provider for his vampire family, is nonetheless depicted as a dedicated and hardworking medical professional. Alice Cullen can use her psychic gifts to play the stock market to bring in money (*New Moon* 12), but this hardly constitutes a worthwhile or employed endeavor. For Edward, his only real purpose in life appears to be found in meeting and marrying Bella Swan. Conversely, and rather atypically within this genre, the shapeshifting characters do not appear to have prolonged life in these texts: they stop aging during their shapeshifting years, but eventually age again once they learn the control to stop shifting (*Eclipse* 106–07).

In Martin Millar's Wolf Girl books, the werewolves live for hundreds of years. Not content with being werewolf royalty, various characters seek stimulation outside the castle walls; Dominil learns ancient languages, Beauty and Delicious attempt to make it in London as musicians, and Thrix establishes a fashion empire. In Glen Duncan's *The Last Werewolf*, the werewolf protagonist Jacob Marlowe is so tired of his existence that he (initially) greets the prospect of his impending death with acceptance. The series *Being Human* (U.S.) similarly points to the negatives of an immortal existence on earth:

> Live forever. Travel the world in a million different ways, know every lover that you could possibly want. Immortality. What's not to love? There's just one thing they leave out of the pitch. Time. That endless sucking time. No closing bell, no quarter, no measure — but memories. Those haunting memories. Slice 'em, dice

'em, rue 'em, do it again. And realize there is only one true thing: it is impossible to live forever perfectly [1.03].

The voiceover is presented over a montage of scenes showing the guilt, sorrow and regret that Aidan, Josh and Sally experience as a vampire, werewolf and ghost.

Du Coudray argues that in some werewolf tales, there is a greater sense of spirituality and sense of holism: "[i]ndeed, this breed of werewolf often finds love, happiness, stability and spiritual growth ... they are more strongly characterized by a focus on circularity, a willing acceptance of embodiment, a recognition of the inevitable cycles of birth and death, a sense of connection with the natural world, and an emphasis on spirituality" ("Cycle of the Werewolf" 58). Yet what we find in so many of these texts is just the opposite: unease with a meaningless immortality and a questioning of faith. However, there is still very much an emphasis on spirituality and religious ideas in many shapeshifting texts, and these are the focus of our discussion in this chapter.

"Past Those Watchful Dragons": Fantasy and Spirituality

We have noted throughout our book that shapeshifting texts can reflect and comment on issues in the real world. For some authors, however, fantasy can go beyond this to reveal truths about spirituality, as C. S. Lewis wrote, the "Fantastic or Mythical is a Mode available at all ages for some readers; for others, at none. At all ages, if it is well used by the author and meets the right reader, it has the same power ... it can give us experiences we have never had and thus, instead of 'commenting on life,' can add to it" (*Essays* 528). This is not to suggest that all authors desire to make a sociopolitical statement in their works, for this is clearly not the case. Yet for some writers, fantasy can allow some themes to be communicated effectively, and this can be particularly true for themes relating to faith and religion:

> I wrote fairy tales because the Fairy Tale seemed the ideal Form for the stuff I had to say.... I thought I saw how stories of this kind could steal past a certain inhibition which had paralysed much of my own religion in childhood. Why did one find it so hard to feel as one ought to feel about God or about the sufferings of Christ? I thought the chief reason was one was told one ought to. An obligation to feel can freeze feelings.... But supposing that by casting all these things into an imaginary world, stripping them of their stained-glass and Sunday school associations, one could make them for the first time appear in their real potency? Could one not thus steal past those watchful dragons? [Lewis *Essays* 527–28].

J. R. R. Tolkien, too, wrote of this potential for the genre where despite the mythologies and impossible creatures or events there are also echoes of reality:

The peculiar quality of the "joy" in successful Fantasy can thus be explained as a sudden glimpse of the underlying reality or truth.... The Gospels contain ... the greatest and most complete conceivable eucatastrophe. But this story has entered History and the primary world.... The Resurrection is the eucatastrophe of the story of the Incarnation ... the joy which the [eucatastrophic] "turn" in a fairy-story gives: such joy has the very taste of primary truth ["On Fairy-Stories" 70–71].

Fantasy has a redemptive quality which places it beyond mere storytelling and above the charge of escapism, for eucatastrophic fantasies allow the writer to assist in the "enrichment of creation" (Tolkien, "On Fairy-Stories" 72). Tolkien rejected the idea that his most famous work, *The Lord of the Rings*, was allegorical (*Fellowship of the Ring* 11), but elsewhere described it as a "fundamentally religious and Catholic work," even if unconsciously so in its initial writing (*Letters* 172). He felt, instead, that the "religious element is absorbed into the story and the symbolism" (*Letters* 172). Thus fantasy literature can accommodate real-life spirituality even if there is no mention made of the religious aspects, because of the rich symbolism of the genre. Fantasy does not escape reality, but rather enhances it. Lewis also took this approach to fantasy, calling the Biblical account of Jesus's birth and resurrection a "true myth" in the sense that while it parallels pagan myths of "dying and reviving gods," the true myth of Christ has "the tremendous difference that *it really happened*" (*Letters* 977).

Lewis considered that Christian beliefs had been encumbered by church dogma which could be removed by placing them in fantasy form. Instead of some of the negative associations of church teaching, Lewis saw fantasy as restoring some of the power of religious truths. This is its "potency," that it acts as a mirror to reality and clarifies that real experience. In his review of Tolkien's *The Lord of the Rings*, Lewis wrote that the "value of the myth is that it takes the things we know and restores to them the rich significance which has been hidden by 'the veil of familiarity.' By putting bread, gold, horse, apple, or the very roads into a myth, we do not retreat from reality; we discover it. As long as the story lingers in our mind, the real things are more themselves" (*Essays* 524–25). Fantasy can take what is familiar and render it unfamiliar by placing it in another context. This has the effect of allowing readers a different perspective on life, and fantasy may therefore be an effective conduit for religious messages because it can "restore" to them their full, "rich significance."

"It Really Is a Curse": Seeking Redemption After (un)Death

There is, then, the potential for fantasy literature to engage with questions of faith and spirituality in intriguing ways, and the texts under discussion in this book are replete with religious and supernatural imagery. We regularly find concepts such as immortality, souls, the life-giving power of blood, sacrifices that save others, resurrection from the dead, apocalypse, curses, forces of darkness, and a defined sense of good and evil. These "undead" or "soulless" characters wrestle with the meanings of their lives in a supernatural context where life and death matters are heightened in every way.

In much of this paranormal genre there is an emphasis on blood: it can be life giving, and the blood of humans can strengthen vampires (*Twilight, The Vampire Diaries*) and vampire blood can also fortify humans (*True Blood, The Vampire Diaries*). The symbolism of blood in Christianity becomes literal in this kind of fiction. As Rickels points out, the "blood and the life have been given a long-standing equation. In the Greek underworld, the spirits could only speak — and thus once more put through a direct connection with life — after they had been granted a drink of blood. And Christ's blood is one of the all-time greatest guarantees of eternal life" (7).

Questions of darkness, death and forgiveness are brought to the foreground in the *Being Human* television series (U.S.), with the opening scenes of the Pilot philosophizing about the place of supernatural creatures in the world: "every human spends a night or two on the dark side and regrets it. But what if you only exist on the dark side?" (1.01). For those creatures who are not human, questions of forgiveness and death linger: "we're all hiding something ... and why not? What's the penalty, what are the consequences, really? I'm only human, you say, and all is forgiven. But what if some cruel twist of fate makes you something else, something other, who forgives you then?" (1.01).

Werewolf Josh takes an apartment with vampire Aidan and ghost Sally in their attempt to live an ordinary life, and much of the series mixes these darker themes with more comedic takes on the supernatural genre and its clichés. The characters are preoccupied with the purpose of their lives in this undead state as ghost, vampire, and werewolf: "[e]very culture has its own way of saying goodbye. Comforts and the rituals that prepare the living for death. They ease the journey into what comes after ... assuming there is an after. In the end, death is a journey you take alone. For some of us, that journey takes us on a hidden path, through a darker forest, or instead of answers, we find a whole new set of questions" (1.05). For Josh, the attraction of a normal life has seemed unobtainable, and he describes his state as a "curse" that haunts him not just once a month but every day, a mark that separates him from normal people (1.01).

Many other werewolf texts reference the idea that lycanthropy is a "curse." For Sive in Holly Bennett's *Shapeshifter*, shapeshifting is both "a gift and a curse" (237). In this retelling of the Irish tale of Finn mac Cumhail, Sive is an Otherworld girl who desires to change into animal form, a deer, but when she is forced to do so to escape the unwanted attention of a villainous druid, too long spent as a deer means she almost loses her humanity (90) and shapeshifting no longer holds the same appeal (237). Glen Duncan's *The Last Werewolf* describes lycanthropy as the Curse, and a state that provokes many questions about the meaning of life:

> The big questions didn't, it turned out, go away. Once a month I transformed into a monster, part man, part wolf. Fair enough.... But where did it all *fit in*? Was my species God's handiwork or the Devil's? Darwin's *Origin*, published four years earlier, had said, effectively, neither, but old habits died hard. What would happen to me when I died? Had I still a soul? [126].

Believing himself to be the last werewolf in existence, Jacob Marlowe concludes there is no God and no meaning to his life, until he meets and falls in love with a female werewolf and finds some purpose in their relationship.

In *The Vampire Diaries*, evil vampires were entombed below the now-gone original Mystic Falls church, in a rather fitting symbol of evil contained underground. In the book series, the township is named "Fells Church," rather than the somewhat more secular and Gothic "Mystic Falls." In the novels, the church is a central location; a space wherein Elena speaks with the town's founder and protector, Honoria Fell. In the *Stefan's Diaries* iteration of the books — a recent addition to the novel franchise, based on the television series and written by an unnamed author — the language used to describe Stefan's angst after his transformation into a vampire and his subsequent reformation from "ripper" to being a morally responsible animal blood drinker is almost Biblical in tone and proportions. He notes that "even though I was destined to live on Earth for eternity, a part of me was always in hell" (Alloy, *Ripper* 10), and he argues that the Originals, who are central to the action of *Dark Reunion* and the television series, come "directly from hell ... had never had a soul, and thus had no memories of what it was like to live, to hope, to cry, to be human. What they did have was a relentless thirst for blood and a desire for destruction" (Alloy, *Ripper* 30). He also notes that he had long since given up praying, because he did not think that "any sort of God would want to hear [his] requests" (Alloy, *Ripper* 46).

Vampirism is configured as a transformation in *The Vampire Diaries*, often out of the victim's control; some seek it (Isobel Flemming) but most are turned against their will or even knowledge (Caroline, Vicki). Lycanthropy, however, is not only restricted by genes but also by actions: those with the lupine gene will never become a werewolf unless they kill someone first. Thus lycanthropy is a kind of penance for the consequences of killing another human being, whether deliberate or otherwise. Although Mason Lockwood's shapeshifting is triggered by killing someone in self defense rather than murder, this seems to be undermined by his later duplicity and association with Katherine.

Yet in *The Vampire Diaries*, ultimately we find a relatively sympathetic portrayal of werewolves where lycanthropy is seen as a curse that werewolves must attempt to overcome. Mason's determination to suppress his dangerous lupine side extends to chaining himself during the full moon and drinking diluted wolfsbane to prevent his attacking anyone. He is anxious to prevent his nephew, Tyler, from succumbing to the same fate and acts as a mentor by giving advice to Tyler. Moreover, he attempts to coexist with Damon and Stefan peacefully, offering peace to Damon, and only acts against them when Damon tries to murder him. His return in ghost form in Season Three to torture Damon is not an act of vengeance, as he explains, but in aid of his nephew, Tyler: "I can't change what happened to me, but maybe I can change what happens to Tyler. I don't need revenge, Damon. I need redemption" (3.07). Even Mason's work against Elena and Bonnie is complicated by its motivation: love for Katherine. Ultimately, Mason becomes a rather tragic figure in his brief narrative arc: he is tortured and killed by Damon, who frames this act as akin to a mercy killing, remarking that "he wants me to kill him anyway, don't you, Mason? It really is a curse, isn't it?" (2.06). This aligns with the similarly sympathetic depictions of Lupin in *Harry Potter* and Sam in *True Blood*, both of whom are given rather tragic back stories as they are rejected by friends and family because of their shapeshifting. For characters such as Lupin, Mason, and Tyler, shapeshifting is a curse or is unsought, and the victim is thus innocent of wrongdoing, for although Mason and Tyler both activated the lycanthropy by killing, it was accidental.

Season Three also makes mention of "the other side" in its episode "Ghost World," when now-ghost Mason explains to Damon that there is little to do: "You know what the other side is like? We're all alone. We watch the people we left behind and we regret our decisions. That's it" (3.07). And if that is the sole explanation of the afterlife in *The Vampire Diaries*, it is perhaps no wonder that immortality is prized in the series mythology. It does not necessarily rule out the concept of a deity, for when Damon asks Mason if he is "all knowing," Mason retorts, "I'm a ghost. I'm not God" (3.07).

The concern over curses and what happens after dying recurs in other texts than *The Vampire Diaries*. Much of the angst over vampire boyfriends in *Buffy, the Vampire Slayer* and *Twilight* centers around their souls, or lack thereof. In *Buffy*, we can find an ongoing interest in religious ideas and imagery. Angel, for instance, is a vampire "cursed" by gypsies with a soul. This soul changed him from villain to hero, giving him, in effect, a conscience and sense of morality that vampires do not have. This enables him to become an ally and romantic interest to Buffy, but the curse has a secondary aspect in that when he experiences a moment of true happiness, he loses his soul and returns to his evil self, Angelus. This element is introduced when Angel loses his soul after sleeping with Buffy and becomes her nemesis. Willow succeeds in restoring his soul but Buffy must still kill Angel to save the world from the demon Acathla and the hellish vortex that he has awakened (2.22). Fellow vampire Spike has no soul but determines to win one in the hopes of proving himself worthy of Buffy, and he embarks on a quest for redemption by undergoing the Demon Trials in Season Six. He is successful, and ultimately sacrifices his life to help Buffy and her friends avert an(other) apocalypse. Angel experiences time in "hell," and Buffy is in "heaven" after dying (for the second time) prior to Season Six, and Buffy and her friends regularly deal with apocalypses, but the series does not, again, propose an explicit version of spirituality.

In *Twilight*, Edward worries that he has no soul and that Bella will lose hers if she seeks vampirism. Shapeshifting has important links to spirituality, given that the Quileute wolf pack see shapeshifting as an important manifestation of their cultural heritage: only those who have the blood connection to the original shifters possess the ability to transform into a wolf (see Jensen for a discussion of Quileute traditions in the series). Beyond the wolves, other characters' beliefs are either absent or rather wishful. Bella says that her life is "fairly devoid of belief" in anything (*New Moon* 32), yet at the same time apparently believes enough to vehemently insist that vampires must have souls and that heaven must accept Edward (*New Moon* 33). Carlisle, meanwhile, declares that he and Edward both believe in God, heaven and hell, but explains that although Edward worries that there is no "afterlife," he himself continues "hoping that there is still a point to this life, even for us…. By all accounts, we're damned regardless. But I hope, maybe foolishly, that we'll get some measure of credit for trying" (*New Moon* 32–33). Although some see little of significance in *Twilight*'s use of religion (such as Hjarvard, as we discuss later), others find more to discuss. Joyce Ann Mercer, for instance, connects the popularity of *Twilight* with readers' desires that the spiritual and physical worlds might meet (272): "As creatures related to humanity and eternity, as well as to sensuality and death, the figure of the vampire long has functioned as a metaphor for such yearnings" (269).

Wilson argues that Edward represents a "celestial" future with Bella, where Edward is a "vampire–Christ incarnate—a white god who has died and come back to life to save Bella, our white lamb/virgin Mary" ("It's a Wolf Thing" 200). Wilson is right in drawing our attention to the numerous ways that Bella constructs Edward and the Cullens in deity-like terms, but the messianic parallels are less clear. Putting aside the difficulties of envisaging the Middle-Eastern–born Jesus of the Christian Bible as a white immortal teenage boy of Meyer's imaginings, or substituting Mary the mother of Jesus with Edward's romantic interest Bella, it is worth pointing out the "lamb" is a term given to Christ (or believers generally) in Biblical accounts, as we discuss later, rather than a romantic interest. Indeed, in some ways it is Bella who brings a kind of secular "salvation" to Edward, allowing him to believe once more that perhaps he has a soul, and giving him purpose in his life.

In *Harry Potter* we do not find a sense that werewolves are excluded from the afterlife because of their curse. Lupin is not exempt from the same after death existence as others simply because of his lycanthropy; Harry sees Lupin after his death with Harry's parents and his godfather, Sirius Black. All seem happy, and they reassure and comfort Harry as he faces his own death. Much like Mason in *The Vampire Diaries* television series, Lupin speaks from beyond the grave to explain that his intentions are pure: "I was trying to make a world in which he [his son] could live a happier life" (*Deathly Hallows* 561). Thus Lupin has not only joined these characters "beyond the veil," but is clearly on the side of good, rather than eternally cursed. His placement among the ranks of family and godfather marks him as one of Harry's moral protectors.

The theme of sacrifice runs deeply throughout Rowling's series, beginning with Harry's mother Lily who gives her own life while shielding her son, an act that protects him throughout his adventures. The series concludes with Harry's decision to give his life to save those around him, although he does not die, and ultimately good triumphs over Voldemort's evil because of sacrifice and love. The importance of blood is also raised, with Lily's blood protecting Harry and, by extension, Voldemort: "He took your blood and rebuilt his living body with it! Your blood in his veins, Harry" (*Deathly Hallows* 568). Voldemort's soul is split into seven pieces, seven Horcruxes. Thus Rowling's series draws on many of the same themes as these other fantasy fictions: good and evil, blood, souls and the afterlife, without offering an explicit representation of faith or religion beyond the underlying themes of courage, love, and sacrifice.

Shifting the Shape of Spirituality

Noll writes of clinical lycanthropy that "throughout history, the legend of the lycanthrope or werewolf has symbolized the dual nature of humankind — the interplay of our spiritual and carnal natures, the struggle between the sacred and profane within the human soul" (92). Fictional lycanthropy and shapeshifting in general can also reflect this interest in the dynamics between spirituality and secularity. Some works use religious imagery only to reject their power, which we can see in modern iterations where vampires are no longer hostages to crosses and holy water.

Despite the modern tendency to reference Christian and other religious imagery only to subvert them, most works in this genre continue to regularly draw on spiritual themes, often blending Biblical and other religious concepts together in a kind of hybrid mix of religions and beliefs. For Mercer, this reflects a growing pluralism in religion and tolerance of different perspectives in the United States (and, presumably, in other Western nations). Partridge, meanwhile, suggests that despite the appearance of increased secularization in the West, there is nonetheless a re-enchantment in the form of occulture, a term he uses to designate the rise of non–Christian spirituality such as paganism and the paranormal, among other things. Popular culture has a particularly effective role in transmitting and transmuting these alternative spiritual ideas, and in Partridge's view, "popular occulture is sacralising the Western mind" (2).

In his discussion of religion and the media, Stig Hjarvard calls this hybridity of beliefs a "banal religion," a term he adapts from Billig's work on nationalism:

> Banal religion may consist of elements taken from institutionalised religion, such as crosses, prayers and cowls as well as elements usually associated with folk religion, such as trolls, vampires and black cats crossing the street.... Banal religion is banal in the sense that it is unnoticeable and does not constitute a highly structured proposition about a metaphysical order of the meaning of life, and it is religion in the sense that it evokes cognitions, emotions or actions that imply the existence of a supernatural agency [128].

These spiritual aspects are often modified and used according to the genre in which they appear, including fantasy, and Hjarvard notes this is evident in the *Indiana Jones* film series, which uses a great variety of symbols from a range of religions, but they "do not constitute a coherent religious narrative, nor are we, the audience, to take them seriously as real religious symbols, practices or meanings" (129). Instead, they simply "serve the conventions of the adventure genre" (129). Hjarvard goes on to note the same is true of the *Twilight* series, which uses Christian and supernatural concepts without any real purpose except to further the romantic plot and imbue it with a sense of epic destiny. Despite the essentially meaningless placement of these elements within these texts, Hjarvard argues that the spiritual concepts show the "continued presence and relevance of religious artifacts, meanings and sentiments" in our society (129). More than this, he suggests that banal religion is not inferior to conventional faith but even "challenges the authority of existing religious institutions by disembedding specific religious meanings from their original context and rearticulating them in new ways" (129). Petersen similarly argues that shows such as *Supernatural* can "renegotiate" religious imagination by providing viewers with "new perspectives on religious concepts" (6.2). However, given that these fantasy fictions are not internally consistent or coherent in their juxtaposition of real-world religious beliefs and practices with mythical creatures, their subversive potential is disputable.

The hybridity, occulture, or "banal religion" is very evident in the texts discussed in this book. The werewolves in Duncan's *The Last Werewolf* both hope and fear that their lives have a spiritual dimension, and their approach collapses different religions into one vague supernatural dimension, asking if lycanthropy might "fit into anything? Anything like God or the Devil or UFOs or voodoo or clairvoyance or life after death? There was no disguising her fear that it did, her hope that it did, her deep suspicion that it didn't" (169). These questions are rarely as explicitly articulated as in *The Last Werewolf*, but most supernatural texts acknowledge them to some extent even if only in their use of religious symbols, whether maintaining or denying the power of religious iconography.

Buffy, the Vampire Slayer, which is arguably the progenitor of the current spate of supernatural texts within pop culture, maintained many of the vampire traditions, including the power of these elements against vampires. In the opening episode of the series, Angel gives Buffy a silver crucifix necklace to protect herself in her role as the Slayer, and crucifixes are used throughout the series as vampire deterrents. Buffy also often arms herself with holy water, in one instance even using it as her weapon of choice against an unstable vampire who is holding her mother hostage.

More recent works have disempowered these icons, however. In *True Blood*, Bill Compton meets with members of the historical society, the Descendants of the Glorious Dead, to share his unique perspective on local involvement in the Civil War. The meeting takes place in a church, and, far from being dangerous to him, he unveils the covered cross, later telling Sookie that crucifixes are just "geometry" (1.05). Bill insinuates that symbols are only imbued with power when one believes in those symbols. Elsewhere, vampires Stefan and Edward present similar arguments. Stefan tells his mortal girlfriend Elena that crucifixes are "decorative" and holy water is "drinkable" (*The Vampire Diaries* 1.16), and Edward explains to Bella that they keep a wooden cross in their house for its "nostalgia" value, acknowledging that it is "ironic" (Meyer, *Twilight* 288). Bill Compton also subscribes to the view that the undead have no souls, for although he holds what Sookie identifies as Christian values, he is emphatic in his use of the past tense when he tells her that he *was* a Christian (1.10).

For most texts, spiritual ideas and references are rather vague, nebulous elements that are not explored in any detail. *The Vampire Diaries*, for instance, does not offer a particularly concrete idea of faith. In one sense the series to date collapses different cultures and beliefs into one apparent myths-of-the-world concept, when Klaus and Elijah faked the Curse of the Sun and Moon to get vampires and werewolves to all search for the moonstone and Klaus refers to Aztec cultures, African tribal etchings, and Roman scrolls: "It's all so Biblical sounding, don't you think?" (2.19). The Sun and the Moon curse in Season Two is framed as not only limiting vampire and werewolf freedoms but also enforcing the enmity: if the vampires break the curse, they can walk in the sunlight but the wolves are still trapped by the full moon; if the werewolves break the curse they can transform at will, "a.k.a. werewolf domination" or even cease shifting entirely (2.14), as a release from the curse of shapeshifting. Despite the false aspects of this mythology, the curse of the sun and moon, which drives much of the narrative arc of Season Two, proves to be genuine for Klaus at least. More than this, John Gilbert articulates a semblance of some kind of faith as he ultimately gives his life to save his daughter Elena's life:

> JOHN: Johnathan journaled the story of a mother who called on Emily's services. The woman's baby was sick; dying. Emily cast a spell that would bind the woman's life force with her child.
> DAMON: Skip to the save Elena part.
> JOHN: Well, the child died, but the mother's life force flowed through her, restoring her to life.
> JEREMY: We already know Elena's going to come back to life but she'll be a vampire.
> JOHN: Not if her soul remains intact.
> DAMON: Her soul, really? You're going to put your faith in some act of God mumbo jumbo?
> JOHN: I refuse to let Elena become the thing I've spent my life protecting her against. And you can call that God or mystical energy, whatever you want, but yes ... I'm putting my faith in it [2.21].

John's reference to faith and God is rather symbolic when we consider his sacrifice to save his daughter. This inferred link between father and child suggests that their souls are somehow entwined, and it is noteworthy that his sacrifice achieves its purpose: Elena lives. However, *The Vampire Diaries* also articulates a kind of neo-pagan approach given the references to witches as "servants of nature" that recur throughout the series, and the emphasis on maintaining "the balance in nature" (3.07) in deference to "the spirits" (3.08).

True Blood attempts to produce a different version of Christianity. From the opening credits, religion is cast as one of the key concerns of the series, and images of baptism are jarringly interwoven with sexually explicit and violent ones. Sookie questions the notion that vampires have no souls, remarking to her Gran that she does not believe that Jesus would hate anyone just because they were a vampire. She self-identifies as a Christian, yet does not accept at face value accepted dichotomies of good and evil; in fact, she is better able than anyone else to see through false perceptions. She recognizes the evil and bigotry of the Fellowship of the Sun anti-vampire church, and she is able to see past the beauty of the fairies and identify their true visages and the ways in which they are influencing humans. She alone is incapable of being glamored by vampires but conversely is able to identify good where it exists in vampiric characters.

Sookie's brother Jason also demonstrates a deeply personalized view of Christianity, and wonders if he is cursed by his association with shapeshifting. He sees his kidnap and sexual assault by the female members of the Hot Shot werepanther pack as penance for his previous morally questionable behavior, particularly with regard to his treatment of women. When Jason imagines God speaking to him to explain his punishment, he includes the kind of colorful language that viewers have come to expect from the conversations between Jason and his best friend, Hoyt. Hoyt, for his part, tells a Fellowship of the Sun protestor that he is a better Christian than the demonstrator, for he has love in his heart, while the church member appears only to have hate in his.

A number of non–Christian belief systems are also canvassed in *True Blood*. Lafayette's love interest, Jesus, for example, is a *brujo* or shaman, drawing on his cultural heritage as a Mexican, a family history of shamanism, and his own interest in learning about and practicing magic. Here, too, hybridity is at play, for Jesus recounts that his Tio Luca had been a powerful healer, whose shamanistic rituals had, on at least one occasion, included a "prayer to the Santa Margarita" (4.07). The show's engagement with religion takes racial overtones at times as well:

> LAFAYETTE: You don't think that maybe we're stepping in on some place where we don't belong?
> JESUS: Black men and magic?
> LAFAYETTE: Yeah.
> JESUS: I don't believe in that.... Don't blame the magic, blame the practitioners. If your soul is dark, it's black magic. If your soul is light, like I know yours is, you got nothing to worry about.
> LAFAYETTE: I ain't never been accused of being overly light before [4.02].

Jesus joins a coven whose leader, Marnie Stonebrook, repeatedly asserts in Season Four that she and her cohort were merely "assembling peacefully to practice their religion" (4.03, 4.05), but this peace is quickly shattered when she is possessed by the spirit of the long-deceased witch, Antonia, who had been burned at the stake in Spain some centuries previously.

Antonia is introduced as a powerful and dangerous necromancer. As the series develops, however, this representation is developed. Antonia, a healer who used her Wiccan powers for the good of her village, is seen to clasp her hands as though in prayer when she is grateful. Antonia's final act had been one of necromancy, luring the vampire priests who had condemned, abused and defiled her into the sun to meet their True Deaths. Using the dark humor which has become one of *True Blood*'s trademarks, the vampire King of Louisiana, Bill Compton, acknowledges the current rise of secularism, explaining to one of his Sheriffs that vampires "have often found it advantageous to maintain a presence in humanity's most powerful institutions. And in the 1600s, that was the Catholic church. And today, as you all know, it's Google and Fox News" (4.05). Towards the end of the season, Antonia is resistant to Marnie's plans to annihilate all vampires, whatever the cost, declaring "I delivered babies with these hands. I did not come back to spill blood" (4.10). Marnie responds by binding their souls so that she can continue to access Antonia's magic; Jesus, accessing his family's shamanic powers and in demonic form, breaks the spell and releases Antonia's spirit (4.10).

Marnie is killed in battle with the vampires that night, but her spirit returns. She possesses medium Lafayette, ties Bill and Eric to a stake, and sets it alight. Wiccan Holly, atheist Tara and Christian Sookie work together on the night of Samahain to lift the veil separating the dead from the living, raising protective spirits from the nearby local cemetery. Chief among them are Antonia, who shares with Marnie her new-found belief that "all creatures have a purpose. Even vampires" (4.12) echoing the deceptively conservative words of Sookie's Gran in Season 1, that "[t]here's a purpose for everything that God creates" (1.03). Adele Stackhouse does indeed take the role of protector, physically pulling Marnie's spirit out of Lafayette's body, and counseling Marnie to let out all her anger because "there's no room for that where we're going" (4.12).

Shamanism and the occult are not the only non–Christian belief systems in Bon Temps, however. In Season Two, the long-lived and shapeshifting maenad Maryann convinces the township of Bon Temps to join her in worshipping Bacchus. Although for her this is clearly a case of religious worship, the other townsfolk are depicted as being possessed and not in control when they participate in the orgies and sacrifices she organizes. It is interesting to note, then, that these alternative religions — bacchanalia in Season Two and witchcraft in Season Four — have thus far been aligned with the villains of the narrative.

Much like *True Blood*, Kristopher Reisz's *Unleashed* YA novel offers a treatment of religious ideas that blends together disparate concepts. Teenagers

Daniel Morning and Misty Sandlin shapeshift into wolves under the influence of hallucinogenic mushrooms. This experience is a ritual of consuming the mushrooms, dancing in a frenzy and chanting, much like a shamanistic trance. The mushroom substance is nicknamed the "rot-eater god," in recognition of its fungal properties as well as early Sanskrit hymns treating the mushroom like a deity (38). Although neither teenager behaves in conventional Christian ways — they take drugs, drink, sleep around, and behave in hostile and demeaning ways to other people — both attend church and there are regular references to spiritual ideas and practices.

For Misty, the shapeshifting ritual has parallels with her church experience: it is a "putrid eucharist" (78), a ceremony that echoes church services:

> Misty had nothing to compare their transformation to except church. She didn't go every week like she should, and when she did she was usually bored and hot. There'd been a few times, though, when Misty had lost herself in the songs and shouts of praise. A trembling ecstasy had welled up inside her until it seemed like her skin would split open, shedding all her fear and loneliness with it. But those moments were few and fleeting, and the transformation had never been as total as what their ritual at the furnace had led to. For a few seconds, Misty had been reborn in body as well as mind and spirit [46].

Misty stops attending church once she becomes a wolf (162), but as their drug-induced shapeshifting ritual continues, she begins to question if there might be an element of evil in the transformation, wondering if the mushroom is actually the Devil and if she and her friends might go to hell (78–79). She even wonders if God knows about their activities and worries about having sincere faith (169). One of her friends, Val, insists that "wolves aren't evil" (79), and another, Eric, tells her that "there's no such thing as good and evil. There's only predators and prey" (269), but Misty struggles to accept this amoral view of the world, believing instead that "hiding under wolf skin made it so easy to do evil things" (216).

Daniel also attends church, but this appears to be more from duty rather than desire. His engagement with faith is limited compared to Misty's in the novel, rather superficial and in line with the facade he shows his family and peers as a successful boy meeting everyone's expectations of him. For Daniel,

> shifting into wolf skin, though, had nothing on the mysterious change that overtook a soul between Saturday night and Sunday morning. In crumbling Birmingham, the churches stood as forts against the rot-eater god. The decay spreading around them only inspired congregations to sing louder, to offer up more, to scrub and polish the Lord's houses until they shone.... Daniel lifted his voice alongside his brothers and sisters in Christ [158].

Daniel hates the rot-eater name his friends use, but sees in it a connection to the general decay around Birmingham: economic downturn, unemployment, trouble (145), which is particularly apt in that their ritual takes place in a now-abandoned industrial part of the city, a city overlooked by a statue of Vulcan, god of fire (73, 320–21). Birmingham is called the Magic City, a name the teenagers treat with derision (45). These connections between gods, industry, religion, rituals, magic and commerce are not unlike the conflation of disparate ideas articulated by a character in Atwater-Rhodes's *Shapeshifters*, a vague catch-all of beliefs and practices: "Magic ... Science. Religion. Whatever you call it. The void. The Ecl" (532), although the shapeshifters of her text do subscribe to particular religious beliefs (311).

Despite the fact that Daniel continues attending church while Misty stops, it is Misty who articulates the most concern about spiritual issues. Her growing questions over the rightness of their shapeshifting parallels their descent into increasingly more dangerous and aggressive behaviors. Finally, when Daniel is hospitalized after being attacked by one of the wolves as he attempts to stop them taking revenge on humans, Misty seeks solace in the hospital chapel. This place is configured as a space of "subtler wonders" in amidst the medical and scientific technologies adorning the hospital (306). The chapel is multi-denominational and does not identify with one particular religion, and Misty takes communion in a Catholic Mass service, and later listens to a family praying with a minister. Misty cannot at this stage reconcile her shapeshifting activities with her faith, finding it difficult to pray or ask forgiveness for what they have done (308), but it is here that she comes to terms with her loneliness and pain and realizes that her inner resilience and fighting spirit can combat pain and loneliness (308). Even Daniel undergoes his own "confession" (316), of sorts, admitting he has cheated on his college admission test, and finding a freedom in his honesty after months of deceptions. Daniel turns his back on the prized admission to an Ivy League college, announcing instead that it is time for him to "learn how to be good.... I have to figure it out by myself" (317). Perhaps ironically, when Misty and Daniel decide to travel overseas, their work supervisor recommends that they visit the Russian city of Tolyatti to "light a candle" for him in the Transfiguration Cathedral (319), the name of which has obvious symbolic links to their own shapeshifting experiences as well as to their psychological journeys to understand themselves better, not to mention the Christian allusions to the transfiguration of Jesus Christ.

Druid Atticus O'Sullivan is another practitioner of transfiguration who sometimes seeks assistance from key figures from Christianity in Kevin Hearne's *Iron Druid* novels. In the opening pages of the first novel he claims that the attraction of modern America is that "it's practically godless" (Hearne, *Hounded* 2), yet this is configured in practical terms — that he does not need to worry about unintentionally committing sacrilege, and it is clearly evident from the outset that he practices his earth-based religion daily and is in contact with a number of Irish deities, including the Morrigan, Chooser of the Slain and Goddess of War, who often appears to him in crow form (*Hounded* 11, 28, 51, 174, 316, 331; *Hexed* 137; *Hammered* 245). Atticus is himself able to change into the shapes of an owl, otter, wolfhound or stag as appropriate through druidic rituals, but he is not isolated by his ability; both his doctor and one of his lawyers are werewolves.

These texts, too, fuse different belief systems; when doing battle against a fallen angel, Atticus enlists the help of Indigenous trickster-spirit, Coyote (*Hexed* 77); when battling the Norse god Thor, the Celtic Morrigan begs him to desist (*Hammered* 247). Her insistence that his course of action will lead to dire consequences echoes earlier counsel he received when sharing a beer with Jesus Christ (*Hammered* 115), who uses the plural term "gods" during the conversation (*Hammered* 113). Earlier, he had asked his Irish and Catholic neighbor, Mrs. MacDonough to visualize the Virgin Mary, so that she would appear and bless his weapons, telling her that visions of the Virgin are manifested by faith and that because Mary has free will, she may choose when and to whom she will appear (*Hexed* 72). These representations of Christ and Mary are constructed as being accepting of religious fluidity and pluralism.

The American series *Being Human* depicts religion as a tool for people wishing to gain power, with the villain, Bishop, explaining that throughout history, political leaders have "used" religion to advance their cause (1.05). Hence, he sees the addition of a vampire priest as invaluable to their plan to increase their numbers so that vampires can live openly in society. Aidan describes the priest's beliefs as "perverted theology" and "unhinged" when the priest compares Jesus to vampires because "Jesus himself rose from the dead," and argues that "if God made everything, then he made vampires too" (1.05). The priest claims a further link between vampirism and religion when he argues that immortality was God's intention for humans anyway.

Transformative Fictions: Shapeshifting and Spiritual Truths

In conventional, epic, high fantasy, spiritual themes are often more explicitly addressed, and the shapeshifting characters in particular often symbolize psychological and spiritual transformation. For example, daemons in Philip Pullman's work can shift shape during childhood to become different animals, only settling to one form in adolescence, as a reflection of the person the adolescent is and will become, as we discussed in Chapter One. Pullman has criticized the use of secondary worlds because of their implicit superiority to the primary one. In "Republic of Heaven," he writes that the only things that matter are in the physical world only, and that the secondary worlds of fantasy are negative and less rich than reality. Rather than this, he proposes a view that is focused on what is material and sensual. Lyra must "trust her body and the truth of what her senses told her" (*Amber Spyglass* 288); out of the "spirit *and* soul *and* body ... the best part is the body" (*Amber Spyglass* 392). This emphasis on the body, however, is interesting when we consider the array of shapeshifting works premised on just the notion that the body cannot be trusted, that there is no control, no volition, and no stability in shifting.

Lewis's *The Chronicles of Narnia* offers a mixed array of shapeshifters; all speak in some way to his own beliefs about faith. Werewolves are present in *The Lion, The Witch and the Wardrobe* as well as *Prince Caspian*; in both novels they appear to be evil: serving the White Witch in battle (*Lion*), and speaking of their blood thirst: "I'm hunger. I'm thirst. Where I bite, I hold till I die, and even after death they must cut out my mouthful from my enemy's body and bury it with me. I can fast a hundred years and not die. I can lie a hundred nights on the ice and not freeze. I can drink a river of blood and not burst" (*Prince Caspian* 143). This "Wer-Wolf" is a "horrible, grey, gaunt creature, half man and half wolf" (*Prince Caspian* 147), and when he attacks the protagonists in *Prince Caspian* and is killed, his dead body is that of a human with a wolf's head. Caspian is bitten but he does not become a werewolf; lycanthropy appears to be genetically oriented rather than contagious. Lupine shapeshifters in Lewis's world are portrayed in the conventional sense of evil: their shifting is a mark of their evil.

Shapeshifting is again linked to deception in *The Silver Chair*, featuring the Lady of the Green Kirtle, also known as the Queen of Underland, who is a witch with shapeshifting powers. The Lady attempts to deceive Eustace, Jill and Puddleglum to make them fail in their quest to rescue Prince Rilian, whom she has taken hostage in an attempt to take over Narnia. Part of her deception is making Rilian believe he himself is a shapeshifter, and this is seen in sinister terms:

> I am bound by a spell, from which my Lady alone can free me. Every night there comes an hour when my mind is most horribly changed, and, after my mind, my body. For first I become furious and wild and would rush upon my dearest friends to kill them, if I were not bound. And soon after that, I turn into the likeness of a great serpent, hungry, fierce, and deadly.... I myself know nothing of it, for when my hour is past I awake forgetful of all that vile fit and in my proper shape and sound mind—saving that I am somewhat wearied [126].

Like Mason and Tyler in *The Vampire Diaries*, Rilian willingly submits to being bound during his transformation, which in his case is a silver chair to which he is tied each night for an hour. Yet in this hour Rilian never actually shifts shape but regains his psychological independence from the Lady's enchantment — he becomes "a man again" (132) and realizes that he has been a captive to the Lady. When Rilian calls on the name of Aslan, he is saved by Eustace, Jill and Puddleglum, and they discover that the real shapeshifter is the Lady, as she transforms into an enormous green snake to attack them, and is killed by Rilian.

Like the Lady, the White Witch appears to be one thing but is in fact another, for she hasn't "a drop of real human blood" in her (*Lion* 76) despite her appearances. These facades are treated with suspicion. As Mr. Beaver tells the Pevensie children, "when you meet anything that's going to be human and isn't yet, or used to be human once and isn't now, or ought to be human and isn't, you keep your eyes on it and feel for your hatchet" (*Lion* 77). Shapeshifting in these examples is linked to deception and danger. This notion that some shapeshifters cannot be trusted because of their deceptive nature is evident in more recent examples, as with some of the shapeshifter villains in *Supernatural*, and also in *Terminator 2: Judgment Day*, where the T-1000 terminator possesses mimetic technologies allowing it to shapeshift into almost any person or object. The goal for this category of evil shapeshifter is to kill its prey, often by mimicking the appearance of those family and friends who might best allow access and make the target vulnerable. Thus instability and lack of physical integrity are villainous aspects because they cannot be trusted.

The deceptive aspect of shapeshifting is linked to evil in Tolkien's *The Silmarillion*. In the tale of Beren and Lúthien, there are several shapeshifters: antagonist Sauron, who is the embodiment of evil under Morgoth, takes the form of a werewolf to attack Lúthien and Huan (a hound), who have come to rescue Beren. Sauron's wolf form is a manifestation of his evil nature, with "the menace of the fell spirit in his eyes and the foul vapour of his breath" (210). Lúthien and Huan battle him, and Sauron transforms from a wolf into a snake, before changing into a vampire bat in his escape. Lúthien, Beren and Huan take the shapes of werewolves, orcs and vampire bats, but this is only for the purpose of gaining entry to dark places to fulfill their quest. Sauron can also take on a "fair and wise" form (345), but after losing his physical body after the fall of Númenor, he can no longer change at will nor can he "appear fair to the eyes of Men" again (338). After this point he can only take the form of his true nature, "an image of malice and hatred made visible" (338). In this treatment of shapeshifting, then, unless the transformation is temporary, as in Lúthien, Beren and Huan, there seems to be a sense that the inner character will eventually determine the outward form, as with Sauron. Thus Sauron, as the manifestation of evil, ultimately takes on a shape closer to his true nature.

In Juliet Marillier's *Wildwood Dancing*, protagonist Jena loses her childhood friend Costi to drowning, and later befriends a frog, Gogu, who travels with her everywhere. When Jena kisses Gogu, he transforms into a boy, and Jena learns that his transformation was caused by a witch to teach him a lesson. Costi's arrogance and desire to be "King of the Lake" led the witch to change him into a frog so he would learn "patience and humility," and that Jena would learn to be compassionate, and that both would learn to love (307). When he transforms back into his human form years later, however, Jena doubts his identity because of visions she has been given from a rival, visions that suggest Costi is actually a monster in disguise. Jena has to learn that those visions are false, and that his true nature is as she always believed. Thus shapeshifting here has implications for learning moral lessons and seeing past appearances to the character within.

In some Narnian cases, shapeshifting is seen in a similar light as an experience that can change characters for good and teach them about spiritual truths. In *The Voyage of the Dawn Treader*, Eustace experiences shapeshifting when his greed for treasure leads to him transforming into a dragon: "He had turned into a dragon while he was asleep. Sleeping on a dragon's hoard with greedy, dragonish thoughts in his heart, he had become a dragon himself" (73). Eustace realizes that his new form gives him the opportunity to take revenge on his companions, whom he despises, but he also sees the isolation from his new shape: "He realized that he was a monster cut off from the whole human race. An appalling loneliness came over him" (74). His companions, however, take pity on him and the shapeshifting leads to positive outcomes; his time in dragon form has matured him spiritually. As the other characters note, "Eustace's character had been rather improved by becoming a dragon" (80). It is only after his encounter with the Christ figure Aslan that he is able to return to his human self, and his transformation back into a human boy reflects Christian beliefs about salvation in that Eustace's own attempts to change himself by pulling away layers of skin achieve nothing; it is only when Aslan intervenes and removes his dragon exterior that he has become whole again. Eustace returns to his former body, but he is at the same time a new person, as the conclusion makes clear: "You'd never know him for the same boy" (189).

The link between shapeshifting and learning is also seen in Lewis's other works. It is evident in Prince Rabadash in *The Horse and His Boy*, whose pride and anger leads to his turning into a donkey (169–71). Aslan allows him the chance to become a man again, but the consequences of Rabadash's actions earlier mean that he may become a donkey again, permanently. Like Eustace, Rabadash lives a more peaceable, good life following his transformation, but his change is rather superficial in comparison. Similarly, the Duffers in *The Voyage of the Dawn Treader* were dwarves who were changed into Monopods, creatures with only one leg, a transformation caused by the Magician Coriakin in punishment for refusing to work. The Duffers are invisible after using a spell to hide because of their dislike for their new appearance, which they see as an "uglifying spell" (108), although Coriakin believes it is an improvement in their looks (126). The mouse Reepicheep teaches them to be more independent by using their enormous feet as boats and they take on a new name in recognition of their new identity, Dufflepuds, itself a hybrid of Duffers and Monopods. Lucy herself experiences the desire to change her own appearance to become more beautiful as she discovers a book of spells in *Voyage*. As she looks through the pictures accompanying the spell, she sees the possibilities of using a spell to transform herself: "the Lucy in the picture now seemed quite as big as the real Lucy; and they looked into each other's eyes and the real Lucy looked away after a few minutes because she was dazzled by the beauty of the other Lucy; though she could still see a sort of likeness to herself in that beautiful face" (119). Lucy sees the consequences of the transformation as being bloodshed and violence in her name as kings and nations fight for her favor, but resolves to perform the spell until she sees Aslan's face in the pictures and is afraid of his response to her plans.

The most notable shapeshifter of the *Narnia* series is Aslan himself, who takes several forms during the series. Like Sauron's eventual form, Aslan's forms reveal aspects of his character, and as the messianic figure of Narnia, his qualities reflect those attributed to Jesus. Aslan is primarily a lion, a figure in the Bible representing Jesus, the lion of the tribe of Judah (Revelation 5:5). Aslan is also seen in the form of a cat in *The Horse and His Boy* as he protects and comforts Shasta. In *The Voyage of the Dawn Treader*, Aslan takes the form of an albatross to guide the Dawn Treader out of darkness into light. The albatross appears initially to be a cross in a "beam of light," and as it draws closer seems to be an aeroplane and a kite. The albatross flies ahead of the boat and the helmsman Drinian follows the albatross out of darkness into light, and Lucy hears it speaking to her in Aslan's voice as he encourages her, and when they follow the albatross into sunlight, "everybody realized that there was nothing to be afraid of and never had been" (143), which recalls New Testament accounts of Christ urging his disciples to trust in him, and the declarations "I am the light of the world. Whoever follows me will never walk in darkness, but will have the light of life" (John 8:12). Later in *Voyage*, Aslan is a lamb, an allusion to the Biblical symbolism of Jesus as the Lamb of God, a sacrifice for the sins of the world as John the Baptist declares in John 1:29: "Look, the Lamb of God, who takes away the sin of the world!" At the conclusion of *The Voyage of the Dawn Treader*, Aslan tells Lucy that although she will not be returning to Narnia, she can know him in her own world by another name (188), which is a more direct statement of the allegorical nature of Aslan. The final scene of the series in *The Last Battle* reinforces this mirroring of Christian faith in Narnia, when "as He spoke He no longer looked to them like a lion" (171). Thus Aslan in his shapeshifting comes to embody in a literal sense several of the key names and imagery of Jesus Christ: the light of the world, the lion, and the lamb.

Shapeshifting and Christianity

Some critics claim there are more literal connections between Christianity and shapeshifting, and lycanthropy in particular. Charlotte Otten, for instance, argues that the imagery in the New Testament relating to false teachers being like wolves (Matthew 7:15) has links to lycanthropy (5), writing that "the image cluster in the Ecclesiastical Ordinances has roughly the following equivalences" (6):

> sheep/flock = Christian parishioners who are vulnerable to spiritual attack by Satanic forces
> shepherds = bishops and priests who are instructed to protect their "flock" from diabolic attack
> werewolf = Satan and his cohorts who wish to destroy the faith of the "sheep" and to damn them to perdition [6].

According to Noll, the medical condition of lycanthropy has been seen as linked to demonic possession. Whether or not people believed the lycanthropy to be delusion or reality, in either way the delusion or transformation was seen as being caused by Satan and the person should therefore be punished (84):

> Although originally viewed as only a mental disorder, during the period of the Great Witch Hunt in Europe (roughly 1500–1650), such individuals were regarded as instruments of Satan, and many were executed as lycanthropes (or *loups garoux* in France), for changing their forms with the Devil's help — that is, literally transforming themselves into animals — and then committing heretical or violent crimes [84].

Otten references St Augustine's work on shapeshifting and suggests that

> Satan is seen as enlisting humans as allies and servants, adding them to his demonic hosts. This is a covert acknowledgment of Satan's capacity to change humans into werewolves; that is, the instigation to werewolfism is Satan's, but the human will collaborates in the spiritual metamorphosis. Bishops and priests are warned about the subtle, undetectable transformations threatening the spiritual life of the flock [6].

Wilson similarly claims that "wolves feature prominently in Christian mythology" ("It's a Wolf Thing" 199).

Yet this seems to focus on lupine imagery more than is warranted by the meaning of the Biblical text, which seems more interested in using the imagery to signify the danger of false teaching to Christian believers. The imagery of shapeshifting is seen elsewhere in the New Testament, however, for in some ways there are symbolic connections between notions of shapeshifting and spirituality. The Bible makes reference to the notion of new, changed bodies following death: "Listen, I tell you a mystery: We will not all sleep, but we will all be changed — in a flash, in the twinkling of an eye, at the last trumpet. For the trumpet will sound, the dead will be raised imperishable, and we will be changed. For the perishable must clothe itself with the imperishable, and the mortal with immortality" (1 Corinthians 15:51–53). In Christian belief, salvation leads to transformation into a new likeness, into the image and likeness of Christ. As 2 Corinthians 3:18 puts it, "And we all, who with unveiled faces contemplate the Lord's glory, are being transformed into his image with ever-increasing glory, which comes from the Lord, who is the Spirit." Colossians depicts this change as a shift in identity: "you have taken off your old self with its practices and have put on the new self, which is being renewed in knowledge in the image of its Creator" (Colossians 3:9–10). These are spiritual changes, metaphorical transformations. The New Testament repeatedly emphasizes the concepts of being a "new creation" (2 Corinthians 5:17), a new life that is engendered by the death and resurrection of the Christ, and in a very symbolic sense this is a spiritual transformation over time.

Given the influence of Christianity in Western culture, it is no surprise to find these themes repeated across a range of texts that explicitly deal with immortality and eternal life. Most contemporary texts seem to remove God from the equation but retain some of the symbols and imagery, emphasizing again and again the life-giving power of blood, the necessity of sacrificing one's life to save others, the importance of finding purpose in one's existence on earth, the existence of evil and the potential for apocalyptic endings and revelations, and the enduring desire that this life may not be all there is. Thus, although there is a shift towards secularism in society more generally, these popular culture texts attempt to accommodate notions of spirituality to various degrees, and often it is in a relatively positive light.

Conclusion

As we have seen, texts featuring shapeshifting characters are undergoing a popular resurgence, and are to be found everywhere from YA novels and top grossing movies to television and even a startling array of merchandise. Shapeshifters inhabit the same pages and screens as vampires and other supernatural creatures, taking an array of forms from monsters and villains to humans and heroes. They are found in drama, in romance, in comedy, and in texts that combine all three.

Most shapeshifters are werewolves, whether bound by the full moon or able to shift at will, but a smaller number take on other human and animal identities. The modern versions can mimic generic traditions by casting shapeshifters as villains whose transformations emphasize their monstrous nature. More often shapeshifters are portrayed sympathetically, as outsiders who have been marked as different and who cannot reconcile their multiple identities and are forced to inhabit life on the edges of society. At times they are treated comedically, in texts that draw on genre conventions only to subvert or mock. Increasingly they are presented in naturalized ways that emphasize cohesion between human and other identities, where their shapeshifting is a mark of power.

This book argues that the genre itself has shifted shape significantly, reflecting popular concerns and becoming particularly relevant in times of social upheaval. As uniquely fluid characters, shapeshifters are deployed in myriad ways to explore contemporary society and how it affects us. An exploration of current shapeshifting figures in popular culture reveals powerful metaphors for many important social issues. Shapeshifters can come to operate as symbols for issues such as ethnic and cultural differences, attempting to explore through the supernatural genre the social and racial politics that can govern our world. The themes of control, the body, pain and exclusion in shapeshifting narratives can become parallels for the experience of ill health, disability and addiction in real life. The genre addresses how our society understands adolescence as an often painful transformation from child to adult, as well as our ideas about gender and sexuality, and our beliefs about life, death, and spirituality.

Are they always used in these ways? As we have discussed, not always. At times shapeshifters remain marginal figures, hostage to confusion over their multiple selves. Like vampires, they have very often moved from outsider to hero, but also often remain subjects to their own condition, unable to fully move beyond social boundaries. There is an irony that shifting characters are in some respects fixed in their state: trapped in a societal stasis that is, in some cases, anachronistic. They can reinforce cultural, racial, and gender stereotypes, their transformative potential overlooked in deference to traditional, white, patriarchal conventions. Sometimes the symbolic power of these creatures is problematic. Attempting to read shapeshifters such as werewolves as akin to the experience of chronic illness, disability or other minority groups can risk equating that group with danger and monstrosity. Alternatively, their enhanced abilities and in some cases increased social status work against such parallels. As we note, the real power of these shifters is in their experience of pain and exclusion in ways that mimic how readers themselves may often feel in their real lives.

In other ways shapeshifting offers the chance to view our world with new eyes and to transform our thinking about our society. Shapeshifters can elude our attempts to define them, to categorize them into distinct and separate groups. They can cross boundaries into new areas and take on fluid identities. They can encourage us to think differently and provoke us to rethink our assumptions. They can help readers and viewers engage with questions about their own identity, about spirituality and the supernatural.

Despite the secularism of much of Western culture, spiritual elements continue to infiltrate popular culture, whether drawing on Biblical figures such as angels and demons, or more abstract concepts such as souls, eternity, redemption, salvation, and the meaning of existence. As the genre continues to transform itself, perhaps the current celebrities of the undead world, vampires, may begin to lose their appeal, as shapeshifters and other figures continue their rise. The paranormal genre is replete with creatures from supernatural traditions: not just vampires but fairies, witches, and zombies. If we accept that fantasy literature can speak to real life, then it is important to keep engaging with the genre to understand what it is saying — and is not saying — about the world in which we live.

As we acknowledged in the Introduction, it is impossible to analyze every shapeshifting text without reducing this book to a bibliographic survey, given the vast amount of works within this genre, which itself continues to transform with new texts produced every month. Our approach here has been instead to discuss a number of key themes with close reference to selected texts. Inevitably we focus on some texts and miss others that would reward study, but we hope that this book encourages more scholarly attention and dialog about shapeshifting to further enrich those already existing works in this field.

We encourage you to join the conversation at our blog, shapeshiftersinpopularculture.wordpress.com, as we continue to explore the shifting shape of this area. We can also be found on Twitter @KMcMahonColeman and @roslynweaver.

Works Cited

Alloy Entertainment. *Bloodlust. The Vampire Diaries—Stefan's Diaries, 2*. New York: HarperTeen, 2011.
_____. *The Craving. The Vampire Diaries—Stefan's Diaries, 3*. New York: HarperTeen, 2011.
_____. *Origins. The Vampire Diaries—Stefan's Diaries, 1*. New York: HarperTeen, 2010.
_____. *The Ripper. The Vampire Diaries—Stefan's Diaries, 4*. New York: HarperTeen, 2011.
Anderson, Ian. "Introduction: The Aboriginal Critique of Colonial Knowing." *Blacklines: Contemporary Critical Writing by Indigenous Australians*. Ed. Michele Grossman. Carlton: Melbourne University Press, 2003. 17–24.
Anderson-Dargatz, Gail. *The Cure for Death by Lightning*. Toronto: Virago, 1997.
Angel. WB. 1999–2004.
Atwater-Rhodes, Amelia. *The Shapeshifters: The Kiesha'ra of the Den of Shadows*. New York: Delacorte, 2010.
Auerbach, Nina. *Our Vampires, Ourselves*. Chicago: University of Chicago Press, 1995.
Averill, Lindsey Issow. "Un-biting the Apple and Killing the Womb: Genesis, Gender, and Gynocide." *Theorizing Twilight: Critical Essays on What's at Stake in a Post-Vampire World*. Ed. Maggie Parke and Natalie Wilson. Jefferson: McFarland, 2011. 224–37.
Barnes, Jennifer Lynn. *Raised by Wolves*. London: Quercus, 2010.
_____. "Sweet Caroline." *A Visitor's Guide to Mystic Falls*. Ed. Red and Vee. Dallas: BenBella, 2010. 143–57.
_____. *Trial by Fire*. London: Quercus, 2011.
Being Human (U.K.). BBC. 2008–.
Being Human (U.S.). Syfy. 2011–.
Bennett, Andrew, and Nicholas Royle. *Introduction to Literature, Criticism and Theory*. Harlow: Person Longman, 2004.
Bennett, Holly. *Shapeshifter*. Victoria: Orca, 2010.
Bereska, Tami M. "Adolescent Sexuality and the Changing Romance Novel Market." *The Canadian Journal of Human Sexuality* 3.1 (1994): 35–44.
Bernhardt-House, Phillip A. "The Werewolf as Queer, the Queer as Werewolf, and Queer Werewolves." *Queering the Non/Human*. Ed. Noreen Giffney and Myra J. Hird. Aldershot: Ashgate, 2008. 159–83.
Billson, Anne. "Things Are About to Get Hairy." *Sydney Morning Herald: Spectrum* 27–28 February 2010, sec. Spectrum: 14.
Buchbinder, David. *Performance Anxieties: Re-producing Masculinity*. St. Leonards: Allen and Unwin, 1998.
Buffy, the Vampire Slayer. WB-UPN. 1997–2003.
Buffy, the Vampire Slayer, Season 8. Dark Horse Comics, 2007–2011.
Bynum, Caroline Walker. *Metamorphosis and Identity*. New York: Zone, 2001.
_____. "Metamorphosis, or Gerald and the Werewolf." *Speculum* 73.4 (1998): 987–1013.

Calhoun, C. *Love You to Death: The Unofficial Companion to* The Vampire Diaries. Toronto: ECW, 2010.
Campbell, Nancy D. *Using Women: Gender, Drug Policy, and Social Justice.* London & New York: Routledge, 2000.
Carter, Margaret. "The Vampire as Alien in Contemporary Fiction." *Blood Read: The Vampire as Metaphor in Contemporary Culture.* Ed. Joan Gordon and Veronica Hollinger. Philadelphia: University of Pennsylvania Press, 1997. 27–44.
Chappell, Shelley. "Contemporary Werewolf Schemata: Shifting Representations of Racial and Ethnic Difference." *International Research in Children's Literature* 2.1 (2009): 21–35.
_____. *Werewolves, Wings, and Other Weird Transformations: Fantastic Metamorphosis in Children's and Young Adult Fantasy Literature.* Sydney: Macquarie University, 2007. Ph.D. thesis.
Cooper, Susan. *The Dark Is Rising.* London: Chatto & Windus, 1973.
Costello, Carrie Yang. "Teratology: 'Monsters' and the Professionalization of Obstetrics." *Journal of Historical Sociology* 19.1 (2006): 1–33.
Craton, Lillian E., and Kathryn E. Jonell. "I Am Sookie, Hear Me Roar!" *True Blood and Philosophy: We Wanna Think Bad Things with You.* Ed. George A. Dunn and Rebecca Housel. Hoboken: John Wiley, 2010. 109–22.
Creed, Barbara. *Phallic Panic: Film, Horror, and the Primal Uncanny.* Carlton: Melbourne University Press, 2005.
CSI. CBS. 2000–.
Davidson, Michael. "Universal Design: The Work of Disability in an Age of Globalization." *The Disability Studies Reader.* Ed. Lennard J. Davis. 2d ed. New York: Routledge, 2006. 117–28.
Davis, Heather. *Never Cry Werewolf.* New York: HarperTeen, 2009.
Davis, Lennard J. "Constructing Normalcy: The Bell Curve, the Novel, and the Invention of the Disabled Body in the Nineteenth Century." *The Disability Studies Reader.* Ed. Lennard J. Davis. 2d ed. New York: Routledge, 2006. 3–16.
_____. "Preface/Introduction." *The Disability Studies Reader.* Ed. Lennard J. Davis. 2d ed. New York: Routledge, 2006. xiii–xviii.
De Leonardis, Fabio. "War as a Medicine: The Medical Metaphor in Contemporary Italian Political Language." *Social Semiotics* 18.1 (2008): 33–45.
Devlin, Ivy. *Low Red Moon.* New York: Bloomsbury, 2010.
Dickens, Charles. *A Christmas Carol.* 1843. New York: W. Morrow, 1996.
Doctor Who. BBC. 1963–1989; 1996; 2005–.
Doctor Who: The End of Time. BBC. 2009–2010.
Dodson, Michael. "The Wentworth Lecture: The End in the Beginning: Re(De)Finding Aboriginality." *Australian Aboriginal Studies* 1 (1994): 2–13.
Doty, Alexander. *Making Things Perfectly Queer: Interpreting Mass Culture.* Minneapolis: University of Minnesota Press, 1993.
Dracula. Dir. Tod Browning. Universal, 1931.
D'Souza, D. C., R. A. Sewell, and M. Ranganathan. "Cannabis and Psychosis/Schizophrenia: Human Studies." *European Archives of Psychiatry and Clinical Neuroscience* 259 (2009): 413–31.
Duclos, Denis. *The Werewolf Complex: America's Fascination with Violence.* 1994. Trans. Amanda Pingree. Oxford: Berg, 1998.
Du Coudray, Chantal Bourgault. *The Curse of the Werewolf: Fantasy, Horror and the Beast Within.* London: I. B. Tauris, 2006.
_____. "The Cycle of the Werewolf: Romantic Ecologies of Selfhood in Popular Fantasy." *Australian Feminist Studies* 18.40 (2003): 57–72.
Duncan, Glen. *The Last Werewolf.* New York: Alfred A. Knopf, 2011.
Edwards, Justin. *Gothic Canada: Reading the Spectre of a National Literature.* Alberta: University of Alberta Press, 2005.
Eliade, Mircea. *Shamanism: Archaic Techniques and Ecstasy.* Trans. Willard R. Trask. Princeton: Princeton University Press, 1964.
Evans, Walter. "Monster Movies: A Sexual Theory." *Journal of Popular Film* 2 (1973): 353–65.

Fogelin, Robert J. "Metaphors, Similes and Similarity." *Aspects of Metaphor.* Ed. Jaakko Hintikka. Dordrecht: Kluwer Academic, 1994. 23–39.
Forbes Irving, P. M. C. *Metamorphosis in Greek Mythology.* Oxford: Clarendon, 1990.
Freaky Friday. Dir. Gary Nelson. Walt Disney, 1976.
Freaky Friday. Dir. Mark Waters. Walt Disney, 2003.
Frye, Northrop. *The Educated Imagination.* Bloomington: Indiana University Press, 1964.
Futurama. Fox. 1999–2003.
Gelder, Ken. *Reading the Vampire.* London: Routledge, 1994.
Gilligan's Island. CBS. 1964–1967.
Ginger Snaps. Dir. John Fawcett. Lions Gate, 2000.
Ginger Snaps Back: The Beginning. Dir. Grant Harvey. Lions Gate, 2004.
Ginger Snaps Unleashed. Dir. Brett Sullivan. 20th Century–Fox, 2003.
Goldman, Marlene. "Coyote's Children and the Canadian Gothic." *Unsettled Remains: Canadian Literature and the Postcolonial Gothic.* Ed. Cynthia Sugars and Gerry Turcotte. Waterloo: Wilfrid Laurier Press, 2009. 51–74.
Gordon, Joan, and Veronica Hollinger. "Introduction: The Shape of Vampires." *Blood Read: The Vampire as Metaphor in Contemporary Culture.* Ed. Joan Gordon and Veronica Hollinger. Philadelphia: University of Pennsylvania Press, 1997. 1–7.
Gray, Claudia. *Fateful.* New York: HarperTeen, 2011.
Green, Amy M. "Revealing Discrimination: Social Hierarchy and the Exclusion/Enslavement of the Other in the Harry Potter Novels." *The Looking Glass: New Perspectives on Children's Literature* 13.3 (2009). Web. 24 Nov. 2011. <http://www.lib.latrobe.edu.au/ojs/index.php/tlg/article/view/162/161>.
Greenburg, Louis. "Sins of the Blood: Rewriting the Family in Two Postmodern Vampire Novels." *Journal of Literary Studies* 26.1 (2010): 163–78.
Hale, Jenny. "The Author." Web. 24 Nov. 2011. <http://www.jatta.com.au/the-author/>.
_____. *Jatta.* Sydney: Scholastic, 2009.
_____. "Re: Jatta." Message to Roslyn Weaver. 9 Mar. 2010. Email.
Hanks, Carole, and D. T. Hanks, Jr. "Perrault's 'Little Red Riding Hood': Victim of the Revisers." *Children's Literature* 7 (1978): 68–77.
Harper, Molly. *The Art of Seducing a Naked Werewolf.* New York: Pocket, 2011.
_____. *How to Flirt with a Naked Werewolf.* New York: Pocket, 2011.
Harris, Charlaine. *All Together Dead.* New York: Ace, 2007.
_____. *Club Dead.* New York: Ace, 2003.
_____. *Dead and Gone.* London: Orion, 2009.
_____. *Dead as a Doornail.* New York: Ace, 2005.
_____. *Dead in the Family.* London: Orion, 2010.
_____. *Dead Reckoning.* London: Gollancz, 2011.
_____. *Dead to the World.* New York: Ace, 2004.
_____. *Dead Until Dark.* New York: Ace Books, 2001.
_____. *Definitely Dead.* New York: Ace, 2006.
_____. *From Dead to Worse.* New York: Ace, 2008.
_____. *Living Dead in Dallas.* New York: Ace, 2002.
_____. "Vampires, Two-Natured, and Fairies, Oh My! Sookie Discusses the Creatures She's Met." *The Sookie Stackhouse Companion.* Ed. Charlaine Harris. London: Gollancz, 2011. 217–25.
_____, ed. *The Sookie Stackhouse Companion.* London: Gollancz, 2011.
Hearne, Kevin. *Hammered.* New York: Del Rey, 2011.
_____. *Hexed.* London: Orbit, 2011.
_____. *Hounded.* New York: Del Rey, 2011.
Hines, Maude. "Second Nature: Daemons and Ideology in The Golden Compass." *His Dark Materials Illuminated: Critical Essays on Philip Pullman's Trilogy.* Ed. Millicent Lenz and Carole Scott. Detroit: Wayne State University Press, 2005. 37–47.
Hinton, M., et al. "Reductions in Cannabis and Other Illicit Substance Use Between Treatment Entry and Early Recovery in Patients with First-Episode Psychosis." *Early Intervention in Psychiatry* 1 (2007): 259–66.

Hirschman, Elizabeth C. "Professional, Personal, and Popular Culture Perspectives on Addiction." *American Behavioral Scientist* 38.4 (1995): 537–52.
Hjarvard, Stig. "The Mediatisation of Religion: Theorising Religion, Media and Social Change." *Culture and Religion* 12.2 (2011): 119–35.
Hodgkin, Paul. "Medicine Is War: And Other Medical Metaphors." *British Medical Journal* 291 (1985): 1820–21.
The Holy Bible. New International Version: The NIV Study Bible. Grand Rapids: Zondervan, 1995.
Horne, Jackie C. "Harry and the Other: Answering the Race Question in J. K. Rowling's Harry Potter." *The Lion and the Unicorn* 34.1 (2010): 76–104.
Howl's Moving Castle. Dir. Hayao Miyazaki. Walt Disney, 2004.
Hubbard, Rita C. "Relationship Styles in Popular Romance Novels, 1950 to 1983." *Communication Quarterly* 33.2 (1985): 113–25.
The Hulk. Dir. Ang Lee. Universal, 2003.
Irwin, W. R. *The Game of the Impossible: A Rhetoric of Fantasy*. Urbana: University of Illinois Press, 1976.
I Was a Teenage Werewolf. Dir. Gene Fowler Jr. American International, 1957.
Jackson, Rosemary. *Fantasy: The Literature of Subversion*. 1981. London & New York: Routledge, 1993.
Jensen, Kristian. "Noble Werewolves or Native Shape-Shifters?" *The* Twilight *Mystique: Critical Essays on the Novels and Films*. Ed. Amy M. Clarke and Marijane Osborn. Jefferson: McFarland, 2010. 92–106.
Jinks, Catherine. *The Abused Werewolf Rescue Group*. Crows Nest: Allen & Unwin, 2010.
Johnson, Barbara E., Douglas L. Kuck, and Patricia R. Schander. "Rape Myth Acceptance and Sociodemographic Characteristics: A Multidimensional Analysis." *Sex Roles* 36.11 (1997): 693–707.
Jones, Diana Wynne. *Howl's Moving Castle*. 1986. London: HarperCollins, 2009.
Jones, Steven Swann. "On Analyzing Fairy Tales: 'Little Red Riding Hood' Revisited." *Western Folklore* 46.2 (1987): 97–106.
Kirk, Connie Ann. *J. K. Rowling: A Biography*. Westport: Greenwood, 2003.
Lai, Larissa. *When Fox Is a Thousand*. Vancouver: Press Gang, 1995.
Latham, Rob. "Consuming Youth: The Lost Boys Cruise Mallworld." *Blood Read: The Vampire as Metaphor in Contemporary Culture*. Ed. Joan Gordon and Veronica Hollinger. Philadelphia: University of Pennsylvania Press, 1997. 129–47.
Lee, Linda J. "Guilty Pleasures: Reading Romance Novels as Reworked Fairy Tales." *Marvels & Tales* 22.1 (2008): 52–66.
Levy, Sophie. "'This Dark Echo Calls Him Home': Writing Father-Daughter Incest Narratives in Canadian Immigrant Fiction." *University of Toronto Quarterly*. 71.4 (2002): 864–80.
Lewis, C. S. *Collected Letters Volume 1: Family Letters 1905–1931*. Ed. Walter Hooper. London: HarperCollins, 2000.
_____. *Essay Collection and Other Short Pieces*. Ed. Lesley Walmsley. London: HarperCollins, 2000.
_____. *The Horse and His Boy*. 1954. London: Lions-Collins, 1980.
_____. *The Last Battle*. 1956. London: Lions-Collins, 1980.
_____. *The Lion, the Witch and the Wardrobe*. 1950. London: Lions-Collins, 1980.
_____. *Prince Caspian: The Return to Narnia*. 1951. London: Lions-Collins, 1980.
_____. *The Silver Chair*. 1953. London: Lions-Collins, 1980.
_____. *The Voyage of the Dawn Treader*. 1952. London: Fontana Lions, 1987.
Lewis, Ioan M. *Ecstatic Religion: An Anthropological Study of Spirit Possession and Shamanism*. Ringwood: Penguin, 1971.
Lima, Maria. "Home Is Where the Bar Is." *A Taste of* True Blood: *The Fangbanger's Guide*. Ed. Leah Wilson. Dallas: BenBella, 2010. 33–44.
Linton, Simi. "Reassigning Meaning." *The Disability Studies Reader*. Ed. Lennard J. Davis. 2d ed. New York: Routledge, 2006. 161–72.
Love, Kathy. *My Sister Is a Werewolf*. New York: Brava, 2007.
Luntz, Stephen. "What Causes Addiction?" *Issues* 74 (March 2006): 6–7.

MacInerney, Karen. *Howling at the Moon*. New York: Ballantine, 2008.
———. *Leader of the Pack*. New York: Ballantine, 2009.
———. *On the Prowl*. New York: Ballantine, 2008.
Marillier, Juliet. *Wildwood Dancing*. Sydney: Pan Macmillan, 2006.
McIntosh, Pat. "Cry Wolf." *Dragons and Warrior Daughters: Fantasy Stories by Women Writers*. Ed. Jessica Yates. London: Lions Tracks, 1989. 166–85.
McKenzie, Kirsten. *Positive Values: The Figure of the Trickster as a Catalyst for Community in Selected Works of Sheila Watson and Tomson Highway*. Michigan: UMI Dissertation Services, 1988.
McMahon-Coleman, Kimberley. *A Comparison of the Writings of the Ainu author Shigeru Kayano and Inuk author Alootook Ipellie*. Wollongong: University of Wollongong, 2000. BA (Hons) thesis.
———. *Indigenous Diasporic Literature: Representations of the Shaman in the Works of Sam Watson and Alootook Ipellie*. Wollongong: University of Wollongong, 2009. Ph.D. thesis.
McWhorter, Ladelle. "Foreword." *Foucault and the Government of Disability*. Ed. Shelley Tremain. Ann Arbor: University of Michigan Press, 2005. xiii–xvii.
Mercer, Joyce Ann. "Vampires, Desire, Girls and God: *Twilight* and the Spiritualities of Adolescent Girls." *Pastoral Psychology* 60 (2011): 263–78.
Merskin, Debra. "A Boyfriend to Die For: Edward Cullen as Compensated Psychopath in Stephanie Meyer's Twilight." *Journal of Communication Inquiry* 35.2 (2011): 157–78.
Meyer, Stephenie. *Breaking Dawn*. 2008. London: Atom, 2009.
———. *Eclipse*. 2007. London: Atom, 2008.
———. *New Moon*. 2006. London: Atom, 2007.
———. "The Story Behind the Writing of New Moon." Web. 20 Sep. 2010. <http://www.stephe niemeyer.com/nm_thestory.html>.
———. *Twilight*. 2005. London: Atom, 2007.
Millar, Martin. *Curse of the Wolf Girl*. London: Piatkus, 2010.
———. *Lonely Werewolf Girl*. London: Piatkus, 2007.
Miller, April. "'The Hair that Wasn't There Before'": Demystifying Monstrosity and Menstruation in *Ginger Snaps* and *Ginger Snaps Unleashed*." *Western Folklore* 64.3/4 (2005): 281–303.
Miller, Melissa. "Maybe Edward Is the Most Dangerous Thing Out There." *Theorizing Twilight: Critical Essays on What's at Stake in a Post-Vampire World*. Ed. Maggie Parke and Natalie Wilson. Jefferson: McFarland, 2011. 165–177.
Modleski, Tania. "The Disappearing Act: A Study of Harlequin Romances." *Signs* 5.3 (1980): 435–48.
Moretti, Franco. *Signs Taken for Wonders: On the Sociology of Literary Forms*. 1983. London: Verso, 2005.
Mudrooroo. *The Indigenous Literature of Australia: Milli Milli Wangka*. South Melbourne: Hyland, 1997.
The Mummy: Tomb of the Dragon Emperor. Dir. Rob Cohen. Universal, 2008.
Natov, Roni. "Harry Potter and the Extraordinariness of the Ordinary." *The Lion and the Unicorn* 25.2 (2001): 310–27.
Noll, Richard. *Vampires, Werewolves, and Demons: Twentieth Century Reports in the Psychiatric Literature*. New York: Brunner/Mazel, 1992.
Otten, Charlotte F. "Introduction." *A Lycanthropy Reader: Werewolves in Western Culture*. Ed. Charlotte F. Otten. Syracuse: Syracuse University Press, 1986. 1–18.
Pappademus, Alex. "We Are All Teenage Werewolves." *New York Times Magazine*. 20 May 2011. Web. 25 Nov. 2011. <http://www.nytimes.com/2011/05/22/magazine/we-are-all-teenage-werewolves.html?_r=1&pagewanted=all>.
Partridge, Christopher. "Alternative Spiritualities, Occulture and the Re-enchantment of the West." *The Bible in Transmission* (Summer 2005): 1–6.
Pearce, Jackson. *Sisters Red*. 2010. London: Hodder, 2011.
———. *Sweetly*. London: Hodder Children's, 2011.
Penson, Richard T., et al. "Cancer as Metaphor." *The Oncologist* 9.6 (2004): 708–16.
Pernick, Martin S. *The Black Stork: Eugenics and the Death of "Defective" Babies in American Medicine and Motion Pictures Since 1915*. New York: Oxford University Press, 1996.

Peter and the Wolf. Dir. Clyde Geronimi. Walt Disney Pictures, 1946.
Petersen, Line Nybro. "Renegotiating Religious Imaginations Through Transformations of 'Banal Religion' in *Supernatural.*" *Transformative Works and Cultures* 4 (2010). Web. 24 Nov. 2011. <http://journal.transformativeworks.org/index.php/twc/article/view/142/145>.
Peterson, Matthew. "An Interview with L. J. Smith." *The Author Hour.* 19 Nov. 2009. Web. 16 Aug. 2011. <www.theauthorhouse.com/l-j-smith>.
Petrone, Penny. *Native Literature in Canada: From the Oral Tradition to the Present.* Oxford: Oxford University Press, 1990.
Plumb. "Cut." *Chaotic Resolve.* Curb Records, 2006.
Poole, Carol. "The Ego, Id and Sookie Stackhouse: True Blood's Freudian Analysis of Intimacy." *A Taste of* True Blood: *The Fangbanger's Guide.* Ed. Leah Wilson. Dallas: BenBella, 2010. 75–88.
Poulakou-Rebelakou, E., et al. "Lycanthropy in Byzantine Times (a.d. 330–1453)." *History of Psychiatry* 20.4 (2009): 468–79.
Prokofiev, Sergei. *Peter and the Wolf.* 1936.
Prowse, Nycole. "Mother Load[ed]: Literary Representations of Addiction and the 'Monstrous' Mother." Web. 24 Nov. 2011. <http://www.inter-disciplinary.net/wp-content/uploads/2011/05/nprowseepaper.pdf>.
Pugh, Tison, and David L. Wallace. "Heteronormative Heroism and Queering the School Story in J. K. Rowling's Harry Potter Series." *Children's Literature Association Quarterly* 31.3 (2006): 260–81.
Pullman, Philip. *The Amber Spyglass.* New York: Random House, 2000.
———. *Northern Lights.* London: Scholastic, 1995.
———. "The Republic of Heaven." *The Horn Book Magazine* 77.6 (2001): 655–67.
———. *The Subtle Knife.* New York: Random House, 1997.
Punter, David, and Glennis Byron. *The Gothic.* Oxford: Blackwell, 2004.
Radway, Janice A. "Women Read the Romance: The Interaction of Text and Context." *Feminist Studies* 9.1 (1983): 53–78.
Rana, Marion. "'Killers Are Sort of Romantic:' The Eroticisation of Sexual and Domestic Violence in Vampire Diaries and Twilight." *Journal of Children's Literature Studies* 8.1 (2011): 87–103.
Red, and Vee. *A Visitor's Guide to Mystic Falls.* Dallas: Smart Pop, 2010.
Red Riding Hood. Dir. Catherine Hardwicke. Warner Bros., 2011.
Reisfield, Gary M., and George R. Wilson. "Use of Metaphor in the Discourse on Cancer." *Journal of Clinical Oncology* 22.19 (2004): 4024–27.
Reisz, Kristopher. *Unleashed.* New York: Simon Pulse, 2008.
Rickels, Laurence A. *The Vampire Lectures.* Minneapolis: University of Minnesota Press, 1999.
Rogers, Paula. "To Live and Die in Dixie: Magical Creatures and Traditional Southern Culture." *A Taste of* True Blood: *the Fangbanger's Guide.* Ed. Leah Wilson. Dallas: BenBella, 2010. 45–60.
Rowling, J. K. *Harry Potter and the Deathly Hallows.* London: Bloomsbury, 2007.
———. *Harry Potter and the Goblet of Fire.* London: Bloomsbury, 2000.
———. *Harry Potter and the Half-Blood Prince.* London: Bloomsbury, 2005.
———. *Harry Potter and the Order of the Phoenix.* London: Bloomsbury, 2003.
———. *Harry Potter and the Philosopher's Stone.* London: Bloomsbury, 1997.
———. *Harry Potter and the Prisoner of Azkaban.* London: Bloomsbury, 1999.
———. "Harry Potter—Harry and Me." *The Scotsman.* Nov. 2002. Web. 24 Nov. 2011. <http://www.accio-quote.org/articles/2002/1102-fraser-scotsman.html>.
———. *The Tales of Beedle the Bard.* London: Bloomsbury: Children's High Level Group, 2008.
———. "Warner Bros. Entertainment and J.K. Rowling V. RDR Books." 14. Apr. 2008. Web. 24 Nov. 2011. <http://cyberlaw.stanford.edu/system/files/Trial+Transcript+Day+1.txt>.
———. "World Book Day Chat." 4 Mar. 2004. Web. 24 Nov. 2011. <www.accio-quote.org/articles/2004/0304-wbd.htm>.
Rudski, J. M., C. Segal, and E. Kallen. "Harry Potter and the End of the Road: Parallels with Addiction." *Addiction Research and Theory* 17.3 (2009): 260–77.

Russ, Joanna. "Somebody's Trying to Kill Me and I Think It's My Husband: The Modern Gothic." *The Journal of Popular Culture* 6.4 (1973): 666–91.
Ryan, Simon. "Inscribing the Emptiness: Cartography, Exploration and the Construction of Australia." *De-Scribing Empire: Post-Colonialism and Textuality*. Ed. Chris Tiffin and Alan Lawson. London: Routledge, 1994. 115–30.
Sabrina, the Teenage Witch. ABC-WB. 1996–2003.
Said, Edward. *Culture and Imperialism*. New York: Vintage-Random, 1994.
Schell, Heather. "The Big Bad Wolf: Masculinity and Genetics in Popular Culture." *Literature and Medicine* 26.1 (2007): 109–25.
Schreiber, Ellen. *Once in a Full Moon*. Millers Point: Murdoch, 2011.
Seifert, Christine. "Bite Me! (or Don't)." *Bitch Magazine*. Web. 24 Nov. 2011. <http://bitch-magazine.org/article/bite-me-or-dont >.
Shakespeare, Tom. "The Social Model of Disability." *The Disability Studies Reader*. Ed. Lennard J. Davis. 2d ed. New York: Routledge, 2006. 197–204.
Silver, Anna. "*Twilight* Is Not Good for Maidens: Gender, Sexuality, and the Family in Stephenie Meyer's *Twilight* Series." *Studies in the Novel* 42.1–2 (2010): 121–38.
Smith, L. J. *The Awakening, The Vampire Diaries, 1*. 1991. New York: HarperTeen, 2009.
———. *The Fury & Dark Reunion, The Vampire Diaries 3 & 4*. 1991. New York: HarperTeen, 2007.
———. *Midnight, The Vampire Diaries—The Return, 3*. New York: HarperTeen, 2011.
———. *Nightfall, The Vampire Diaries—The Return, 1*. New York: HarperTeen, 2009.
———. *Phantom, The Vampire Diaries—The Hunters, 1*. New York: HarperTeen, 2011.
———. *Shadow Souls, The Vampire Diaries—The Return, 2*. New York: HarperTeen, 2010
———. *The Struggle, The Vampire Diaries, 2*. 1991. New York: HarperTeen, 2009.
Sontag, Susan. *Illness as Metaphor and Aids and Its Metaphors*. London: Penguin, 1991.
Squires, Claire. *Philip Pullman's His Dark Materials Trilogy: A Reader's Guide*. New York: Continuum, 2003.
Stiefvater, Maggie. *Forever*. New York, Scholastic, 2011.
———. *Linger*. New York: Scholastic, 2010.
———. *Shiver*. New York: Scholastic, 2009.
Stoker, Bram. *Dracula*. 1897. Aerie, 1988.
Summers, Sarah. "'*Twilight* Is So Anti-Feminist That I Want to Cry:' *Twilight* Fans Finding and Defining Feminism on the World Wide Web." *Computers and Composition* 27.4 (2010): 315–23.
Supernatural. WB-CW. 2005–.
Sutton, Roger. "An Interview with Patty Campbell." *Horn Book Magazine*. 1 Sep. 2010. Web. 24 Nov. 2011. <http://periodicals.faqs.org/201009/2125383421.html>.
Swan, Susan Z. "Gothic Drama in Disney's Beauty and the Beast: Subverting Traditional Romance by Transcending the Animal-Human Paradox." *Critical Studies in Mass Communication* 16.3 (1999): 350–69.
Taussig, Michael. *Shamanism, Colonialism and The Wild Man*. Chicago: University of Chicago Press, 1987.
Teen Wolf. MTV. 2011–.
Teen Wolf. Dir. Rod Daniel. Atlantic, 1985.
Teen Wolf Too. Dir. Christopher Leitch. Atlantic, 1987.
The Teratology Society. "What Is Teratology?" Web. 18 Aug. 2010. <http://teratology.org/comm/defs.htm>.
Terminator 2: Judgment Day. Dir. James Cameron. Tristar, 1991.
Thompson, Ronda. *Confessions of a Werewolf Supermodel*. New York: St. Martin's, 2007.
Tolkien, J.R.R. *The Fellowship of the Ring*. 1954. London: Grafton, 1991.
———. *The Letters of J.R.R. Tolkien*. 1981. New York: Houghton Mifflin, 2000.
———. "On Fairy-Stories." In *Tree and Leaf, Smith of Wootton Major, the Homecoming of Beorhtnoth Beorhthelm's Son*. London: Allen & Unwin, 1975.
———. *The Silmarillion*. 1977. London: George Allen & Unwin, 1979.
Torkelson, Anne. "Violence, Agency, and the Women of *Twilight*." *Theorizing Twilight: Critical*

Essays on What's At Stake in a Post-Vampire World. Ed. Maggie Parke and Natalie Wilson. Jefferson: McFarland, 2011. 209–23.
Tremain, Shelley. "Foucault, Governmentality, and Critical Disability Theory: An Introduction." *Foucault and the Government of Disability.* Ed. Shelley Tremain. Ann Arbor: University of Michigan Press, 2005. 1–24.
Tressider, Virginia. "Follow the Yellow Brick(Bat) Road." *Disparity: Policy and Argument* 4.2 (2007): 4–9.
True Blood. HBO. 2008–.
Twilight. Dir. Catherine Hardwicke. Summit Entertainment, 2008.
The Twilight Saga: Breaking Dawn (Part I). Dir. Bill Condon. Summit Entertainment, 2011.
The Twilight Saga: Eclipse. Dir. David Slade. Summit Entertainment, 2010.
The Twilight Saga: New Moon. Dir. Chris Weitz. Summit Entertainment, 2009.
Underworld. Dir. Len Wiseman. Columbia Tristar, 2003.
Underworld: Evolution. Dir. Len Wiseman. Lakeshore, 2005.
The Vampire Diaries. CW. 2009–.
van Roosmalen, E. "Forces of Patriarchy: Adolescent Experiences of Sexuality and Conceptions of Relationships." *Youth and Society* (2000): 202–27.
Violato, Claudio, and Arthur J. Wiley. "Images of Adolescence in English Literature: The Middle Ages to the Modern Period." *Adolescence* (Summer 1990): 253–64.
Wagar, W. Warren. *Terminal Visions: The Literature of Last Things.* Bloomington: Indiana University Press, 1982.
Ward, Renée. *Cultural Contexts and Cultural Change: The Werewolf in Classical, Medieval, and Modern Texts.* Edmonton: University of Alberta, 2009. Ph.D. thesis.
_____. "Shape-Shifting, Identity and Change in Harry Potter and the Prisoner of Azkaban." 2005. Web. 24 Nov. 2011. <http://accio.zymurgy.org/proc/reneeward.pdf>.
Whatley, Mark A. "The Effect of Participant Sex, Victim Dress, and Traditional Attitudes on Causal Judgments for Marital Rape Victims." *Journal of Family Violence* 20.3 (2005): 191–200.
Wilcott, Becca. *Truly, Madly, Deadly: The Unofficial* True Blood *Companion.* Toronto: ECW, 2010.
Williams, Andrew, and Michael Farrell. "Substance Use and Psychosis." *Psychiatry* 6.1 (2007): 19–22.
Wilson, Natalie. "It's a Wolf Thing: The Quileute Werewolf/Shape-Shifter Hybrid as Noble Savage." *Theorizing* Twilight: *Critical Essays on What's At Stake in a Post-Vampire World.* Ed. Maggie Parke and Natalie Wilson. Jefferson: McFarland, 2011. 194–208.
_____. *Seduced by* Twilight: *The Allure and Contradictory Messages of the Popular Saga.* Jefferson: McFarland, 2011.
The Wolf Man. Dir. George Waggner. Universal, 1941.
Workman, Jane E., and Elizabeth W. Freeburg. "An Examination of Date Rape, Victim Dress, and Perceiver Variables within the Context of Attribution Theory." *Sex Roles* 41.3 (1999): 261–77.
X-Men Origins: Wolverine. Dir. Gavin Hood. 20th Century–Fox, 2009.
Zipes, Jack. "A Second Gaze at Little Red Riding Hood's Trials and Tribulations." *The Lion and the Unicorn* 7/8 (1983–1984): 78–109.

Index

abilities, enhanced 118, 139, 160, 185
abject 68, 151, 158
abnormal development 129–130, 143, 145–146; *see also* disability
aboriginal *see* indigenous
abortion 118
abstinence 18, 20, 34, 39, 58, 69–70, 91, 156–157
The Abused Werewolf Rescue Group 15–17, 26–27
academia 7, 107, 135
addiction 11, 13–14, 23, 140–160, 184; alcohol 14, 143, 147–149, 152, 155, 157; biopsychosocial model 146; causes 142–143, 146, 148; drugs 23, 141–146, 148–160; eating 150; gambling 150; magic 150; and mental illness 142–143; recovery 14, 153–156; relapse 155, 157; religion 149; sex 150–151; shopping 150; social 150; symptoms 150; types of, blood 14, 58, 140, 153, 155–157; *see also* blood; drugs
adolescence 3, 5, 11–12, 15–41, 43–45, 50, 62, 64, 83, 91, 100, 106, 108, 111, 137, 161, 177; isolation 11, 15; rebellion 17, 30, 159–160; sex 11, 19, 21, 24, 37, 80, 83, 143; *see also* puberty
Aesop: "Wolf in Sheep's clothing" 6
Africa 150, 172
African American characters 72, 107, 109, 149, 156
afterlife 167–169, 171; *see also* heaven
agency 17, 20, 26, 39, 48, 52, 69, 80, 88, 125, 141
AIDS 13, 125, 133, 136; *see also* illness
albatross 181
alcohol 14, 27, 141, 143–145, 147–149, 152, 157
All Together Dead 76, 78
allegory 164, 181–182
Alpha 21–22, 26, 44–45, 47, 50, 52–56, 64, 86, 90–91, 96, 106, 118–120

alpha male 26, 42, 64, 118
alter ego 33, 69, 156
Amanita muscaria 158
The Amber Spyglass 29–30, 178
Anderson-Dargatz, Gail: *The Cure for Death by Lightning* 5, 11, 15, 23–26, 110–111, 129
Angel 81; *see also Buffy, the Vampire Slayer*
angels 177, 185
anger 34, 42–43, 49, 152
Animagi 107, 134–135
animal nature 33–34, 39, 78, 81, 87
animal self 28–29, 81–82, 89–90, 95, 135
anthropology 2, 9
antiquity 8
anxiety 138, 142–146; *see also* fear
aphrodisiac 140, 151
apocalypse 165, 168, 183
The Art of Seducing a Naked Werewolf 42
Asia 112
assimilation 104
atheism 168, 174
Atwater-Rhodes, Amelia: *Falcondance* 95; *Hawksong* 95; *The Shapeshifters* 12–13, 54, 68, 85–86, 92, 95–97, 108, 118, 122, 126–128, 176; *Snakecharm* 95; *Wolfcry* 12, 68, 85–86, 91, 95; *Wyvernhail* 95
Auerbach, Nina 69, 74, 80
Australia 3, 7, 137
The Awakening 18, 20, 26
Aztec culture 172

bacchanalia 174
Ball, Alan: *True Blood* 3, 5–6, 9, 12–14, 18, 41, 57, 68, 70, 73–74, 79–80, 85, 91–92, 94, 98, 115, 122, 124, 140, 148–154, 161, 165, 167, 171–174; *see also* Harris, Charlaine: The Sookie Stackhouse novels
baptism 172
Barnes, Jennifer Lynn: *Raised by Wolves* 6, 12, 41, 53–57, 59, 66, 93, 114, 120–121,

161–162; "Sweet Caroline" 18–19, 30–31; *Trial by Fire* 41, 45, 53–56, 61, 66, 96–97, 118–120, 123
bat 10, 179
bear 6, 23, 72, 104, 158
beauty 1, 48–49, 64, 100–101, 118, 138, 173, 181
Beauty and the Beast 38, 57–58, 61
beetle 135
Being Human (U.K.) 3, 13, 41, 120, 140–141
Being Human (U.S.) 13, 41, 105, 119–120, 124–126, 130, 141, 162–163, 165, 177
Bennett, Holly: *Shapeshifter* 45, 165–166
Bible 168–170, 172, 181–183
Big Bad 46
Big Bad Wolf 46, 52
bigotry 74, 136, 173; *see also* prejudice
Bildungsroman 17, 26
binaries 69, 106; *see also* dichotomies
bisexuality *see* sexuality, bisexuality
blood 14, 20, 25, 31, 50, 71, 74, 107, 121, 140, 151, 153, 155, 157–158, 165–166, 169, 174, 178–179; animal 120, 140, 156; artificial 153; Christian symbolism 165; as drug 58, 71, 73, 151–152, 155, 157, 160; fairy 80, 153; human 14, 18, 58, 115, 120, 140, 153, 155–157, 165, 179; of Jesus 165; as life giving 165, 183; mixed 96–97, 115, 126, 143; as protection 169; royal 22, 97, 153; vampire 73, 80, 115, 120, 140, 151, 153, 165; *see also* addiction; drugs; pureblood
bloodlines 93, 95–96, 98, 109, 126, 153, 168
bloodlust 84, 107, 124, 166, 178
bodies 8, 10–11, 13, 15–16, 18, 21–22, 27, 31, 44, 63, 65–67, 76–77, 108, 112, 114, 117, 121–123, 125, 128, 131, 135, 140, 175, 178, 180, 183–184; modified 10, 84; replacement 10
Breaking Dawn 65, 99, 102, 104–105, 112–113, 115
brujo 149–150, 173; *see also* shaman; witches
Buffy, the Vampire Slayer 2–3, 6, 10, 12, 16, 41–43, 45–46, 52, 58–59, 61, 68, 71, 80–83, 85, 88, 92, 103–104, 123–124, 141, 167–168, 171
Bulgaria 28

Callisto 6
Canada 3, 6–7, 23–26, 84, 111–112, 157
cancer 124–125, 136; *see also* illness
capitalism 7, 102–103, 119
Carmilla 69
cat 78, 89, 126, 135, 170, 181
catatonia 126
Catholicism 164, 174, 176–177

Celtic traditions 28, 177
chick lit 12, 42
children 46, 52–53, 55–56, 65–66, 76, 89, 106, 125, 132
children's literature 8, 10, 43, 62, 93, 132
chimera 108
China 6, 112
Christ 163–164, 168–169, 173, 175–177, 180–182
Christianity 14, 70, 79, 164–165, 170, 172–176, 180, 182–183
The Chronicles of Narnia see Lewis, C.S.: *The Chronicles of Narnia*
church 164–166, 168–169, 171, 173–176, 180–182
Civil War (American) *see* war, Civil War
civilization 106, 143, 152
civilized 8, 68, 106, 142, 158
class 5, 7–8, 12–13, 70, 79, 88, 92, 97–99, 101–104, 108, 112, 115–116, 130, 158
Club Dead 73–75, 153
colonial gaze 104–105
colonization 7, 63, 100, 104–105, 110–111, 114; neo-colonization 105–106; *see also* postcolonialism
comedy 59, 165, 184
commerce 176
condition 27, 64, 119, 121–126, 130–131, 133–134, 136–138, 182; *see also* illness; infection
confession 176
Confessions of a Werewolf Supermodel 42
congenital defects 129–130; *see also* disability
conquest 103
conservatism 70
consumerism 102–103, 118
contagion *see* infection
contamination 100, 107, 125, 130; *see also* infection
control 14, 16, 23, 42–44, 50–55, 57, 59–60, 62, 76, 82, 84, 86, 88, 95, 106–107, 113–114, 120–122, 125, 127, 134–136, 140, 142–143, 148, 152–153, 156–157, 162, 166, 174, 178, 184
Cooper, Susan: *The Dark Is Rising* 28
coping 13–14, 27, 140–141
Coyote 5, 23–25, 111, 129, 177
crocodile 6
crow 95, 155–156, 177
crucifix 14, 76, 92, 170–171, 181; *see also* religion
"Cry Wolf" 122
CSI 125
cultural traditions 13
cure 34, 38, 80, 87, 123, 131–132, 134, 153, 155; for shapeshifting 34, 123, 139, 158

The Cure for Death by Lightning 5, 11, 15, 23–26, 110–111, 129
curse 14, 26, 44–45, 58, 62, 66, 80, 109–110, 125, 128, 137, 142, 154, 158, 164–167, 169, 172–173
Curse of the Wolf Girl 11, 13, 15, 22–23, 140–142, 145–148, 162

daemon 7, 10, 28–30, 177
dangers of shapeshifting 62, 85, 126–130, 135, 137, 179
The Dark Is Rising 28
Dark Reunion 18, 166
Darwin, Charles 166
Davis, Heather: *Never Cry Werewolf* 6, 11, 15, 22, 36, 39–40, 46, 52–53, 57–58, 96
Dead and Gone 70, 73, 76
Dead as a Doornail 75–77
Dead in the Family 73
Dead Reckoning 74
Dead to the World 75
Dead Until Dark 71–72
deception 62, 160, 176, 178–179
deer 166
Definitely Dead 70, 76–78
definitions 6, 10
deformity 111, 118, 130; *see also* disability
demons 7, 44, 59, 82–83, 89–90, 154, 168, 174, 182, 185
depression 65, 127, 143, 145, 153
desirability of shapeshifting 1, 9, 13, 42, 63, 118–120, 135, 139
detoxification 123, 157; *see also* drugs
developmental delay 24; *see also* disability
Devil 166, 171, 175, 182; *see also* Satan
Devlin, Ivy: *Low Red Moon* 11, 15, 36, 38–39, 85, 91
Diazepam 142, 144
dichotomies 8, 173; *see also* binaries
difference 8, 11, 13, 22–23, 27, 75, 91, 93, 100, 115–118, 120, 129, 131–132, 135, 137–139, 141–142, 146, 149
disability 2, 3, 5, 11, 13–14, 70–71, 117–118, 120, 125, 128–139, 141, 161, 184–185; as inspirational 136; intellectual 129; medical model 131; in popular culture 130; rights 118; social model 117, 131–133, 137, 139; *see also* passing
disease *see* illness
dissociative disorder 126
Dr. Jekyll and Mr. Hyde *see* Hyde
Doctor Who 10
dog 29, 62, 71–72, 88, 94, 105, 122, 126, 128, 135, 177, 179
donkey 180
Doppelgänger 18, 31, 63, 109
dormancy 33, 109, 125

Dracula 3, 5, 12, 68–69, 80, 100, 102–103
dragon 43, 108, 163, 180
drama 118, 184
drugs 15, 23, 27, 34, 71, 77, 101, 123, 142–143, 146–153, 155, 157–160, 175; animal blood 14, 120, 140, 156, 166; and gender 143; human blood 14, 18, 58, 140, 153, 155–157; laudanum 13, 23, 140–146; marijuana 88, 149, 158; overdose 89, 145, 148; in sport 151–152; substitution 156; twelve-step program 157; vampire blood 14, 73, 80, 140, 149–154, 160, 165; *see also* addiction; blood
druid 158, 162, 166, 176–177
duality 7–9, 61, 95, 103, 122, 141, 159, 169
Duncan, Glen: *The Last Werewolf* 7, 126, 162, 166, 171
dwarf 180

eating disorder 142, 144–145
Eclipse 63–65, 99–101, 104–107, 112–114, 162
Eclogues 6–7
erotica 87
eternity 161–162, 166, 168, 185
ethnicity 3, 5, 7–8, 11–14, 16, 25, 78–79, 90–118, 120, 126, 129–131, 133, 136, 141, 152, 155–156, 158, 161, 173, 180, 184–185; *see also* blood, mixed; hybridity; pure-blood
eucharist 175
eugenics 105, 118, 131, 152
Europe 100, 103–104, 106, 110, 112, 182
evil 7, 47, 79, 83, 100, 132, 136–139, 143, 147, 149, 152, 155–156, 165–166, 168–169, 171, 173, 175, 178–179, 183
evolution 63, 105
exclusion 13, 63, 117–118, 136–139, 169, 184–185
existential angst 161–162; *see also* meaning of life
extinction 104

fairies 77, 80, 153–154, 173, 185
fairytales 1, 23, 46–47, 50, 57–59, 83, 99, 163
faith 14, 161, 163–164, 168–170, 172, 175–178, 182; *see also* religion; spirituality
falcon 86, 95–96, 118, 122, 126–127
Falcondance 95
family 11, 15, 18–19, 22, 26, 30–32, 37, 39–40, 57, 65–66, 98–101, 109–112, 114–115, 123, 129, 141–150, 153–154, 157–160, 162, 167, 169
fantasy 10, 14, 17, 21, 28, 63, 75, 92, 118, 136, 161, 163–164, 171, 177–178, 185
Fateful 6

fear 2, 9, 127, 131–134, 136–138, 150, 152, 156, 159, 171; *see also* anxiety
The Fellowship of the Ring 164
females 44, 50, 57, 64; beauty 49–50; matriarchy 23–24, 111; as moral compass 59; sexuality 60; as victims 50–51, 59; *see also* gender; menstruation
feminism 26, 49, 57, 79, 111
First Nations *see* indigenous
flock 182
fluidity 12, 65–66, 70, 73–74, 85, 91, 108, 112–114, 116, 184–185
folklore 28, 37, 107, 123; *see also* mythology
Forever 17, 31, 34–36, 41
forgiveness 165, 176
fox 6, 13, 18, 84, 111–112; *see also* kitsune
freak 138
Freaky Friday 10
frog 1, 58, 180
From Dead to Worse 70, 76–78
The Fury 18
Futurama 10

Gelder, Ken 80, 100
gender 3, 8, 11–14, 24, 29, 41–75, 78–79, 84–85, 93, 98, 111, 130, 143, 161, 185
genetics 10, 14, 16, 21, 27, 47, 53, 60, 65–66, 70, 74–75, 93, 95–97, 99, 109, 125, 130, 133–134, 148, 166, 178
ghosts 1, 36, 56, 163, 165, 167
Ginger Snaps 6, 43, 45, 60, 84, 119, 122–123, 138, 140, 157–158
Ginger Snaps Back: The Beginning 157
Ginger Snaps Unleashed 157–158
God 166–168, 171–173, 175–176
gods 164, 176–177
good and evil 79, 132, 143, 165, 169, 173, 175, 178, 183
Gothic 7–8, 68–69, 80, 98, 166; American 48; contemporary 7, 58, 69
Gray, Claudia: *Fateful* 6
Great Britain *see* United Kingdom
Grimm, Brothers 51; *see also Little Red Riding Hood*

Hale, Jenny: *Jatta* 5–6, 11, 13, 45, 62, 124, 137–139
Halloween 36, 46; *see also* Samahain
hallucinations 89, 150, 158
hallucinogens 126, 150, 158, 175; *see also* peyote
Hammered 120, 162, 177
Hansel and Gretel 47
Hardwicke, Catherine: *Red Riding Hood* 12, 44, 60, 68, 82–83, 128–129
harm minimization 156
Harper, Molly: *The Art of Seducing a Naked Werewolf* 42; *How to Flirt with a Naked Werewolf* 42
Harris, Charlaine: *All Together Dead* 76, 78; *Club Dead* 73–75, 153; *Dead and Gone* 70, 73, 76; *Dead as a Doornail* 75–77; *Dead in the Family* 73; *Dead Reckoning* 74; *Dead to the World* 75; *Dead Until Dark* 71–72; *Definitely Dead* 70, 76–78; *From Dead to Worse* 70, 76–78; *Living Dead in Dallas* 70–73; The Sookie Stackhouse novels 3, 9–10, 12, 68–70, 74, 78–80, 94, 124, 150–151, 153; *see also* Ball, Alan: *True Blood*
Harry Potter and the Deathly Hallows 117, 133–134, 169
Harry Potter and the Goblet of Fire 135
Harry Potter and the Half-Blood Prince 125, 133
Harry Potter and the Order of the Phoenix 134
Harry Potter and the Philosopher's Stone 135
Harry Potter and the Prisoner of Azkaban 8, 132–135
haunting 23–24, 66, 141, 165
hawk 85–86, 95–96, 104, 122
Hawksong 95
Hearne, Kevin: *Iron Druid* novels 6–7, 120, 162, 176–177; *Hammered* 120, 162, 177; *Hexed* 177; *Hounded* 162, 176–177
heaven 37, 168; *see also* afterlife
hell 166, 168, 175
heredity *see* genetics
heroism 8, 63
heteronormativity 8, 12, 68–69, 74, 85–86; *see also* sexuality
heterosexuality *see* sexuality, hereterosexuality
Hexed 177
hierarchies 22, 54–56, 64, 67, 69, 94–95, 97–100, 107–108, 115–116, 135
His Dark Materials see Pullman, Philip: *His Dark Materials*
HIV *see* AIDS
Hollywood 100, 118, 138
holy water 14, 92, 170–171; *see also* religion
home 23–33, 94, 111, 114
homosexuality *see* sexuality, homosexuality
hormones 15, 27, 45; *see also* puberty
horror 10, 37, 44, 75, 121, 151, 158
The Horse and His Boy 180–181
Hounded 162, 176–177
How to Flirt with a Naked Werewolf 42
Howling at the Moon 88–90
Howl's Moving Castle (film) 62
Howl's Moving Castle (novel) 62, 128
The Hulk 14
The Hunters 18, 156

hunters of wolves 28, 47, 52–60, 144, 148
hybridity 80, 85–86, 93, 95–96, 108–109, 115, 120, 126, 140, 154–155, 173, 181; of religion 14, 170–171; *see also* ethnicity
Hyde 69

I Was a Teenage Werewolf 16
id 82
identity 2, 8–11, 13–14, 16–17, 24, 26–30, 32–36, 46, 49, 52, 60, 62, 66, 68–70, 72–73, 82, 88–89, 91, 95, 100–101, 105–106, 108–109, 112–116, 122–123, 126–128, 130, 132–133, 135, 137, 144, 159–160, 180–181, 183, 185
Idylls 6
illness 13, 34, 110, 117, 120, 122–125, 129–133, 136–137, 139, 184–185; *see also* infection
immigrant 13, 25, 111
immortality 112, 125, 161–163, 165, 167, 177, 183
imprinting 31, 54, 64, 112, 115; *see also* soul mates
incest 25, 153
indigenous 1, 13, 23–26, 98–100, 103–106, 108, 111–114, 177; American 13, 63, 98–100, 104–106, 112; Australian 105, 150; Canadian 23, 25–26, 111, 150; *see also* Quileute
infection 9, 33–34, 52, 60, 71, 96–97, 99–100, 106, 123–125, 131, 133–135, 158; *see also* contamination; illness
insects 18
internet 107
intimacy 69, 74, 156
Inuit *see* indigenous
Ireland 165, 177
Iron Druid (novels) *see* Hearne, Kevin: *Iron Druid* novels
isolation 11, 13, 15–16, 22–23, 30, 86, 88, 117–118, 132–134, 136–137, 142, 146, 180

Jackson, Rosemary 17
Japan 6, 19, 84
Jatta 5–6, 11, 13, 45, 62, 124, 137–139
Jesus Christ *see* Christ
Jinks, Catherine: *The Abused Werewolf Rescue Group* 15–17, 26–27
Jones, Diana Wynne: *Howl's Moving Castle* 62, 128
jungle animals 6

kitsune 18–19, 84, 155; *see also* fox

Lai, Larissa: *When Fox Is a Thousand* 13, 111–112
lamb 168–169, 181–182

language: medical 27, 119, 123–126; war 124–125
The Last Battle 182
The Last Werewolf 7, 126, 162, 166, 171
Leader of the Pack 90–91, 118
Le Fanu, Joseph: *Carmilla* 69
Lewis, C.S.: *The Chronicles of Narnia* 10, 178–182; Essays 163–164; *The Horse and His Boy* 180–181; *The Last Battle* 182; *Letters* 164; *The Lion, the Witch and the Wardrobe* 178–179; *The Silver Chair* 178–179; *The Voyage of the Dawn Treader* 180–181
liminality 16, 25, 29, 75, 143, 145
Linger 17, 31, 33–35, 41, 70
lion 181–182
The Lion, the Witch and the Wardrobe 178–179
Little Red Riding Hood 36–37, 39, 46–48, 50–53, 60; *see also* Red Riding Hood (film)
Living Dead in Dallas 70–73
Lonely Werewolf Girl 3, 11, 13, 15, 22, 97, 118, 140–148
longevity 88, 161–162
The Lord of the Rings 164
The Lost Boys 118
Love, Kathy: *My Sister Is a Werewolf* 12, 68, 87–88
Low Red Moon 11, 15, 36, 38–39, 85, 91
lunar cycle 42, 45, 76, 82, 144, 154; *see also* moon
lycanthropy (medical condition) 126, 128
Lycaon 3, 6

maban reality 23–24, 111
MacInerney, Karen: *Howling at the Moon* 88–90; *Leader of the Pack* 90–91, 118; *On the Prowl* 89–90; *Tales of an Urban Werewolf* 12, 42, 68, 88, 118
madness 22, 126–127, 142; *see also* mental illness
maenads 72, 79–79
magic 10, 58, 62, 78, 86, 107, 126–127, 134–135, 141, 145, 148–151, 173–174, 176, 181
Maker 57, 73–74, 77, 87, 153
malach 84, 155
Marillier, Juliet: *Wildwood Dancing* 58, 179–180
marriage 21, 28, 35, 40, 69, 73, 79, 83, 86, 88–89, 91, 95–96, 102, 133
Marx 102
masculinity 6, 8, 26, 41–44, 50–51, 53–54, 57–58, 61, 63–64, 118
masking 13, 23, 39, 140–141
mate 54, 68, 85–88, 90–91
matriarchy 23–24, 111

McIntosh, Pat: "Cry Wolf" 122
meaning of life 162, 166, 170, 185; *see also* existential angst
meditation 82
menstruation 45, 64–65, 84, 140, 145, 157–158
mental health 14, 117, 126, 129, 161
mental illness 13, 58, 117, 126–129, 132, 134, 139, 141–143, 145, 148–150, 160; *see also* madness
messianic figure *see* Christ
Metamorphmagi 134–135
Metamorphoses 6
metamorphosis: dual-bodied 10, 70; facial 80–81, 150; modified 10, 43, 50, 63, 77, 84–85, 122, 128; multi-bodied 10, 70; terminal 10; unidirectional 10
metaphors 1, 3, 7, 11, 13, 16–17, 26, 43, 51, 58, 80–81, 87, 93, 103, 108, 117, 124–125, 129–133, 136–137, 139, 168, 183–184
methadone 156
Mexico 89, 150, 173
Meyer, Stephenie: *Breaking Dawn* 65, 99, 102, 104–105, 112–113, 115; *Eclipse* 63–65, 99–101, 104–107, 112–114, 162; *New Moon* 21–22, 64, 99, 101, 104, 106, 112, 162, 168; *Twilight* 57, 100–101, 107, 162, 171; the *Twilight* series: 2–3, 5–6, 11–13, 15–18, 21, 26, 31, 34–35, 41–42, 54, 57, 59, 61, 63–66, 69, 85, 91–92, 98–108, 112–116, 118–122, 162, 165, 167–171
Midnight 18
Millar, Martin: *Curse of the Wolf Girl* 11, 13, 15, 22–23, 140–142, 145–148, 162; *Lonely Werewolf Girl* 3, 11, 13, 15, 22, 97, 118, 140–148; the Wolf Girl novels 3, 11, 13, 15, 22–23, 97, 118, 140–145, 147–148, 162
minority 74, 92–94, 100, 108, 130–133, 185
miscarriage 76, 130
miscegenation 75–76, 85, 95, 126; *see also* blood, mixed
Mr. Hyde *see* Hyde
Miyazaki, Hayao: *Howl's Moving Castle* 62
monkshood *see* wolfsbane
monogamy 69, 76, 85–87, 91
mononucleosis (mono) 64
monsters 2, 7–8, 10, 13, 15–16, 42, 44, 48, 52, 57–59, 70, 92, 98, 100, 105, 115, 118, 123, 129–132, 137, 139, 145, 166, 180, 184
monstrosity 92–93, 99, 117, 123, 129–131, 136, 138–139, 185
moon 6, 9, 22, 28, 37–38, 42, 45, 53, 60, 62, 64, 70, 75, 82, 89, 92, 94, 104, 109, 121, 124, 130, 132–133, 135, 137, 142, 144, 167, 172, 184; *see also* lunar cycle
morality 21, 52, 59–60, 69, 74, 79, 86, 113, 128, 139, 148, 166–167, 169, 175, 180

Morrigan (Irish deity) 177
multiple sclerosis 132
The Mummy: Tomb of the Dragon Emperor 43
mushrooms 158–160, 175
mutation 125
My Sister Is a Werewolf 12, 68, 87–88
mythology 6–7, 15, 26, 93, 107, 109–111, 125, 144, 154–155, 163–164, 167, 171–172, 182; *see also* folklore

narcotics *see* drugs
Native Americans *see* indigenous, American; Quileute
Native Canadians *see* indigenous, Canadian
natural world 38–39, 44, 63, 65, 105–106, 109–110, 114–115, 123, 152, 163, 172
Navajo *see* indigenous, American
Nazi Germany 118, 152
necromancy 174
neo-colonization *see* colonization, neo-colonization
neopagan *see* paganism
Never Cry Werewolf 6, 11, 15, 22, 36, 39–40, 46, 52–53, 57–58, 96
New Moon 21–22, 64, 99, 101, 104, 106, 112, 162, 168
New Testament *see* Bible
Nightfall 18–20, 84
normality 8, 15, 19, 27, 32, 47, 49, 86, 129–132, 134–135, 137–138, 143–146, 157, 165
Norse history 6–7, 177
Northern Lights 29–30
Nosferatu 80

occult 14, 174
occulture 170–171, 191
Odin 7
On the Prowl 89–90
Once in a Full Moon 11, 15, 17, 36–38, 85, 91
orc 179
Other 1–2, 8, 12, 17, 23, 49, 68, 74–75, 83, 86–87, 93, 100–101, 108, 114, 132–134, 141, 143, 146, 148–149, 165, 184–185
Otherworld 166
otter 177
overdose *see* drugs
Ovid: *Metamorphoses* 6
owl 177

pack 3–4, 9, 21–23, 26–27, 31–32, 35–36, 38, 47–48, 50, 53–56, 63–64, 66, 70, 76–77, 87–91, 99, 101, 106, 115, 119–120, 152, 160, 168, 173

Index

paganism 14, 164, 170, 172
pain 13, 34–35, 45, 52, 120–123, 127, 132, 139–140, 142, 176, 184–185
pansexuality *see* sexuality, pansexuality
panther 70, 75–76, 104, 153, 173
passing 13, 124, 133, 140–141, 144; *see also* disability; ethnicity
patriarchy 54, 56, 64–66, 69, 143, 185
Pearce, Jackson: *Sisters Red* 6–7, 11–12, 15–17, 28, 41, 47–53, 66; *Sweetly* 41, 47–52, 66
Perrault, Charles 51; *see also* Little Red Riding Hood
Peter and the Wolf 43–44
pets 78, 105
peyote 89, 150
Phantom 20, 24, 156
Plec, Julie: *The Vampire Diaries* 5–7, 9, 11–19, 26, 30–31, 41–43, 58–63, 66, 68, 80, 84, 91–95, 98, 100, 102–107, 109–110, 118, 120–122, 140–141, 154–157, 161, 165–167, 169, 171–172, 178
pluralism 170, 177
postcolonialism 14, 25, 99, 103–105, 107–108, 110–111, 116; *see also* colonization
postmodernism 1, 31
predators 42, 50–51, 57, 60, 80, 175, 179
pregnancy 65–66, 76, 84–85, 87, 136; *see also* reproduction
prejudice 66, 74, 88, 103; *see also* bigotry
Prince Caspian 178
Progeny 74, 77
Prokofiev: *Peter and the Wolf* 43
psychic 7, 39, 54–55, 70, 76, 88, 90, 113, 120, 123, 162
psychopathy 7, 57
puberty 11, 15–16, 21, 45, 74, 88, 137; *see also* adolescence; hormones
Pullman, Philip: *The Amber Spyglass* 29–30, 178; *His Dark Materials* 7, 10–12, 15, 28–30, 177–178; *Northern Lights* 29–30; "The Republic of Heaven" 177–178; *The Subtle Knife* 29
pure-blood 74–75, 86, 95–97, 109, 126, 143–144, 153; *see also* blood, mixed

queer theory 8, 69–74, 132
Quileute 13, 21, 41, 63–64, 98–102, 104–107, 113–115, 168; *see also* indigenous, American

race *see* ethnicity
Raised by Wolves 6, 12, 41, 53–57, 59, 66, 93, 114, 120–121, 161–162
rape 26, 30, 46, 51, 77, 84–85, 153; myths 51–52, 59; *see also* sexual assault
rat 135

raven 95
reanimation 111
Red Riding Hood (film) 12, 44, 60, 68, 82–83, 128–129; *see also* Little Red Riding Hood
redemption 57, 59, 130, 136, 164, 167–168, 185
rehabilitation 131, 158
reincarnation 111
Reisz, Kristopher: *Unleashed* 158–160, 174–176
religion 9, 14, 126, 149, 161–183; symbols 149, 167, 169–171, 183; *see also* crucifix; holy water; spirituality
reproduction 65–66, 99, 118; *see also* pregnancy
resurrection 150, 164–165, 183
The Return trilogy *see* Smith, L.J.: *The Vampire Diaries* novels
The Ripper 166
rituals 99, 154, 159, 165, 173, 175–177
Roman mythology 6, 172
romance 6, 11–12, 15, 18–21, 25, 30–34, 36–40, 42, 44, 47, 49–50, 52, 54, 56–62, 64, 69, 74–75, 83–91, 99, 112–113, 115, 121, 129, 133, 149, 151, 156, 167, 169–170, 184
Romulus and Remus 6, 53
Rowling, J. K.: *Harry Potter and the Deathly Hallows* 117, 133–134, 169; *Harry Potter and the Goblet of Fire* 135; *Harry Potter and the Half-Blood Prince* 125, 133; *Harry Potter and the Order of the Phoenix* 134; *Harry Potter and the Philosopher's Stone* 135; *Harry Potter and the Prisoner of Azkaban* 8, 132–135; *Harry Potter* novels 2, 5, 7–8, 13, 41, 59, 63, 103, 106–107, 115, 117, 124–125, 130–138, 140–141, 167, 169; *The Tales of Beedle the Bard* 134–135

sacrifice 24, 63, 109, 112, 154–155, 165, 168–169, 172, 174, 181, 183
salvation 14, 160, 168–169, 172, 180, 183, 185
Samahain 174; *see also* Halloween
Satan 126, 149, 182; *see also* Devil
scarecrow 62
schizophrenia 150
Schreiber, Ellen: *Once in a Full Moon* 11, 15, 17, 36–38, 85, 91
science 42, 107, 118, 125–126, 176
science fiction 10, 118, 124, 130
Scotland 22, 141–143, 146, 156
screen shapeshifting 5, 9, 19, 42, 118, 155, 161, 184
secularism 14, 166, 169–170, 174, 183, 185
self harm 19, 25, 58, 144–147

self-medication 13, 140–160; *see also* drugs
seventh son 27–28, 47
sexual assault 23–24, 30, 85–86, 173; *see also* rape
sexuality 8, 11–12, 19–21, 24, 29, 32, 34–35, 37–39, 44, 46, 50, 59–60, 68–91, 95, 98, 111, 143, 161, 185; bisexuality 3–74, 79, 82, 86, 129; heterosexuality 12, 69–70, 73, 82, 85–86, 91; homosexuality 31, 70–74, 79, 85–86, 148–149; orientation 73–74, 130; pansexuality 74, 80
Shadow Souls 18, 20, 84
shaman 9, 149–150, 173–175
Shapeshifter 45, 165–166
The Shapeshifters 12–13, 54, 68, 85–86, 92, 95–97, 108, 118, 122, 126–128, 176
Shiver 6, 17, 31–33, 41
shyness 62, 138
The Silmarillion 179
silver 9, 39, 53, 60, 71, 76, 92, 123, 140, 171, 178–179
The Silver Chair 178–179
Sisters Red 6–7, 11–12, 15–17, 28, 41, 47–53, 66
Skinwalkers (Navajo legend) 94
Smith, L.J.: *The Awakening* 18, 20, 26; *Dark Reunion* 18, 166; *The Fury* 18; *The Hunters—Phantom* 20, 24, 156; *The Return—Midnight* 18; *The Return—Nightfall* 18–20, 84; *The Return—Shadow Souls* 18, 20, 84; *The Struggle* 18; *The Vampire Diaries* 3, 5, 7, 10–21, 26, 43, 59, 61, 68, 83–84, 91, 140, 155–156, 165–166
snake 122, 179
Snakecharm 95
social model of shapeshifting 131–137, 139
Sookie Stackhouse novels *see* Harris, Charlaine: The Sookie Stackhouse novels
sorcerer *see* wizards
sorceress *see* witches
soul mates 64, 91, 112; *see also* imprinting
souls 14, 29–30, 38, 47, 61, 80, 114, 124, 165–169, 171–175, 178, 185
the South (United States) 50, 70, 73, 79, 149
South America 150; *see also* Mexico
sparrow 95
species *see* ethnicity
speculative fiction 10
speech disorder 138
spirituality 3, 11, 14, 20, 24–25, 111, 114, 146, 161–183, 185; *see also* religion
sport 36, 43, 123
stability 23, 31, 39, 67, 69, 80, 93, 95, 114–115, 122, 129, 132, 163, 178–179
stag 135, 177
Stefan's Diaries novels 166

Stiefvater, Maggie: *Forever* 17, 31, 34–36, 41; *Linger* 17, 31, 33–35; *Shiver* 6, 17, 31–33, 41; *The Wolves of Mercy Falls* 3, 6, 11, 15, 31, 34, 41, 63, 91, 98
stigma 75, 133, 136
Stoker, Bram: *Dracula* 3, 5, 12, 68–69, 80, 100, 102–103
The Struggle 18
subaltern 25
The Subtle Knife 29
sun 48, 106, 109, 137, 172–174
sunlight 71, 80, 92, 124, 153, 172, 181
super race 105, 109, 118, 120, 152
superhuman 102, 118, 139, 143
Supernatural 71, 171, 179
Sweetly 41, 47–52, 66

taboo 30, 93, 151, 158
Tales of an Urban Werewolf see MacInerney, Karen: *Tales of an Urban Werewolf*
Tales of Beedle the Bard 134–135
Taoism 111
Taussig, Michael 9
technology 7, 107, 176, 179
Teen Wolf (films) 6, 12, 15–16, 28, 41, 43, 63, 119, 122
Teen Wolf (TV series) 6, 12, 15–16, 41, 43–46, 52, 58, 60, 63, 96, 105, 107, 118–119, 122, 138
teenagers *see* adolescence
teratology 129–130
Terminator 2: Judgment Day 179
terrorism 7
Theocritus: *Idylls* 6
Thompson, Ronda: *Confessions of a Werewolf Supermodel* 42
Thor 177
tiger 6, 70, 72, 76–78
Tolkien, J.R.R.: *The Fellowship of the Ring* 164; *Letters* 164; *The Lord of the Rings* 164; "On Fairy-Stories" 163–164; *The Silmarillion* 179
Tourette's Syndrome 129
transfiguration 107, 135, 176
Trial by Fire 41, 45, 53–56, 61, 66, 96–97, 118–120, 123
trickster 19, 23–25, 84, 111, 177
triggers of shapeshifting 10, 15–16, 21, 26, 29, 31–34, 39, 43, 47, 50–53, 60, 62, 66, 81, 94, 96, 104, 106–107, 125, 135, 166–167, 182; *see also* control; infection
True Blood see Ball, Alan: *True Blood*
Twilight (films) 3, 5–6, 11–12, 15–18, 30, 63, 100, 102, 118
Twilight (novel) 57, 100–101, 107, 162, 171
Twilight (novels) *see* Meyer, Stephenie: The *Twilight* series

UFOs 171
uncanny 16, 23–25, 31, 33, 44, 93, 145
underworld 165
Underworld 3, 93, 96, 98, 104, 108, 120, 125, 162
Underworld: Evolution 3, 108
United Kingdom 3, 7, 13, 22, 41, 69, 110, 120, 140–141
United States 3, 6–7, 20, 37, 41, 48, 53, 55, 100, 103–104, 106, 110, 118–120, 124, 130, 141, 162, 165, 170, 176–177
Unleashed 158–160, 174–176
utopia 108, 110

The Vampire Diaries (novels) *see* Smith, L.J.: *The Vampire Diaries*
The Vampire Diaries (TV series) *see* Plec, Julie: *The Vampire Diaries*; Williamson, Kevin: *The Vampire Diaries*
vampires 1–3, 5–7, 9–10, 12–14, 16–21, 26, 28, 31, 42, 46, 57–61, 63–66, 68–75, 77–81, 84, 87–88, 92–110, 112–116, 118, 120–121, 124–125, 138, 140, 149, 151–157, 161–163, 165–168, 170–174, 177, 184–185
Victorian England 69, 80
Vikings 72, 158
village idiot 24, 129
villain 6, 42, 46–47, 63, 79, 109, 130, 140, 152, 154, 166–167, 174, 177, 179, 184
Vinvocci 10
violence 18, 21, 26, 42–46, 48, 53, 55–60, 62, 79, 81, 83, 85–87, 93, 102–103, 108, 121, 142, 144, 147, 151, 157–159, 176, 181–182; *see also* sexual assault
Virgil: *Eclogues* 6–7
Virgin Mary 168–169, 177
virus *see* infection
vixen lit 12
The Voyage of the Dawn Treader 180–181

war 92–93, 95–97, 124–125, 130, 171; Civil War 171; werewolf-vampire 9–10, 42, 92–94, 97–98, 103–104, 115, 121, 172; World War II 111
warlocks *see* wizards
When Fox Is a Thousand 13, 111–112
whiteness 13, 25, 98, 100, 104, 106, 108–112, 114, 116, 149, 168, 185; *see also* ethnicity
Wicca *see* witches
Wildwood Dancing 58, 179–180
Williamson, Kevin: *The Vampire Diaries* 5–7, 9, 11–19, 26, 30–31, 41–43, 58–63, 66, 68, 80, 84, 91–95, 98, 100, 102–107, 109–110, 118, 120–122, 140–141, 154–157, 161, 165–167, 169, 171–172, 178; *see also* Plec, Julie: *The Vampire Diaries*
witches 18, 31, 37–38, 47, 62–63, 75, 78, 81–82, 85, 88–89, 107, 109–110, 126, 128, 139, 149, 151, 154, 156, 172, 174, 178–180, 182, 185
wizards 62, 109–110, 117, 128, 133–134, 137, 141
The Wolf Girl novels *see* Millar, Martin: The Wolf Girl novels
"Wolf in Sheep's clothing" 6
wolf in sheep's clothing 82
wolf man 3, 6, 44
wolf pack *see* pack
Wolfcry 12, 68, 85–86, 91, 95
wolfsbane 88–89, 121, 123, 158, 167
The Wolves of Mercy Falls see Stiefvater, Maggie: *The Wolves of Mercy Falls*
wyvern 85–86, 108
Wyvernhail 95

X-Men Origins: Wolverine 63

Young Adult (YA) 10–11, 16–17, 20–22, 28, 46, 62, 68–69, 91, 98, 174, 184
youth 17, 100, 106, 113, 118–119, 139, 143

Zeitgeist 69
Zeus 6
zombies 7, 98, 105, 185

www.ingramcontent.com/pod-product-compliance
Ingram Content Group UK Ltd.
Pitfield, Milton Keynes, MK11 3LW, UK
UKHW042006140426
5217IPUK00015B/1017